D0722071

Not Invited to the Party

James T. Bennett

Not Invited to the Party

How the Demopublicans Have Rigged
the System and Left Independents
Out in the Cold

 Springer

James T. Bennett
Department of Economics
George Mason University
Fairfax, VA
USA
jbennett@gmu.edu

ISBN 978-1-4419-0365-5   e-ISBN 978-1-4419-0366-2
DOI 10.1007/978-1-4419-0366-2
Springer New York Dordrecht Heidelberg London

Library of Congress Control Number: 2009928094

Printed on acid-free paper

Springer is part of Springer Science+Business Media (www.springer.com)

Acknowledgments

Politics, says the old adage, makes strange bedfellows, and this book is a testament to the truth in that claim. Surely, readers must be surprised (shocked may be a more appropriate word) to find a book with a Foreword by Ralph Nader, an activist well known for his liberal views and his advocacy of government regulation, and with an Afterword by William Redpath, Chairman of the Libertarian National Committee, whose views are at the opposite end of the political spectrum. When left and right, liberal and libertarian are in complete agreement on the same issue, something clearly is seriously wrong with the status quo that must be fixed. In this instance, the status quo involves the virtual exclusion of third parties and independent candidates from effective participation in elections for local, state, and federal offices. Governmental regulations have effectively guaranteed the dominance of the Demopublican duopoly in virtually every election. In 1968, when George Corley Wallace ran for president as a third-party candidate, he made a statement that I have long remembered – "there's not a dime's worth of difference" between Democrats and Republicans. Arguably, history has more often than not proved Wallace correct: thus this book.

I am grateful to many for their assistance with and support of the research and editing of this work. The research would not have been possible without the generous financial support of the Sunmark Foundation and help from the Locke Institute. Research assistance was provided by Steven M. Davis. I also owe profuse thanks to my editor, Bill Kauffman, for I am indebted to him for significant contributions to this study.

Finally, I must express my unbounded gratitude to my wonderful wife of more than 40 years, Sally, to whom I dedicate this book. Only a saint could have put up with my ranting and raving about politics and economics (and life in general) for more than four decades. Equally important, she has never read any book that I have written, and that for me is a true blessing – the last thing that I want to do after work is to come home and debate my views and defend my work. Sally is the inspiration for much of what I do well and is blameless for the rest. If only every husband were so lucky, the world would be a much happier place.

Fairfax, VA   James T. Bennett
                                                    George Mason University

Foreword

I wrote my first article on ballot access obstacles to small political starts and candidates in 1959 for the *Harvard Law Record*. Little did I anticipate that 50 years later the political bigotry, the Jim Crow-type laws against a competitive electoral process, and the shared monopoly of the Republican and Democratic duopoly would be more obstructive and more deeply ingrained than ever in our history. The intolerant legal and political systems and practices continue to intensify. The grotesque word "spoiler" continues to be applied to dissenters, even though dissent is the mother of assent over time, even though the cash register political rackets themselves are the ones spoiled to the core.

Nor did I anticipate personally experiencing the relentless obstructions of wildly varying state laws with their numbing ambiguities, and even county tripwires, through three presidential campaigns in 2000, 2004, and 2008. As my campaign manager in the first two, Theresa Amato, recounts in her recent book, *Grand Illusion*, the daily drumbeat of these choreographed impediments with all their short deadlines, phony lawsuits, harassments, and their drain on time and resources must be engaged in order to demonstrate more fully this tragic mockery of democratic elections.

"Freedom," wrote Marcus Cicero, "is participation in power." That is what voters are supposed to be doing when they participate in elections. The transgression of voter rights in so many ways recalls some of the struggle of the civil rights movement. Still, there are new violations and confusions to replace the racialist laws of the past. Even accurately counting the votes has become a many-sided challenge in numerous jurisdictions. Yet, fundamental to voter rights are candidate rights to be on the ballot and to compete fairly by offering more choices, differing agendas, and broader debates.

While voter rights often command media, scholarship, and intensive public controversies involving the major parties, comparable questions affecting smaller parties and independent candidates remain largely in the shadows with the repressed and excluded crying in the wilderness. However, those who do stay the course inside the manipulated electoral arena are documenting the tyranny, winning some cases in court, and providing the necessary pulses for an ascendant public recognition of how valuable a function they could perform in an otherwise converging two-party dominance.

Speaking around the country for the Nader/Gonzalez 2008 presidential ticket, I discussed major, often majority-supported, redirections that Senators McCain and Obama either ignored or opposed. These included full Medicare for all; an inflation-adjusted minimum wage from 1968; subordination of fossil and nuclear fuels energy to energy conservation and solar and geothermal energy; crackdown on corporate crime, fraud, and abuse; an end to corporate welfare and corporate personhood; military withdrawals from Iraq and Afghanistan; addressing forthrightly the two-state solution for the Israeli–Palestinian conflict; an end to civil liberties violations post-9/11; and an adherence to constitutional checks and balances, due process, and habeas corpus. Also argued was the impeaching of Bush and Cheney; a carbon and derivatives speculation tax; helping to reduce taxes on labor; cutting the bloated, wasteful military budget; and several procedural ways to advance the empowerment of voters, candidates, consumers, taxpayers, and workers through the "facilities of democracy."

None of these important subjects was raised or discussed on the three presidential debate stages occupied only by McCain and Obama.

The above considerations are reason enough to welcome the entry of a powerful new voice and scholar – Professor James T. Bennett – into this rising protest against the exclusion and silencing of candidates other than those identified as Republicans and Democrats. In his historically and analytically informative book, *Not Invited to the Party: How the Demopublicans Have Rigged the System and Left Independents Out in the Cold*, driven by an empirically based moral indignation, Professor Bennett guides the engrossed reader through the history of how the cartelized duopoly obstructs small starts. But renewal comes primarily from small starts given a chance to compete. The crushing of competitors by the two-party duopoly, if it occurred in the marketplace, would lead to indictment and conviction under the antitrust laws. Without entrepreneurs in the marketplace or seeds in nature, neither would be revitalized. Instead, there would be decay or stagnation, as there is year after year in the theatre of politics. Our country will never know, for the most part, the great talent, integrity, and electoral commitment of Americans who were deterred or blocked from attaining, in Lincoln's words, "a new birth of freedom" for "a government of the people, by the people and for the people."

Not Invited to the Party starts with the Founders' deep skepticism and dread over the prospect of political parties controlling the Republic. Even the Federalists or Republicans were, in historian Richard Hofstadter's words, "men who looked upon parties as sores on the body politic." As with the word "corporation," the words "political parties" are not once mentioned in our Constitution. Yet, these two extra constitutional forces control our nation's political economy.

To his credit, Professor Bennett — an informed libertarian and econo-mist — provides an astute analysis of concentrating power, starting with the adoption of the Australian ballot in the late nineteenth century and how subsequent statist absorptions of the electoral process — in the name of reform — served to cartelize the country's politics as a "Democrat–Republican duopoly." The symbiosis between this cartel and state authority tightens with each passing decade — garnished by a closed system of politi-cal debates and taxpayer subsidies that reach all the way to the two parties' national conventions. Imagine, if you will, Congress deemed these predict-able outcomes of the conventions and their extravagant corporate hospital-ity soirees "educational" enough to make you pay over $30 million for them every four years.

So averse to competition are the Republicans and the Democrats that they go to great lengths to gerrymander one or the other from any prospect of contention. At the congressional and state legislative levels, one-party domi-nation prevails beyond anything seen in the early decades of our country. And, once again, the big parties use governmental authority to install authori-tarian controls that deny voters choice. After all, an election implies a contest, and a contest implies at least two viable contestants. Instead, over 90% of the voters for the House of Representatives are confronted with a coronation — for the incumbent.

James Bennett shows that all these restrictions on voter choice and candi-dates' rights keep getting worse compared to our nation's earlier history, when small parties paved the way against slavery, the denial of women's right to vote, and labor, farmer, and minority needs, so that they share more in the power and benefits of the land. His next to last chapter sobers any vestige of political jingoism by showing how other western countries surpass us in pro-viding for a more fluid and competitive politics.

There is much to ponder in this book. It makes one wonder just how the voters, given the ultimatum that only one of two candidates — if that — can win the elections – can ever escape their chattled desire to vote for "winners" while they – the people – keep losing.

It also makes one wonder about the insidious genius of a straight-jacketed electoral system that leads otherwise intelligent people to vigorously oppose smaller candidates they largely agree with because of the winner-take-all, least-worst syndrome. Because this attitude has no discernible breaking point, it becomes a trap that regularly prevents them from utilizing even a pre-election political lever on a variety of issues over their intransigent least-worst choice.

This wonder argues for the widest readership of this book and should attract many Americans who want to escape the two-party trap and break out of their leg irons and handcuffs into a world of free and imaginative possibilities for our presently demeaned politics.

Washington, DC   Ralph Nader
                                                                             Public Citizen

Contents

Chapter 1

The Issue

Few institutions in America are held in such uniformly and consistently low esteem as our political parties. Opinion polls show that Americans regard the parties as less trustworthy than used car salesmen, union officials – even lawyers. (Yes, lawyers!) The parties are thought to be corrupt, unprincipled, and interested only in achieving and maintaining power, not in "the public good," whatever that amorphous concept may be. They are, in short, despised.

Yet, when we speak of "parties" in America, we are really talking about only two parties: the Democrats and the Republicans. The former have their roots in Thomas Jefferson's Democratic-Republican Party of the early republic; the latter grew in the mid-1850s from the remains of the Whig, Anti-Masonic, Liberty, and Free Soil parties. The very recitation of those Republican forerunners suggests the tumultuous and colorful history of the early party system. The Whigs were distinguished by their sponsorship of the "American System" of Henry Clay, which envisioned government support of internal improvements (roads, canals, waterways) and a national bank as a means to economic growth. The Anti-Masonic Party, on which so many Republican strategists cut their eyeteeth, stood for an end to secret societies and for openness in government. The Liberty Party was abolitionist; it saw slavery as the great stain on the American escutcheon, and sought to erase that stain by emancipating African slaves. The Free Soil Party combined a determination to stop the spread of slavery into the western territories with a plan to encourage the settlement of those western lands by free farmers who would form the backbone of frontier society.

These parties were fueled by ideas, by passions, by visions of what America could and should be. They were not perfect, of course: the Whigs

J.T. Bennett, *Not Invited to the Party*, DOI 10.1007/978-1-4419-0366-2_1,
© Springer Science+Business Media, LLC 2009

were cautious to a fault, avoiding the issue of slavery as futilely as a man might avoid the 900-pound gorilla romping through his trophy room, smashing everything in sight. "The Whig Party died of too much respecta-bility and not enough people," said Edward Stafford, a Mississippi Republican newspaper editor.[1] The Anti-Masons, born in the furor surrounding the apparent murder of an apostate member of the Masonic Order who had threatened to go public with the fraternity's secrets, were too narrowly focused on a specific historic incident to retain any kind of long-term rele-vancy. The Liberty Party was perhaps too radical: abolition seemed too great a step into the unknown to most voters in the 1840s. And the Free Soil Party was too sectional, too tied to New England and the Northwest to generate the nationwide appeal necessary for a national party. But despite these weak-nesses, these inevitable flaws, the parties stood for something. What a con-trast they make with the Democrats and Republicans of our day. And what is more, those parties waned and waxed, fought and won and lost, in what was a relatively free marketplace of ideas and politics. They had unobstructed access to the ballot: indeed, any party could and did run candidates, without having to jump through hoops or beg the favor of the ruling party. They operated without public subsidy, as did their opponents: none of the parties even dreamt of having their conventions, their candidates, and their cam-paigns financed by the federal treasury.

Today, of course, the spectrum of political opinion is forcibly channeled into two government-sponsored, government-protected national parties, the Democrats and the Republicans. They constitute a duopoly – that is, a situ-ation in which economic or (in this case) political power is lodged in only two actors. These actors use every means at their disposal, first and foremost the coercive and financial powers of the state, to forbid or punish competi-tors. Our duopoly has succeeded in suffocating debate, striking dumb other voices, and reducing a once-vibrant arena of political discussion and argu-mentation to the anemic, lifeless, contentless politics we have today.

In *Not Invited to the Party*, I examine the history and array of laws, regula-tions, subsidies, and programs that benefit the major parties and discourage even the possibility of a challenge to the Democrat–Republican duopoly. The book synthesizes political science, economics, and American history in a man-ner that is frankly generalist.

The Founders – supreme generalists – distrusted political parties. Nowhere in the Constitution are parties mentioned, much less given legal protection or privilege. As historian Richard Hofstadter has written, "the creators of the first American party system on both sides, Federalists and Republicans, were men who looked on parties as sores on the body politic."[2] And yet the sores festered, despite the warning of John Adams that "a division of the republic into two great parties … is to be dreaded as the greatest political evil."[3]

This book explores how the Democrats and Republicans, who by the end of the Civil War were established as the two major parties, guaranteed their continued dominance by means to which the Founders would have objected with the greatest vigor. For instance, I explore the seldom-visited history of how the two parties fortified their positions through such reforms as the Australian ballot, which transferred the design of the ballot from private political parties to the government. The widespread adoption in the 1890s of the Australian ballot gave the dominant parties an opening through which they could suppress challengers. This led, in short order, to ballot access laws, bans on cross-endorsements, and other artificial boosts to the Democratic and Republican parties.

Over the years, the Democrats and Republicans in the states became very skilled at devising a truly ingenious array of regulations and restrictions that keep competitors off the ballot and present voters with Tweedledum-Tweedledee choices.

In time, a range of methods developed to protect the duopoly: ballot access laws, restrictions on strategic activities often used by minor parties, and even direct subsidies to the parties. Most critically in modern times, the Federal Election Campaign Act (FECA) of 1971 (as amended in 1974 and 1976), which was sold to the public as an act of good government reformism that only the most hopelessly corrupt politico or deep-pocketed lobbyist could object to, actually reinforced the dominance of the two parties. By placing strict limits on campaign contributions, subsidizing the Democratic and Republic conventions, and filling the tills of major party candidates, FECA further protected the two-party system – despite that system's obvious lack of any constitutional mandate. The parties have become almost unassailable, thanks in large part to the subsidies and protections offered them by the government – subsidies and protections, it should be noted, that are written into law by Democratic and Republican legislators.

The Federal Election Campaign Act of 1974 was a frank and blatant subsidy of the major parties, whose campaigns and conventions are now federally subsidized upfront. Third parties, meanwhile, are eligible for subsidy – but only if they attracted more than 5% of the vote in the previous election. Insurgents get relative pittances, but they must obey the FECA limits on individual and Political Action Committee (PAC) contributions, leading three leading scholars of American party politics to write that "The FECA is a major party protection act."[4]

In the concluding chapter, I examine what might happen if the government withdrew from the field, neither subsidizing nor prohibiting a wide variety of political parties and activities. The political scientist Theodore Lowi has said: "One of the best-kept secrets in American politics is that the two-party system has long been brain dead – kept alive by support systems like state electoral laws that protect the established parties from rivals and by Federal subsidies and so-called campaign reform. The two-party system would collapse in an instant if the tubes were pulled and the IV's were cut."[5] Now wouldn't *that* be interesting?

The wave of anti-party alienation seems to crest every 20 years or so. It last swept over the shorelines of American politics in 1990–1992, culminating in the Perot campaign, and we seem to be on the verge of something similar. If nothing else, the Iraq War, supported as it has been by both parties, has revealed the essential sameness of the two wings of the duopoly.

Establishment pundits (such as David Broder of the *Washington Post*) explicitly support subsidization of the two-party system as a necessary condition of American republicanism – despite the admonitions of the Founders against the spirit of party and faction. Third parties are consistently demeaned and derided in the mainstream media – witness the mockery of such figures as Perot and former Minnesota Governor Jesse Ventura – while the eminences of the Republican and Democratic parties are treated with wholly undue respect. A rather odd figure like Al Gore, raised in a Washington hotel, a pompous recycler of environmentalist clichés, wins Nobel Prizes and Academy Awards; a much more substantial man of the regulation-happy left, consumer activist Ralph Nader, who, whatever his faults and misconceptions about capitalism, has actually thought hard about American democracy and put forth propositions worth debating – is reviled by the establishment that formerly revered him, and all because he had the temerity to challenge the duopoly.

The two-party system has become a sacred cow against which no one in respectable Washington breathes a word of criticism – but in the sticks, voters are sick and tired of the duopoly. Their restlessness, their unhappiness with the status quo, is not a sign of immaturity or unsophistication, as establishment theorists would have it. Instead, it is evidence that the philosophical assumptions of the American Founders and the spirit of the American revolutionaries of 1776 are not dead. They may be latent, they may be underground, they may not be visible on the six o'clock news, but they are not dead.

Political scientists and good government types are aware of the general contempt for the duopoly. They can see the evidence every election day, when so many Americans stay home, declining to exercise what they are incessantly told is the precious right of voting. The response from too many academics is the proposal of ridiculous gimmicks (lotteries, direct payments to voters) to boost turnout. How about presenting us with more choices instead?

Rather than relying on Rube Goldberg schemes, the simplest and most effective reform would be to abolish the many hidden and not-so-hidden subsidies that keep the two-party system alive. The two parties have rigged and benefitted from the system for so long that few observers even bother to complain, and few voters even notice. Observing – noticing – and informing the reader just how we got here and what we might do get out of this mess is the purpose of this book.

Notes

1. Michael F. Holt, *The Rise and Fall of the American Whig Party: Jacksonian Politics and the Onset of the Civil War* (New York: Oxford University Press, 1999), p. 951.
2. Richard Hofstadter, *The Idea of a Party System: The Rise of Legitimate Opposition in the United States, 1780–1840* (Berkeley: University of California Press, 1969), p. 2.
3. John Adams to Jonathan Jackson, October 2, 1780, *Works of John Adams, Second President of the United States, with a Life of the Author*, edited by Charles Francis Adams, Vol. 9 (Boston: Little, Brown, 1854), p. 511.
4. Steven J. Rosenstone, Roy L. Behr, and Edward H. Lazarus, *Third Parties in America: Citizen Response to Major Party Failure* (Princeton, NJ: Princeton University Press, 1984, second edition), p. 26.
5. Theodore J. Lowi, "Toward a More Responsible Three-Party System: Deregulating American Democracy," in *The State of the Parties: The Changing Role of Contemporary American Parties*, fourth edition, edited by John C. Green and Rick Farmer (Lanham, MD: Rowman & Littlefield, 2003), p. 354.

Chapter 2

The American Suspicion of Parties

The political scientist E.E. Schattschneider, whose seminal work *Party Government* (1942) set the terms of scholarly debate for decades, defined the beast: "A political party is an organized attempt to get control of the government."[1] There is nothing pretty or glossed-up in this definition. There is no high-minded rumble-bumble about American ideals or liberty or justice. Reduced to its essentials, the party is merely an instrument in the naked scramble for raw power.

For this reason, those earliest and most sagacious political scientists, the Founding Fathers, did not put their faith or trust in political parties. In fact, they spurned them as inimical to republican liberty. They agreed with the satirist Jonathan Swift, who remarked: "Party is the madness of many, for the gain of the few."[2]

On June 2, 1787, as the Constitutional Convention was just beginning its summer-long labor in Philadelphia, Benjamin Franklin, venerated delegate from Pennsylvania, rose to speak. Or, rather, to have someone speak for him, for as James Madison records, "being very sensible of the effect of age on his memory, he had been unwilling to trust to that for the observations [he wished to make] ... and had reduced them to writing, that he might with the permission of the Committee, read instead of speaking them." His Pennsylvania colleague, James Wilson, offered to the read the paper for Franklin, and the doctor accepted.

Franklin said very little over the course of the convention, so his rare remarks reflected his greatest concerns. And among these concerns was party, or, in the parlance of that time, faction. Men, Franklin told the convention, are powerfully motivated by "ambition and avarice; the love of power, and the love of money."

J.T. Bennett, *Not Invited to the Party*,
DOI 10.1007/978-1-4419-0366-2_2, © Springer Science+Business Media, LLC 2009

Unite these — as is the case in prominent positions in government — and the "struggles for them are the true sources of all those factions which are perpetually dividing the Nation, distracting its councils, hurrying sometimes into fruitless & mischievous wars, and often compelling a submission to dishonorable terms of peace."

The typical men who seek such positions "will not be the wise and moderate, the lovers of peace and good order, the men fittest for the trust. It will be the bold and the violent, the men of strong passions and indefatigable activity in their selfish pursuits. These will thrust themselves into your Government and be your rulers."

The instrumentality which they will use to achieve rulership will be party. Their unseemly arena will be "the bustle of cabal, the heat of contention, the infinite mutual abuse of parties, tearing to pieces the best of characters."[3]

Franklin's was not a lonely voice. The men who drew up the Constitution were not party hacks. They weren't even party loyalists, or party members. But they were acting in a long tradition of anti-party thought.

It's not that these early republicans valued unanimity of thought or uniformity of philosophy; no, they desired a rich, full, robust exchange of ideas and debate, from tavern halls to the halls of Congress. But why, they wondered, must this debate be channeled through parties, which are organizations dedicated not to truth or liberty or the common good but rather to seizing, holding, consolidating, and extending political power.

They had been anticipated by John Trenchard and Thomas Gordon, English libertarian authors of the influential *Cato's Letters*, which historian Clinton Rossiter called "the most popular, quotable, esteemed source of political ideas in the colonial period."[4] *Cato's Letters* had been read avidly in the colonies since 1720; they were incisive, trenchant, and a major carrier of the ideas of liberty throughout America.

On the subject of parties, Trenchard and Gordon were merciless: "How apt Parties are to err in the Choice of their Leaders: How little they regard Truth and Morality, when in Competition with Party. The terrible Consequences of all this; worthy Men decried and persecuted; worthless and wicked Men popular and preferred; Liberty oppressed and expiring."[5]

"'Tis worth no Man's Time to serve a Party, unless he can now and then get good Jobbs by it," as Cato quoted Lord Chancellor William Cowper. Party business was for abject hacks, squalid opportunists, men who had no principles other than a willingness to climb the slimy pole of self-advancement.

Of party leaders the authors of *Cato's Letters* said, "They all professed to have in View only the Publick Good; yet every one shewed he only meant his own;

and all the while the great as well as little Mob … contended as fiercely for their Leaders, as if their Happiness or Misery depended on the Face, the Cloaths, or Title of the Persons who robbed and betrayed them."[6]

The followers of these leaders were pathetic indeed: they were "the Tools and Instruments of Knaves and Pick-pockets."[7]

The American colonists read this. It accorded with their instincts, with the evidence of their own senses, with what they had heard from the Old World and even seen in the colonial governments. They were not eager to import this foul system into the New World.

Parties are "extralegal"[8]; that is, their existence was not prescribed (or proscribed) by the writers of the Constitution. The Framers in Philadelphia never mentioned Democrats, Republicans, Whigs, Federalists, Libertarians, Greens, or Anti-Masons. In the careful notes that Virginia delegate James Madison kept at the Philadelphia convention, there is no evidence that political parties were ever contemplated. The governmental structure that these men created was to be filled by regular elections, but nowhere in the Constitution or the convention in which it was composed is there so much as a jot or tittle that authorizes parties. The candidates who would run for the offices established in the Constitution were to be, presumably, men (and later women) of standing in their communities. They would present themselves for election, standing on character and general principles, and the voters would make their decision. The middle-man – the party – was not necessary. It certainly was not provided for in the founding document.

The *Federalist Papers*, those classic short essays in which James Madison, Alexander Hamilton, and John Jay explained the Constitution to their country-men, are filled with warnings of the danger of "faction," that is, the tendency of public men to divide into sects or groups that are based on self-aggrandizement and the pursuit of power rather than the general good of the community. (In the late eighteenth century, *faction* and *party* were synonyms.) These factions were probably inevitable, for as Madison wrote in *Federalist 10*, "The latent causes of faction are thus sown in the nature of man."[9] The Constitution of which Madison was the chief, though certainly not the sole, author sought to curb the baneful effects of faction through a system of widely distributed powers and checks and balances. It did not propose a role for parties in curbing faction; indeed, parties were viewed warily as a probable source of factiousness, for as Madison wrote, "the public good is disregarded in the conflicts of rival parties."[10]

Yet contrary to the expressed wishes of the drafters and defenders of the Constitution, parties arose. As the historian Richard Hofstadter wrote in *The*

Idea of a Party System (1969), the Founders "did not believe in political parties as such, scorned those that they were conscious of as historical models, had a keen terror of party spirit and its evil consequences, and yet, almost as soon as their national government was in operation, found it necessary to establish parties." This is the paradox of early American politics. As Hofstadter writes, "the creators of the first American party system on both sides, Federalists and Republicans, were men who looked upon parties as sores on the body politic."[11]

George Washington, for instance, despaired that independent-minded Americans were subordinating their own good sense to the demands of party loyalty. The historian of the Founding Era Gordon Wood writes of Washington: "In this new democratic era of party politics, he said, 'personal influence,' distinctions of character, no longer mattered. If the members of the Jeffersonian Republican party 'set up a broomstick' as candidate and called it 'a true son of Liberty' or 'a Democrat' or 'any other epithet that will suit their purpose,' it still would 'command their votes in toto!' But even worse, the same was true of the Federalists. Party spirit now ruled all, and people voted only for their party candidate."[12]

This complaint was picked up by Washington's successor in the executive branch, John Adams, who said that party "wrought an entire metamorphosis of the human character. It destroyed all sense and understanding, all equity and humanity, all memory and regard to truth, all virtue, honor, decorum, and veracity."[13] Like Madison, Adams was resigned to the existence of parties. They must be firmly controlled, however, and not permitted to plunder the treasury.

Adams was not at the Constitutional Convention and so cannot bear any responsibility (or credit) for the extraordinary accomplishment in Philadelphia, but the system itself is in some sense the father of the duopoly. Or rather the system as it developed. For a fairly large body of evidence suggests that the first cause of the bifurcation of American politics into two parties was the single-member district system. In fact, Hofstadter writes that "The American two-party system is the direct consequence of the American election system, or system of representation."[14]

The Constitution apportions representation to the states on the basis of population: as ratified, it provided that "the number of representatives shall not exceed one for every thirty thousand" in population. It does not, however, dictate how those representatives shall be chosen, leaving that up to the states in Article I, Section 4: "The times, places and manner of holding elections for senators and representatives, shall be prescribed in each state by the legislature thereof;

but the Congress may at any time by law make or alter such regulations, except as to the places of choosing Senators."

In the early republic, states and districts therein elected U.S. representatives by different methods. The myth of the single-member district election had yet to take hold. Some districts sent multiple representatives to Washington. "The first five federal apportionment laws (1792–1832) simply prescribed the specific numbers of representatives for each state,"[15] writes Stephen Calabrese of the Department of Government and International Affairs of the University of South Florida. Various electoral systems were used to select U.S. House members over the first half-century of the American Republic: the single-member district elections we know today; statewide elections of multimember delegations; multimember elections in discrete districts within a state; and a combination of the aforementioned. In the first Congress, every state selected at least part of its delegation in multimember districts. The method that eventually became the accepted – or rather mandated – standard helped to determine the number of serious political parties that would compete in American elections.

Multimember districts were part and parcel of the legacy of British democracy. Knights and burgesses of the British past were elected in pairs or triplets. This began as a pragmatic measure; as Maurice Klain of Western Reserve University wrote in his classic 1955 study of multimember legislative districts, "In the thirteenth century roads to London were lonely, rough, and bandit-ridden – two or three men would afford each other company and protection."

The American colonists were often represented by multimember delegations from a single district, as was the case with the Virginia House of Burgesses. "Multiple districts were the rule, single ones the exception," writes Klain.[16]

In 1842, according to Tory Mast of the Center for Voting and Democracy, "six states were electing representatives at-large and twenty-two states were electing representatives by single-member district." The other three had but one representative.

At-large elections were sharply restricted by the Apportionment Act of 1842, which set the size of the House at 233 members and required that congressmen be elected in single-member districts. The law directed that members of the House "be elected by districts composed of contiguous territory equal in numbers to the number of representatives to which said state may be entitled, no one district electing more than one representative."[17] This would seem to encroach on the Constitution's grant of such authority to the states, a point that President John Tyler made, but the measure passed anyway. Single-member districts would, in theory, produce representatives who embodied the best qualities of the district, whereas statewide at-large elections merely sent party-line slates of candidates to Washington, sometimes depriving whole sections of a state of effective representation.

The 1842 law ruled out anything other than single-member districts, but a number of states – Georgia, Mississippi, New Hampshire, Missouri – simply ignored it, going right on electing members at-large. The House, after some discussion, seated the members thus elected, and for the next 125 years a handful of states continued to elect persons to the U.S. House of Representatives by methods other than the single-district election.

At-large elections for Congress were finally and fully banned in 1967. The putative reason was protection of the rights of African Americans. This was part of the wave of civil rights legislation, because elections other than single-member were seen as one way that Southern states might dilute minority representation. The fact that only Hawaii and New Mexico, states with negligible black populations, held at-large elections in 1966 did not make an impression on the legislators. A more potent reason for the law's passage was suggested by Tory Mast: Many members were concerned that the courts might order at-large elections in states with intractable redistricting problems, and "such elections could have threatened the position of incumbents whose district seats were considered safe for re-election."[18]

Why does it matter to parties whether congressmen are elected in single districts or multimember districts?

American voters, at least in congressional races, now cast a single vote for a single candidate. The candidate who wins a plurality of votes within the district is that district's sole congressional representative. This "first past the post" system is simple to understand and easy to administer. But it has the stifling effect of funneling political energies into a two-party system. In a system in which several representatives are elected from each district, a rational voter may well cast her vote for a long-shot candidate or a candidate from a minor party, since that candidate may well come in third or fourth or in a position high enough to win a seat. In a single-member district, the voter is discouraged from "wasting" a vote on a long shot. If she wishes for her "vote to count" – and this is largely an illusion, given the current 635,000-member congressional districts – she will vote for one of the two top candidates: in practice, a Democrat or Republican.

The single-member congressional district, which is nowhere mandated in the Constitution but has been adopted by all of the states, is a bulwark of the two-party system. The link between method of election and number of parties is so strong, so incontrovertible, that political science has endowed it with a name: Duverger's Law, after the French sociologist Maurice Duverger, who contended that "the simple-majority single-ballot system favors the two-party system."[19] In other words, political systems in which representatives are those who place first in single-member districts are conducive to the development of two-party systems. A corollary – not a law, at least according to Duverger – is that systems in which multiple representatives are selected from single districts will tend toward multiparty systems. The most-discussed alternative to the single-member district is proportional representation, in which each district produces multiple winners. Not coincidentally, the Green Party, acting out of self-interest, has pushed proportional representation in recent years.

Multimember districts survive and thrive at the state and municipal level and in school boards, union locals, condominium associations, and such. The majority of city council members in America are still elected in this way. Multimember districts are "natural and spontaneous,"[20] writes Josep M. Colomer, and ensure that all voices, not only those of the dominant majority, are heard. They were the rule in the state legislatures for much of our history. The original 13 states "established popular assemblies wholly or predominantly on a multi-member basis."[21] As late as 1954, 12% of the state senate seats and 45% of the state house seats in the 48 states were filled in multimember districts. Most of these districts sent two or three members to the state legislature, though one Detroit district was represented by a boatload of 21 members. Only 12 states had no multimember districts.[22] In 2000, more than one-quarter of all state legislators were still elected in multimember districts.

As with most laws, there are conspicuous exceptions to Duverger's: India and Canada most prominently. Strong regional parties, à la the Parti Québécois, operate outside the French sociologist's law. The American political scientist William H. Riker, in assessing Duverger's Law, considered the brief lives of most American third parties. Why, he asked, do they begin with such hope and die such quick deaths?

"I believe the answer is that donors and leaders disappear," wrote Riker. "A donor buys further influence and access, and many donors are willing to buy from any party that has a chance to win. (In the United States, at least, many donors give to *both* parties.) But as rational purchasers they are not likely to donate to a party with a tiny chance of winning, and in a plurality system, most third parties have only that chance, because plurality rules give large parties a large relative advantage over small parties. ... Similarly a potential leader buys a career, and as a rational purchaser he has no interest in a party that may lose throughout his lifetime. So the answer to the question of failure is that third parties are rejected in the rational calculus of expected utility especially by leaders, though also in the calculus by many simple voters."[23] (Note, however, that not all political scientists accept Duverger's Law. Josep M. Colomer, for instance, is among those who assert that Duverger gets this flip-flopped, and that "it is the parties that choose electoral systems and manipulate the rules of elections."[24] More on that later.)

In the American context, the electoral college has also encouraged the development of a two-party system. The electoral college's winner-take-all practice, under which the victor in a state receives all of its electoral votes, is not constitutionally mandated, but only Maine and Nebraska currently allocate their electors by district.

The electoral college has penalized the likes of Ross Perot (19% of the popular vote in 1992 but no electoral votes), though it "does favor regionally based third-party candidates,"[25] for instance Strom Thurmond in 1948, who won 39 electoral votes, or 7.3% of the total, with just 2.4% of the popular vote nationally – but 22.4% in the South. On the other hand, Henry Wallace, the leftist Progressive Party candidate of that year, won almost as many votes as Thurmond – 2.38% of the national total – but did not come close to winning a single electoral vote.

In the 48 states other than Maine and Nebraska, the winner-take-all system makes voting for a third-party presidential candidate an act of conscience rather than practicality.

Or does it? In fact, the likelihood that an individual vote will determine the outcome of a state's presidential vote is as close to nil as can be. It's more likely that you the reader will begin dating Angelina Jolie or George Clooney than that your vote will provide the winning margin for a candidate in the next presidential election. So in a way, voting one's conscience – which at least provides a measure of inner satisfaction – is a more rational choice than voting for the lesser of two evils.

The primary system, which "has channeled dissent into the two major parties,"[26] according to political scientists John F. Bibby and L. Sandy Maisel, has also given us the duopoly. Leftists, libertarians, and right-to-lifers can work within the system in the belief (or under the illusion) that they can be heard within the two parties. Dissenters are absorbed; their dissent is tamped down, tamed, as once their protest candidate loses they are expected to meekly support the nominee of their party. This doesn't always happen: witness Senator Eugene McCarthy, whose insurgent antiwar candidacy in the Democratic primaries of 1968 drove President Lyndon B. Johnson from the race. When LBJ's slavishly loyal vice president Hubert Humphrey finagled the nomination in Chicago and refused to break with the Johnsonian Vietnam War, McCarthy sat the race out, issuing only a halfhearted endorsement. McCarthy would break finally and fully with the Democrats in 1976, in an independent candidacy that won few votes but succeeded in overturning restrictive ballot access laws and offering a philo-sophical justification for staying outside the party system. But McCarthy was a rarity. Most in-party "rebels" are pretty well housebroken.

Going back to the early republic, a two-party system had begun to develop in the United States in the 1790s, as blocs formed around the towering figures of Thomas Jefferson and Alexander Hamilton. James Madison, author of the cel-ebrated *Federalist 10* essay and keen analyst of the ills of party, which he called *faction*, went on to help Jefferson found the Democratic-Republican Party. Inconsistent? Yes. But times change.

And even though parties were coming into being, writes the political scien-tist Austin Ranney, in the early years of the republic, "most right-thinking people regarded political parties and party conflict as evil in intent and disas-trous in effect — epidemic diseases of the body politic to be quarantined and stamped out wherever possible."[27] They believed that "political parties are inherently and irremediably destructive of popular government."[28] They are not amenable to reform or melioration. But they were here. They were grow-ing. They were also taking on various forms, different names, particular com-plexions. By the 1820s, Andrew Jackson was the titular head of the "Democratic Republicans" against John Quincy Adams and Henry Clay and their "National Republicans": the parties were, in many ways, descendants of Jeffersonian Republicans and Hamiltonian Federalists, respectively.

The Anti-Masonic Party held the first national political nominating conven-tion in American history in Philadelphia in September 1831. (Prior to this, the parties' congressional caucuses chose the candidate for president.) The National Republicans, following the lead of the Anti-Masonic Party, held a convention in Baltimore in December 1831 which nominated Henry Clay. Jackson's "Democratic Republicans" followed suit in Baltimore in May 1832. Now, it should be noted, in light of discussion later in this book, that the National Republicans, the Democratic Republicans, and the Anti-Masons paid for their own conventions. For instance, the National Republicans appointed a committee to help defray the expenses of the delegates. Although the National Republicans had a more expansive view of the role of government than did Jackson's Democratic Republicans, the National Republicans emphatically did *not* ask the federal government to pay for their Baltimore shindig.

Over the first three-quarters of the nineteenth century, the parties were sepa-rated by something more than petty disputes over which loyalists would get which government sinecures. While in the early party system the contending factions actually stood for principles, for philosophies, as expressed by substantial men such as Jefferson and Hamilton, by the late nineteenth century the English observer Lord Bryce told readers of his magisterial *The American Commonwealth* (1888) that "Neither party has anything definite to say on these issues; neither party has any principles, any distinctive tenets. Both have traditions. Both claim to have tendencies. Both have certainly war cries, organizations, interests enlisted in their support. But those interests are in the main the interests of getting or keeping the patronage of the government. Tenets and policies, points of political doctrine and points of political practice, have all but vanished. They have not been thrown away but have been stripped away by Time and the progress of events, fulfilling some prophecies, blotting out others. All has been lost, except office or the hope of it."[29]

Bryce was merciless. The parties were mental and philosophical corpses, and he did not avert his eyes from the gruesome remains. His forensic examination still packs a punch: "When life leaves an organic body it becomes useless, fetid, pestiferous: it is fit to be cast out or buried from sight. What life is to an organism, principles are to a party. When they which are its soul have vanished, its body ought to dissolve, and the elements that formed it be regrouped in some new organism. ... But a party does not always thus die. It may hold together long after its moral life is extinct."[30]

This, of course, is the situation of the Democratic and Republican parties of the early twenty-first century. But much as we like to think of the past as a golden age, a century ago Lord Bryce was calling the parties "two bottles, each having a label denoting the kind of liquor it contains, but each being empty."[31]

Yet there were other bottles on the shelf. Outside the South, a party other than the Democrats or Republicans received at least 20% in an election between 1874 and 1892 in a majority of states.[32] The Democrats and Republicans might dominate, but they had not yet cemented their duopoly through manipulation of election laws and the erection of great subsides. Those acts were still to come.

But the push to regulate the parties, to bring them under great government control — which in turn enabled the parties to bring the government under control — was on. American political parties began as wholly private organizations, unregulated but also unsubsidized. Not until the post-Civil War era did state governments regulate the doings of parties — at first, passing anti-bribery laws or requiring advance notice of caucuses and such. The Progressive Era fully brought the parties under the thumb of the states — or was it the other way around? State governments now regulated party meetings, state committees, and of course the nominating process, especially the direct primary, by which voters selected the party's nominee directly, at the ballot box, rather than entrusting that decision to a caucus or convention or smoke-filled room crammed with insiders. The direct primary seems to have been born in 1842 in Crawford County, Pennsylvania, though it didn't become widespread until the early years of the twentieth century, when Populists and Progressives sought to break down the power of the political bosses. "By 1917, forty-four of the forty-eight states had primary laws of some kind," writes Austin Ranney. The hope was that it "would end boss rule once and for all."[33] But that hope, oft expressed, failed to take into account the possibility that the new boss might be just as bad as the old boss.

The critique of parties took on an extra bite as the interlocking directorate of corporations and government strengthened during the 1870s and 1880s. During the "Great Barbecue," that post-Civil War era marked by economic boom but also the flourishing of corrupt urban political machines, some reformers again pinpointed party as the cause of the rot. Albert Stickney opined that "party, instead of being a machinery necessary to the existence of free government, is its most dangerous foe."[34] He and others, dubbed "abolitionists" by political scientist Austin Ranney, sought ways to purge politics of partisanship. They were naïve, perhaps, and proposed measures of dubious wisdom (outlawing parties, adopting a system of direct rather than representative democracy), but they understood that political parties are not benign clubs for the civic-minded but power-seeking organizations that must be watched with the utmost vigilance lest they empty the treasury to fill the pockets of their friends and allied interest groups.

William Graham Sumner, the great 1890s individualist sociologist and defender of "The Forgotten Man" – that is, the middle-class man who pays his bills and supports the local civic life and for his trouble is shaken down by governments eager for revenue – denied that the parties are benign forces: "I cannot trust a party; I can trust a man. I cannot hold a party responsible; I can hold a man responsible. I cannot get an expression of opinion which is single and simple from a party; I can get that only from a man. A party cannot have character, or conscience, or reputation; it cannot repent, nor endure punishment or disgrace."[35]

The party can only seek power. In this pursuit it is not bound by the usual moral scruples that shape human behavior. If, in order to achieve power, it needs to cheat, it will cheat. If it needs to hamper or cripple the opposition, it will do so without a second thought. If it needs to seize taxpayer money from the public treasury in order to further its goals, it will do so.

The Russian-born political scientist M.I. Ostrogorski, who wrote widely on American parties in the early twentieth century, believed that they drained the taproot of American democracy. "Local self-government," he wrote, "which in Anglo-Saxon communities had, from time immemorial so to speak, set in motion the whole political machinery, has subsided" due to the control of political life by the parties. The Democrats and Republicans in combination have caused "a harmful centralization, which by stifling self-regulated local life and by enfeebling men's initiative and volition, dries up the sap of a political community and preys upon the very roots of its existence."[36]

The party values conformity. It places a premium on docile obedience. Its scourges mavericks; it despises independents. The worst rise within a party; the best are thwarted – or, more often, don't even try.

Ostrogorski charged that "the life of the party is, consequently, only one long school of servile submission. All the lessons the citizen receives in it are lessons in cowardice."[37] Republican virtue, democratic initiative: these traits were hard, if not impossible, to cultivate in a political system dominated by parties. The Founders realized this, though they were unable to prevent the development of factions, and thus parties.

Ostrogorski, convinced that parties mar the character of those who are its instruments and, in time, kill the very possibility of democratic self-government, proposed an alternative: nonpartisan elections. Without the necessity of enlisting under a party banner, people would, Ostrogorski believed, coalesce with the like-minded on issues of the day, but these coalitions would be ad hoc, finite, and based on philosophy, not the pursuit of power. Party operatives, petty functionaries, selling out one's principles to win an endorsement – these would belong to the corrupt past.

Was this naïve? Did Ostrogorski understimate what James Madison, among others, held to be the natural propensity of men to divide into factions? Or was it a way out, an alternative to a political world run by bosses, controlled by two parties, and eventually, some decades later, effectively closed to dissenters who chose not to belong to those two parties?

Ostrogorski's vision never materialized at the national level. What chance did it have in a world of Mark Hanna, James Farley, and other strategists, fixers, and backroom bosses? But it made serious headway in the cities and towns of the fruited plain.

Nonpartisan elections are still held at the local level in many states, usually for offices such as a district board of education. Political scientists Brian F. Schaffner, Matthew Streb, and Gerald Wright estimate that perhaps three-fourths of all elections to municipal office are nonpartisan.[38] There is an exception to the general run of nonpartisan races for school board and sewer commissioner, however, and a significant one it is, out on the prairies. The state of Nebraska, by a 1934 amendment to the state constitution, became the only member of the union to have a legislature that is (1) unicameral and (2) nonpartisan. The measure, which set Nebraska very much apart from her 47 sister states, was approved in a statewide citizen initiative by a vote of 286,086 to 193,152.[39]

Other states – Alabama, Arizona, California, Colorado, Kansas, Minnesota, New York, Ohio, Oklahoma, Oregon, South Dakota, Tennessee, and Washington – manifested varying degrees of interest in a one-house legislature during the first three decades of the twentieth century, but only in Nebraska did the idea gain legs.

U.S. Senator George Norris, the Nebraska progressive whom even his political opponents conceded to be a man of great integrity, was the most influential sponsor of the amendment. He argued for unicameralism, or a one-house legislature, on two grounds: (1) economy, since one house is cheaper than two; and (2) honesty in government, since the conference committee, that oft-mysterious conclave wherein leaders of the two houses meet to iron out differences between the bills they have passed, had become a corrupt bazaar at which favors and subsidies were granted.

Unicameralism delivered, at least on these two grounds. Administrative costs were reduced. The legislative jungle was cleared: the number of committees, for instance, fell from 61 to 18. And with but one house, the conference committee was eliminated. Opponents complained that the lack of a second house deprived Nebraskans of the cool consideration and thoughtful deliberation that would-be laws deserved. In practice, unicameralism has been a qualified success. It introduced certain efficiencies into the process – though whether or not efficiency is an undiluted virtue in government is a thorny question – but it has not chased the lobbyists or the pork barrel out of the Cornhusker State, for as long as there is loot to be divided, there will be flies buzzing around the pile. The one-house legislature has faded in the reformist imagination. In 1936, the University of Nebraska political scientist John P. Senning predicted that "other states seem likely to follow [Nebraska's] example and discard their bicameral lawmaking bodies," but that prophecy has all the force and accuracy of Marx's prediction that under communism, the state would wither away.[40]

Our interest in this particular case, however, is not in the unicameral nature of Nebraska's legislature but in its less-studied counterpart reform: nonpartisanship. The 1934 amendment to the Nebraska State Constitution that established the one-house legislature also stipulated that "Each member shall be nominated and elected in a nonpartisan manner and without any indication on the ballot that he is affiliated with or endorsed by any political party or organization."[41]

The foremost justification for this fairly radical measure was, as the engaged political scientist Senning wrote, "In election on a nonpartisan ticket the machine control of the majority party is eliminated and subjects of legislation can be decided on their merits."[42] Politicians, relieved of the burden of party expectations, are liberated to act as statesman — or at least that's the hope, perhaps naïve, of nonpartisan-election advocates. Voters, meanwhile, are asked to judge candidates on their merits. Deprived of the "cue" of party identification, they must assess the men and women who ask for their votes on other criteria — including, ideally, merit.

Candidates for the "unicam" do not run as representatives of a political party. They are listed on the ballot with no identifier other than their name. A primary winnows the field to the top two candidates, who then face off in the general election. Not that parties have been banished from the Great Plains: most — but not all — state senators (as unicam members are called) are affiliated with a party. But they do not organize by party within the unicam, and in fact Nebraska seemingly has more of a place for independents than does any other legislature. (In 2008, three of the unicam's 49 members were independents; the rest professed membership in the Democratic or Republican parties.)

Senator Norris, father of the nonpartisan unicam, was, for most of his lengthy political career, a Republican, but he followed his own path and was about as far from a party-liner as one can find. He took on a Democratic President (Woodrow Wilson) in opposing U.S. entry into the First World War and then became one of the staunchest Senate supporters of the next Democratic president's New Deal. Parties, he had found, distorted the relationship between a representative and his constituency. They introduced a third and foreign element into this relationship: the national political party. Instead of representing his district or state, bringing its particular wisdom and point of view into the debate over public questions, a partisan legislator also had to answer to his party: a machine, usually based far away, that for reasons having nothing to do with local concerns wanted a legislator to act in certain ways. That these ways might often be quite contrary to the true interests of the district, Norris had seen all too well: in 1917, he had watched as Senate Democrats who had no appetite for involvement in a foreign war voted against the wishes of the folks back home and in allegiance to the Democratic President and his national party.

Norris, though, was not your typical Republican. The nonpartisan nature of Nebraska's unicam has rankled regular party officials for decades now. The Republicans formally came out for repeal of nonpartisanship in 1954. Conceding that it was a "noble experiment," the GOP platform of 1974 – the Watergate year, no less – called for a return to a partisan legislature, where "effective government and responsible leadership" could flourish.

Nebraska Democrats, too, chafed under the nonpartisan bit. Their state platforms began calling for a return to party politics in the unicam in 1956. Typically, the 1964 platform urged the reappearance of Rs and Ds as way of "establish[ing] greater political responsiblity."[43] Note well that 1964 was also the year in which Democratic President Lyndon B. Johnson had obtained the blank check to escalate the war in Vietnam via the Gulf of Tonkin Resolution, which was based on an alleged attack on U.S. destroyers that even the National Security Agency later admitted did not occur. A Democratic president was dishonestly leading his country into a disastrous war, and the pressures of party loyalty led even the professed doves in his party to swallow their doubts and give LBJ his resolution, which he was fond of waving, symbolically, at congressmen who later expressed even mild doubts about the course of the Vietnam War. The vote in the House was 416–0; in the Senate it was 88–2, with only Oregon's Wayne Morse and Ernest Gruening of Alaska dissenting. How many more Democrats might have voted "no" if partisan obligations were not weighing on them? We'll never know. But the claim of Nebraska Democrats in 1964 that party-dominated legislatures lead to "greater political responsibility" was shown up as the sort of inanity that not even the most gullible Democratic stamp-licker could swallow.

Frequent attempts to dislodge nonpartisanship from the constitution have been unsuccessful. (They were successful in Minnesota, however, which from 1913 to 1973 had nonpartisan elections to its two-house legislature.) Nebraskans seem satisfied to go to the polls and not be guided in their decisions by the attachment of an *R* or *D* to a candidate's name. Politicians, however, have been known to grumble. "Turnover is quite high" in the unicam, as one political scientist has written.[44] It's hard to launch a spectacular national career from a nonpartisan house: the institutional infrastructure by which one wheels and deals and does favors and obeys party instructions is harder to find in Nebraska. A hack can't stake his claim to advancement by voting the party line and carrying water for the party when there is no party! As political scientist Carol A. Cassel writes, "nonpartisan elections are viewed negatively [by many political scientists] because it is believed they do not provide a channel for recruitment to higher partisan office."[45]

Critics point to another alleged flaw of the nonpartisan system: absent parties, the leadership is weak and power is decentralized. This is not a flaw from the point of view of those who distrust the adjective "strong" when applied to government. Indeed, it is a major selling point. Similarly, liberals in the mid-twentieth century often turned against nonpartisan elections because they assumed – though the evidence is mixed – that nonpartisan elected officials were less likely to tax and spend to please interest groups. One undeniable effect of nonpartisan municipal elections is a lowering in turnout, since urban party machines, or what passes for urban machines these days, do not have an incentive to get supporters to the polls. Using data from Champaign-Urbana, Illinois; Asheville, North Carolina; and the adjacent states of Nebraska and Kansas, Schaffner, Streb, and Wright found that "nonpartisanship depresses turnout," though they point out that the early reformers, who were skeptical of unreflective party-line voters, might not be dismayed by that fact.[46]

In the end, though, the "differences between partisan and nonpartisan systems appear to be less than both the proponents and critics of nonpartisanship argue."[47] Ostrogorski's arguments against partisanship still pack a punch, but his remedy – nonpartisan elections – appears to have a limited rejuvenescent effect on the democratic or republican spirit of those who no longer have to vote Democratic or Republican.

In national elections and in the 49 states other than Nebraska, our choices are limited to two, and for years have been limited to two, excepting the occasional flare-up around a charismatic or controversial political maverick who has something different to offer – Teddy Roosevelt in 1912, Bob LaFollette in 1924, George Wallace in 1968, Ross Perot in 1992. Other democracies, such as Canada and Great Britain, have long been dominated by two major parties, but their systems are also enlivened by vigorous third parties that contest and sometimes even win regional elections (the Parti Québécois in Canada, the Scottish National Party in Great Britain, and even such non-regional parties as Reform in the Canada of the 1990s and the Liberals earlier in twentieth-century Britain). It is a cruel paradox that the United States of America, home of the most inspiring revolution ever won against distant power and tyranny, today offers its citizens fewer electoral choices than almost any other nation in the industrial world. The two-party duopoly has replaced a once-lively political marketplace in which radicals and conservatives, constitutionalists and collectivists, utopians and hard-headed realists, formerly competed for attention and votes.

In their study of third parties, Steven J. Rosenstone, Roy L. Behr, and Edward H. Lazarus write, "Children grow up learning about the president, the Congress, and the Democrats and Republicans. Most have never even heard about

Libertymen, Greenbacks, or Prohibitionists. Voters are socialized into a two-party norm that is constantly reinforced by the common portrayal of elections as contests between Democrats and Republicans."[48]

Voting third party seems vaguely subversive to many, raised as they have been on the pabulum and gruel of Republicans and Democrats. It is done furtively, silently, behind closed voting-booth curtains. So effectively have Americans been bred into the assumptions of two-party dominance that the whole thing has about it the air of disloyalty. Un-Americanness. And besides – you're throwing away your vote! (The old "throwing away your vote" syndrome persists even though in fact the chances of an individual's vote determining the outcome of his state's presidential race is… well, it has never happened in the history of the republic, not even in Florida in 2000. And is it really throwing away your vote to cast a ballot for, say, the Liberty Party, which faced the slavery issue foursquare in 1840 while Whigs and Democrats hid?)

Although third parties are sometimes credited, grudgingly, as "safety valves"[49] for discontent, the Republicans are the only minor party ever to displace a major party (in their case, the Whigs), and it happened over 150 years ago. Since 1854, Democrats and Republicans have been the two dominant parties, to the exclusion – often coerced – of others. "A host of barriers, disadvantages, and strategies block the path of would-be third-party supporters," write Rosenstone, Behr, and Lazarus. "So formidable are these hurdles that third-party voting occurs only under the most extreme conditions." Indeed, the authors write that "it is an extraordinary act that requires the voter to reject explicitly the major parties."[50]

"Minor" parties were well represented in many of the early Congresses. The Anti-Masonic Party dominated Upstate New York and Vermont in the early 1830s before folding into the Whig Party. Anti-Masons even served as governors of Vermont and Pennsylvania. The American Party, or the Know Nothings, as they came to be derisively called for their penchant for secrecy, rode an anti-immigrant platform to a showing of 43 members of the 34th Congress, including Speaker of the House Nathaniel Banks, before being effectively absorbed by the new Republican Party. The Know Nothings won the state house and both houses of the Massachusetts state legislature in 1854 – thanks to fear of the Irish. The People's Party, or Populists, of the late nineteenth century, sent senators and representatives to Washington and cross-endorsed the Democrat William Jennings Bryan in 1896.

The Populists were "the last important minor party to sustain a working national, state, and local organization over the course of several elections,"[51] a distinction that the present-day Libertarians and Greens would like to someday claim but cannot as yet. As a rule, the third parties of the twentieth century were personality-based: Teddy Roosevelt's Progressive, or Bull Moose, Party; Fighting Bob LaFollette's Progressives; Henry Wallace's Progressives and George Wallace's American Independent Party; John Anderson's National Unity Party; Ross Perot's Reform Party – though we make a mistake if we insist on too sharp a delineation between personality-based and ideology-based parties, for candidates such as Perot, Wallace, Ralph Nader, Pat Buchanan, and others often stand for a set of principles or ideas that are far better defined than the "principles" allegedly undergirding the Democrats and Republicans.

Roosevelt and Perot were the best financed of the lot: TR by Wall Street, and Perot by himself. Money can buy exposure – but it can't always buy the media. As a rule, third-party candidates get bad press. They are sometimes treated kindly or as curiosities at first (Anderson 1980, Perot 1992), but by campaign's end they are slagged, ridiculed, and demonized (especially Wallace in 1968). They are usually barred from debates, though Anderson did share a stage (poorly, it must be said) with Reagan in 1980 and Perot enlivened the three presidential debates of 1992.

Political parties may be lionized by a segment of the political science community but among ordinary folk – those who have to live with the mess the parties create – they are widely regarded as a source of the problem, not the solution. This was driven home with a ramrod velocity in 2004 by the extensive *Transparency International Global Corruption Barometer 2004*, a massive public-opinion survey that asked more than 50,000 people in 64 countries about their experience and perception of corruption in all facets of life – public, private, business, the judiciary, the media, the military, religious institutions, the police, the tax collectors, the medical system, and others. It was an extraordinary undertaking. And for those who have watched too much TV over the years and think that sleazy businessmen or perverted priests are the most insidious evils stalking the world, it was an eye-opener.

In its report detailing its global survey, Transparency International put forth as its first, and central, finding, that: "*Parties and political corruption are the main problem. The Global Corruption Barometer 2004 paints a picture of people around the world gravely concerned about corruption in political life. The general public believe that political parties, followed by parliament/legislature, are the institution most affected by corruption in their country.*"

This result was hardly localized to the most famed cesspools of political thievery. "In 36 out of 62 countries surveyed," the authors write, "political parties were rated by the general public as the institution most affected by corruption, followed by parliament/legislature (second) and the police and the legal system/judiciary (tied for third)." Respondents were asked to rate institutions on a corruption scale, with 1 being "not at all corrupt" and 5 being "extremely corrupt." *Political parties topped all other sectors* with an average corruption score of 4.0. Parliament/legislature was second at 3.7. In last place – that is, the sector of community life that is viewed around the world as the least corrupt – was "religious bodies" with an average score of 2.7.[52]

Remember, these political parties are the very bodies that in our own country have been praised by political scientists as the indispensable glue that holds the system together. They have been given subsidies and favors and even the power to effectively ban competition. And they are, according to this comprehensive survey of world opinion, "clearly perceived by the public at large to be the institution or sector most affected by corruption."[53]

And it's not like the United States is an exception to this pattern. Among the 36 countries in which political parties are regarded as the single most corrupt institution or sector in the nation is the United States, where parties score a 3.6 on the corruption scale. (The American media come in second at 3.5.)

The American political parties have company in the corruption pool: other nations wherein parties were scored the most corrupt include Argentina, Austria, Bolivia, Bosnia and Herzegovina, Brazil, Canada, Costa Rica, Czech Republic, Denmark, Ecuador (which, at 4.9, takes first place with an almost perfect storm of corruption), Estonia, Finland, France, Germany, Guatemala, Iceland, India, Indonesia, Ireland, Israel, Italy, Japan, Latvia, Luxembourg, Mexico, Peru, Poland, Portugal, Romania, South Africa, Spain, Switzerland, Ukraine, United Kingdom, and Uruguay.

How did the parties fall to so low an estimation? Why do no-money-down used-car hawkers look down on the American political parties as pits of corruption beneath their contempt? Perhaps it has something to do with the way that two parties – the Democrats and Republicans – have banned competition when they were able, and enriched themselves with audacious reaches deep into the public purse. We now turn our attention to the ways in which the duopoly has girded itself against any challenge.

Notes

1. E.E. Schattschneider, *Party Government* (New York: Holt, Rinehart and Winston, 1942), p. ix.
2. Quoted in Hofstadter, *The Idea of a Party System*, p. 2.

3. Max Farrand, editor, *The Records of the Federal Convention of 1787*, Vol. I (New Haven: Yale University Press, 1911), p. 82.

4. Quoted in Leonard W. Levy and Alfred Young, Foreword, *The English Libertarian Heritage: From the Writings of John Trenchard and Thomas Gordon* in *The Independent Whig and Cato's Letters*, edited by David L. Jacobson (Indianapolis: Bobbs-Merrill, 1965), p. viii.

5. *The English Libertarian Heritage*, p. xliv.

6. Ibid., p. 45.

7. Ibid., p. 47.

8. Schattschneider, *Party Government*, p. 11.

9. James Madison, Alexander Hamilton, and John Jay, *The Federalist Papers*, Federalist 10 (New York: New American, 1961 [1788]), p. 79.

10. Ibid., p. 77.

11. Hofstadter, *The Idea of a Party System*, pp. viii, 2.

12. Gordon S. Wood, *Revolutionary Characters: What Made the Founders Different* (New York: Penguin, 2006), p. 62.

13. Charles Francis Adams, *The Works of John Adams, Second President of the United States, with a Life of the Author*, Vol. I (Boston: Little, Brown, 1856), p. 80.

14. Hofstadter, *The Idea of a Party System*, p. 69.

15. Stephen Calabrese, "Multimember District Congressional Elections," *Legislative Studies Quarterly* (Vol. 25, No. 4, November 2000), p. 611.

16. Maurice Klain, "A New Look at the Constituencies: The Need for a Recount and a Reappraisal," *American Political Science Review* (Vol. 49, No. 4, December 1955), p. 1111–1112.

17. Tory Mast, "History of Single Member Districts for Congress," http://www.fairvote.org/reports/1995/chp2/mast.html.

18. Ibid.

19. William H. Riker, "The Two-party System and Duverger's Law: An Essay on the History of Political Science," *American Political Science Review* (Vol. 76, No. 4, December 1982), p. 754.

20. Josep M. Colomer, "On the Origins of Electoral Systems and Political Parties: The Role of Elections in Multi-Member Districts," *Electoral Studies* (Vol. 20, 2006), p. 2.

21. Maurice Klain, "A New Look at the Constituencies," *American Political Science Review*, p. 1113.

22. Ibid., p. 1107–1108.

23. William H. Riker, "The Two-party System and Duverger's Law," p. 765.

24. Colomer, "On the Origins of Electoral Systems and Political Parties," p. 1.

25. Rosenstone, Behr, and Lazarus, *Third Parties in America*, p. 17.

26. John F. Bibby and L. Sandy Maisel, *Two Parties. Or More? The American Party System* (Cambridge, MA: Westview, 2003), p. 62.

27. Austin Ranney, *Curing the Mischiefs of Faction: Party Reform in America* (Berkeley: University of California Press, 1975), p. 30.

28. Ibid., p. 33.

29. James Bryce, *The American Commonwealth*, Vol. I (New York: Putnam's, 1959 [1888]), p. 151.

30. Ibid., p. 153.

31. James Bryce, *The American Commonwealth*, Vol. 2, new edition (New York: Macmillan, 1914), p. 29.

32. Peter H. Argersinger, "'A Place on the Ballot': Fusion Politics and Antifusion Laws," *American Historical Review* (Vol. 85, No. 2, April 1980), p. 289.

33. Ranney, *Curing the Mischiefs of Faction*, pp. 122–123, 124.

34. Quoted in ibid., p. 36.

35. Quoted in Austin Ranney, *The Doctrine of Responsible Party Government: Its Origins and Present State* (Urbana: University of Illinois Press, 1962), p. 14.

36. Quoted in ibid., p. 121.

37. Quoted in ibid., p. 124.

38. Brian Schaffner, Matthew Streb, and Gerald Wright, "Teams without Uniforms: The Nonpartisan Ballot in State and Local Elections," *Political Research Quarterly* (Vol. 54, No. 1, March 2001), p. 7.

39. See Adam C. Breckenridge, "The Origin and Development of the Nonpartisan Legislature," pp. 11–27, in *Nonpartisanship in the Legislative Process: Essays on the Nebraska Legislature*, edited by John C. Comer and James B. Johnson (Washington, DC: University Press of America, 1978).

40. John P. Senning, *The One-House Legislature* (New York: McGraw-Hill, 1937), p. vii.

41. Ibid., pp. 108–109.

42. Ibid., p. 80.

43. Breckenridge, "The Origin and Development of the Nonpartisan Legislature," p. 20.

44. John C. Comer, "The Nebraska Legislature: An Evaluation," in *Nonpartisanship in the Legislative Process*, p. 123.

45. Carol A. Cassel, "The Nonpartisan Ballot in the United States," *Electoral Laws and Their Political Consequences*, edited by Bernard Grofman and Arend Lijphart (New York: Agathon, 1986), p. 234.

46. Schaffner, Streb, and Wright, "Teams Without Uniforms," p. 7.

47. Carol A. Cassel, "The Nonpartisan Ballot in the United States," p. 239.

48. Rosenstone, Behr, and Lazarus, *Third Parties in America*, p. 3.

49. Ibid., p. 9.

50. Ibid., p. 15.

51. Ibid., p. 75.

52. Transparency International, "Report on the Transparency International Global Corruption Barometer 2004," (Berlin: Transparency International, December 9, 2004), p. 3.

53. Ibid., p. 11.

Chapter 3

No Competition Allowed or He Who Controls the Ballot Controls the Election

James Madison, in *Federalist* 10, explained that "Liberty is to faction what air is to fire, an aliment without which it instantly expires."[1] Parties depend on liberty to exist. Free, robust debate is healthy in a republic. But what happens when two parties assert their right to exist and suppress competitors?

We are living with the consequences of such suppression. When voters are forced to choose between lookalike and soundalike candidates who are distinguished only by the R on one's lapel and the D on the other's, something is horribly amiss.

Lacking choices, many Americans decide not to vote. In recent years, the typical presidential election has attracted to the polls at best half the eligible voters. In off-year elections, when the 435 members of the Peoples' House are up for selection, the figure is closer to 40%.

"Voter turnout has not exceeded two-thirds of the eligible electorate since 1900," writes Mark Lawrence Kornbluh in *Why America Stopped Voting: The Decline of Participatory Democracy and the Emergence of Modern American Politics* (2000). Tens of millions of otherwise engaged and intelligent Americans do not bother to vote. Yet as Kornbluh notes, voter turnout for presidential races in the nineteenth century in the North often exceeded 80% – and this in an age when getting to the polls was not an easy and warm-and-dry car ride away.[2] Turnout remained extraordinarily high – or healthy, to use a better word – into the 1890s. With the coming of the new century it dropped: to 60% in the teens and, in more recent years, to the pathetic 50% (or even lower) level.

There are many reasons for this dispiriting decline. Elections mattered more with a smaller electorate. Voters were less alienated from the system.

J.T. Bennett, *Not Invited to the Party*, DOI 10.1007/978-1-4419-0366-2_3,
© Springer Science+Business Media, LLC 2009

They had yet to have been made to feel insignificant by a massive bureaucracy and remote central government. The parties offered a sharper ideological choice. William Jennings Bryan vs. William McKinley is a much clearer choice than, say, Bill Clinton vs. Bob Dole.

But this is not the whole story. The election of 1888 featured an incredibly high turnout, and while Democrat Grover Cleveland and Republican Benjamin Harrison had many fine qualities, especially Cleveland, they did not make for all that compelling of figures. Between 1880 and 1896, as Kornbluh notes, nation-wide voter turnout in presidential elections averaged 79.2%. It exceeded 90% in places: in New Jersey, for instance, 96.4% of eligible voters cast ballots in the race between James Garfield and Winfield Scott Hancock (with a spirited race also by Greenback-Labor candidate James Baird Weaver). In Kansas, 96.5% voted in the Cleveland–Harrison race of 1888, and turnout in Indiana in the epochal McKinley–Bryan battle of 1896 reached an unbelievable 97.6%. Even in sparsely populated Rocky Mountain states with relatively new populations and often great distances between neighbors, turnout exceeded 75%.[3]

As Kornbluh explains, the Southern states had similarly high turnout rates until the enactment of poll taxes, literacy tests, and other obstacles to voting, especially by African-Americans, depressed voting. In South Carolina, for example, turnout fell from a robust 83.1% in 1880 to 35% in 1888.[4] Those who set the rules for voting and elections can manipulate the results. Southern Democrats learned this early. Northern progressives soon took this lesson to heart.

Turnout rates were high in off-year elections, too, and for positions rang-ing from governor to justice of the peace. Voters cared. They felt as if their ballot made a difference. They had choices, they had options spanning a range of political views, and they exercised the franchise. This extended through virtually every conceivable subgroup of the white male population: rural men voted and so did urbanites; immigrants voted and so did natives; merchants and farmers and working men all voted at rates that we would today find astronomically high. By the final decades of the nineteenth cen-tury, Kornbluh summarizes, "practically all who were eligible to vote *and able to do so* cast their ballots."[5]

Adding to the excitement surrounding off-year elections was the fact that congressional races were far more competitive than they are today. The pro-fessional politician had yet to come into full flower; the average representative served for 5 years, in contrast to the tenure of the lifers a century later. (By 1990, the average congressman had served over 10 years.) In state legisla-tures, turnover reached near-universality. The Nebraska legislature of the late nineteenth century boasted "between 80 and 90% . . . newcomers each term." This was also a heyday of third parties, which had yet to be barred from ballots by the bipartisan administrators. Greenbackers, Populists, and Prohibitionists: all played critical roles in the politics of the day. Between 1880 and 1896, third parties held the "balance of power" – that is, their vote exceeded the difference between the Republican and Democratic candidate – in 23% of the states in presidential elections, 32% in gubernatorial elections, and 26% of congressional elections. Dissent mattered. As Kornbluh writes, "the effect of minor-party challenges was to heighten partisan competition and to guarantee that no state was safe for either party." This was an era of intense competition: "control over government was always contested, frequently divided, and never secure."[6]

The parties had good reason to contend with ferocity and ruthlessness for control of Washington. In a quarter of a century, the number of federal employees boomed from 51,000 in 1871 to 190,000 in 1896.[7] Despite the ballyhooed civil service reform of the 1880s, most of these jobs were patronage plums, to be dispensed by the party in power to its eager lackeys and loyal soldiers. Vicious and unprincipled men had good reason to fight for political power. And they would use any means at their disposal – even something so seemingly mundane as a change in the way voters cast their votes.

Voters prior to the 1890s cast their ballots by a method that seems utterly foreign to us today. This is critical, and an often overlooked fact in the decline of voting in America. Until the 1830s, most voting was done either orally or by handwritten ballot. Thereafter, and for the rest of the century, when men – and, in a few states, women – traveled to the polls in the nineteenth century, they did not enter voting booths or examine voting lists manufactured by the government at government expense. Rather, they voted by a "party strip" ballot. That is, they deposited in the polling box a ticket bearing the names of those candidates for whom they were voting. This ticket they obtained at some time previous to casting their vote: perhaps a week ago, or maybe even minutes ago, from a "party hawker" outside the polling station. The tickets were printed and distributed by the parties themselves. By all the parties. There were no monitors to determine which parties had the "right" to run candidates; any party, whether of venerable vintage or spanking new, could nominate persons for office.

Parties often distinguished their tickets from others by color, logo, or shape: Democrats might hand out blue ballots, Republicans red, Populists green, and so on. The long narrow tickets typically listed candidates for offices across the board. Hand in the party-strip ticket uncorrected and you'd be voting a straight ticket. And indeed, most of those who voted cast a straight party-line ballot. Ticket-splitting for federal and high state offices was not common. But it was possible: one simply had to cross off the name of a candidate one did not support and write above it the name of one's favored candidate. Or the ticket-splitter could mark up two or more different ballots, circling or x-ing out candidates, and drop them into the box.

Any system of voting is liable to corruption, especially if the stakes – in the form of the riches taken by the government in taxes and then distributed to the most influential interests –are high enough. Unscrupulous partymen might "counterfeit their opponents' tickets, substituting one or two of their own for the names listed on the regular ticket."[8] Because the party-strip tickets were variegated in color, and the voter usually dropped his ticket into a ballot box in the center of a room, the ballot was not all that secret, so in some instances intimidation may have played a part. But this crookery was limited in scope, certainly far more modest than anything Mayor Daley came up with in Chicago, or Lyndon B. Johnson used to launch his own political career in Texas.

Widespread reports of election-day mischief, including bribery and fraud, marred the 1888 election and goaded states into spurning the private ballot-strip system and imposing the "Australian ballot." In this scheme, gestated in New South Wales and come to prominence down under in 1856, the government drew up and supplied a single, consolidated ballot listing all candidates for all offices. It was, in theory, "an impartial, multiple-choice instrument."[9] Unquestionably it was the latter: a multiple-choice instrument that laid out the options before the voter in a relatively explicable way. As for being impartial . . . well, the parties would have something to say about that.

The Australian ballot spread first to Australia's British cousins: New Zealand adopted it in 1870, Britain in 1872, and Canada followed in 1874.

With the arrival of the Australian ballot on these shores, the provision of ballots – and the determination of who was and who was not to be included on those ballots – would, if not in the blink of an eye then in the turn of an election cycle, become the province of the state governments. What had theretofore been a privately furnished good – ballots – was now monopolized by government. Mischief, to put it mildly, ensued. And democracy did not flourish.

The first noted campaigner for the Australian ballot in America was the land-reformer Henry George, who took up the cause in 1871. Those upper-class good government reformers known as the Mugwumps fell in behind the Australian ballot movement in the 1880s, as did, for different reasons, segregationists of the Southern States. "One of the advantages of the Australian ballot," according to some Southern segregationists, "was that it . . . disfranchised illiterates, who were mostly Negroes."[10] Not legally disfranchised but practically disfranchised, for the ballot was intimidating to those who could not read. How much easier it was to ask for a brightly colored ballot representing one's favored party. Mugwumps, who moved within a circle in which everyone could read, never quite understood the consequences of their reform for the poorest and most ill-educated voters. (The Populists did not usually oppose the Australian ballot but they did ignore it as largely irrelevant to their main concerns.)

The first Australian ballot law in the United States was enacted in Louisville, Kentucky, in February 1888. After Louisville came the deluge.

The first state to adopt this reform, as with so many other reforms, both wise and wicked, was Massachusetts, which opted for the Australian ballot in 1888. "By 1892," writes Mark Lawrence Kornbluh, "thirty-two states had eliminated party-strip balloting, and by 1896 another seven had followed suit."[11] Within 8 years, all but a handful of states had changed, quite radically, the way that people vote. "Rarely in the history of the United States has a reform movement spread so quickly and successfully," marveled Jerrold G. Rusk of Purdue University.[12] By 1910, Georgia and South Carolina were the only holdouts from the Australian ballot, though five other places – New Jersey, the New Mexico territory, Missouri, Tennessee, and North Carolina – permitted some party-supplied ballots. South Carolina, in a remarkable display of bullheadedness, did not adopt the government-printed ballot system until 1950.

Two-term New York Democratic Governor David Bennett Hill, who succeeded to the office as Lt. Governor when Governor Grover Cleveland was elected President in 1884, was among the public officials who resisted ballot reform. In 1888, the New York legislature had passed an early reform bill that took away from the private sector the right to manufacture and distribute ballots and transferred that responsibility to the public sector. To be listed on the new public ballot, a party must have either won 3% of the vote in the previous election or have submitted a petition of 1,000 signatures.

Braving the sanctimonious huffing and puffing of the Mugwumps of the ballot-reform movement, Hill vetoed the bill as "an unnecessary burden upon the taxpayers." The taxpayers? What did they have to do with anything? Playing to American pride, he called the Australian ballot a "mongrel foreign system."[13] If paper ballots were good enough for grandpa, they were good enough for Governor Hill.

To some extent, Hill, a loyal Democrat, was doing his party's bidding. Urban Democrats feared that a comprehensive ballot listing all parties and candidates on one sheet would confuse the immigrant voters who constituted a Democratic base of support. But in expressing a preference for private instead of public provision of ballots, he was defending a time-honored tradition against the encroachment of the progressive state. The progressive state, as is so often the case, won that battle. And it won it with smugness and conceit. One political scientist even ventured to say in 1891 that the adoption of the Australian ballot "constitutes a decided advance in the moral sense of the people."[14]

Yet as is typically the case with hastily ratified measures, the Australian ballot was signed, sealed, and delivered before its less obvious ramifications had been explored. Or even guessed at. Advancing the moral sense of the people was not quite the simple proposition it had seemed to be.

The Australian ballot did make ticket-splitting easier, and empirical studies have confirmed a rise in this practice after its adoption. It was somewhat easier for the typical voter to cast his vote for, say, a Republican for governor and a Democrat for Congress. But if he wanted to vote Populist for state senate or Prohibition for City Council, well, soon enough he would be out of luck.

The high hopes for the Australian ballot, which was to eliminate boss rule in the cities and redeem the promise of democracy, fell far short. In fact, Mugwump sponsors soon realized that "the law recognized the parties and deliberately obstructed the independent candidates."[15] Democratic and Republican political pros, whose very livelihoods depended on their parties remaining in power, were fairly quick to grasp the possibilities in election law – and so much the better if naked power-grabs could be rouged and burnished and sold as good government "reforms."

Not coincidentally, by the early twentieth century, the voting boom had ended. Turnout for the first five presidential elections of the new century averaged 65%, or 15% lower than the figure for the final five races of the previous century.[16] The decline was sharpest – precipitous, really – in the South due to the passage of laws intended to keep African-Americans from the polls, but turnout in every other region declined, too. There were many factors in this decline. The inclusion of women as eligible voters in many states depressed the percentage of eligible voters casting ballots because women, who had not been acculturated to politics, did not immediately vote in large numbers. Elections, which had once been grand social events, complete with torchlight parades and free booze and bonfires and speeches to which a family might take a picnic lunch, became "merchandising campaigns that did not require the active participation of voters."[17] Elections just weren't as much fun anymore. Many local offices became appointed rather than elected, as the progressive zeitgeist held that credentialed experts could do any job better than a mere elected man.

But there was another reason, one that until recently political historians almost wholly ignored: government had taken over the ballot. When the state took over the provision of election ballots in the late nineteenth century, it also acquired the power to keep parties or persons off the ballot – to limit the voters' choices, to frame their choices, to narrow the range of options and protect the established parties from competition.

Transferring control of the ballot to the government did not remove partisanship from politics; instead, it narrowed the partisanship so that effective control shifted to the two parties, which proceeded to essentially prohibit opposition. In the earliest years of state-controlled ballots, access to parties other than the Democrats and Republicans remained fairly open. A two-party system had developed, but Americans were used to various choices every November, and most would not have taken kindly to a sweeping reform that swept those alternative choices from the landscape. Ballot restrictions would advance at their own deliberate speed.

Elections also became more expensive because of ballot reform. Not only did the government have to manufacture the ballots or election machines, but it also assumed a greater role in the regulation of the parties themselves, for instance setting rules by which primaries would be held. This all cost money – a great deal more money than the old system, under which the parties printed the ballots and all the government had to do was hire competent counters. So the number of elections was reduced; with races that much less frequent, the habits of democracy eroded. Unintended consequences flowed like sewage from a busted pipe.

Assessing the Australian ballot in 1968, L.E. Fredman concluded that "It has not opened doors for poor, independent and third-party candidates."[18] This was among the goals of that early Australian ballot advocate Henry George, but George did not reckon on the duopolists.

Ballot-access expert Richard Winger has sketched the history of ballot restrictions in America. When parties supplied their own ballots, there were no such restrictions. Greenbackers, Prohibitionists, and the abolitionists of the Liberty Party: all were welcome to enter the lists. Of course they were not "equal" in the sense that each had access to the same resources, the same war chest, the same cadre of committed volunteers, or the same newspaper support, but they did have an equal right to run candidates. The state did not cripple them before the race had even begun.

Access laws have never troubled the major parties. Their nominees are generally guaranteed a spot on the ballot each time around as a result of the party's showing in the previous election. Although laws vary by state, the threshold for automatic ballot status is usually set low enough so that the Republicans and Democrats qualify without breaking a sweat but high enough as to keep fringe parties off and make the more popular or established third parties expend whatever limited resources they possess in money and manpower just to make the ballot.

The nominating petition is a *sine qua non* of ballot access. Usually a state will require the signatures of a certain percentage of the registered voters in the previous election. Ohio, which has often seemed to take a sadistic pleasure in tormenting third parties, set its minimum at an impossible-to-obtain 15% until that was struck down by the Supreme Court in *Williams v. Rhodes* (1968). The Buckeye State's Republican-Democratic establishment then reset the standard at 7%, which a U.S. District Court threw out. Yet the Supreme Court approved Georgia's 5% rule in *Jenness v. Fortson*, thus setting, solomonically, the golden mean somewhere between 5 and 6%. You can guess what happened next. After *Jenness v. Fortson*, states rushed to *increase* their minimums to 5%. No good ruling goes unexploited.

The judicial history of ballot access laws makes for a depressing, if illuminating, story. The political establishment in a state sets the bar as high as possible, third parties fail to clear the hurdle, littering the track, and then lawyers for the insurgent parties file suit. If the bar is set ridiculously high – as when Arkansas insisted that an independent statewide candidate must obtain the signatures of 15% of registered voters, a virtual impossibility – the Supreme Court may strike it down (*Lendall v. Bryant*, 1975). But shave a few points off that percentage and the Court will rule that even a stiff, near-unmeetable standard falls "within the outer boundaries of support the State may require."[19]

This may sound like mere squabbling among percentages, quibbling at the margins: one state requires 3% of registered voters to sign a petition, another requires 4%. What, really, is the difference?

The difference is that before states took over the ballot the requirement was zero percent. In the days of privately supplied ballots, there were no thresholds, no petitions, no steep demands for signatures. This was America: anyone who wished to run for public office could run.

Richard Winger compares access to the ballot before and after 1930. His cutoff date is not chosen arbitrarily: after 1930, most states made it far more difficult for third parties to make the ballot. In 1924, as Winger explains, insurgent U.S. Senator Robert LaFollette of Wisconsin easily made the ballot in 47 of the 48 states. (Louisiana was the exception: its petition requirements were not onerous, but only independents could sign, and the state had very few voters who had not registered with a party affiliation.) The total number of signatures required to put LaFollette and his running mate, Senator Burton K. Wheeler (D-MT), on the ballot of every state was about 50,000. A relative pittance, at least compared to the later herculean efforts necessary to achieve a nationwide presence. Moreover, the deadlines were sensibly late: as of July 1924, not a single deadline had passed.[20]

The result of these choice-friendly state laws was a political world in which men like LaFollette or parties such as the Socialists, the Prohibitionists, or more regionally based movements such as the Liberal Party of Pennsylvania (which was anti-prohibition) or the populist Nonpartisan League of North Dakota were very real presences. As Winger notes, in 1912 the Socialist Party was on the ballot in every state. Its presidential candidate, railway union leader Eugene V. Debs, won 6% of the popular vote nationally and hit double figures in seven Western states. It ran candidates in a majority of congressional districts. It even elected the odd congressman and members of state legislatures.

So did the Prohibition Party, which was on the ballot used by 95% of Americans in 1912 and whose presidential candidate, Eugene Wilder Chafin, won 1.47% of the popular vote. Four years later, the Prohibitionists would even elect a governor of Florida, Sidney J. Catts, who is still spinning in his grave every year at spring break time.

In 1912, Theodore Roosevelt, the former president itching for a return to the White House, won 27.4% of the nationwide popular vote (and 88 electoral votes) as the standard-bearer of the Progressive, or Bull Moose, Party. This was the best showing ever by a third party in a presidential race. The party elected 17 congressmen in that third-party watershed year of 1912.

Beginning in the 1930s – which was, not coincidentally, also the beginning of unprecedented growth in the size of the national government – states began sharply restricting access to the ballot. The restrictions came in waves, and these were, in most cases, big increases in the number of signatures required to place a candidate on a state's presidential ballot. For instance, in 1931, Illinois jacked up its demand from 1,000 signatures to 25,000. In 1937, California boosted its requirement from 23,610 signatures to the rather more exhausting – which in this case is a synonym for impossible – 236,608 signatures. Two years later, Massachusetts increased the standard 1,000 signature requirement to 52,977 signatures. Something was in the air – and it wasn't freedom.

"Most restrictive changes in the 1930s were made to thwart the Communist Party,"[21] writes Winger. Unlike the Socialist Party, which achieved some real if limited electoral successes, the Communists never fared well at the polls anywhere in America, with the very partial exception of certain precincts in New York City. The Communists never elected a candidate to federal office, though the long-time New York Congressman Vito Marcantonio had close ties to the Communist Party. Nor did the party ever elect a single state legislator or a member of any city council in any city or town in America with one exception – New York City Council in the early 1940s. The party's best showing in a presidential election was in 1932, when the Stalinist hack William Z. Foster won 103,253 votes, or about one-fourth of 1% of the total votes cast. The Socialist, Norman Thomas, won more than eight times as many votes.

Rather than defeat the relatively tiny number of American Communists in the battle of ideas – for instance, by pointing to the vast prison camp that Joseph Stalin was creating in the Soviet Union – legislators preferred to use legal means to snuff what was, in any case, a virtually non-existent threat. The Illinois law mentioned earlier, for instance, not only changed the signature minimum from 1,000 to 25,000, it also mandated that a statewide candidate submit not less than 200 voter signatures from not less than 50 counties. (The federal courts were unsympathetic to a Communist lawsuit on the matter.)

Southern Illinois was not, to put it mildly, fertile ground for the overwhelmingly urban and often foreign-born Communists, so the Commies could kiss the Land of Lincoln goodbye. Yet this was all much ado about nothing: even if the Communists had been guaranteed a prime spot on every election ballot, they would never have elected so much as a single Illinois legislator, let alone member of Congress. These restrictions, ironically, permitted the Communist Party USA (CPUSA), which was an apologist for a murderous totalitarian regime, to claim, with justification, that it was being oppressed in the United States of America.

Winger records in gruesome detail the story of the Communist exclusion, state by state. In 1931, the Florida state legislature "repealed all procedures by which a new party or an independent candidate could get on the ballot."[22] That was simple: if you don't like 'em, just outlaw 'em. The voters dissatisfied with the Democratic or Republican candidates in solidly Democratic Florida had no other than a Hobson's choice. (Write-ins, that most seldom employed tactic – has anyone actually ever seen a pen or pencil inside a voting booth? – remained legal.)

In Florida, as elsewhere, what began as a punitive measure against the undeniably wicked and anti-American Communist Party applied, in equal measure, to other third parties. Florida was the only Southern state in which the Dixiecrat Strom Thurmond failed to make the ballot in 1948, though he (and the left-wing Democrat Henry Wallace, who ran as the candidate of the Communist-friendly Progressive Party) was placed on the ballot by special act of the legislature.

Thurmond also needed the assistance of the Georgia legislature, which in 1943, as the victorious war for democracy overseas was being fought, instituted a grueling ballot marathon in which new parties, if wishing to run a full slate of statewide candidates, needed 80 separate petitions signed by 1% of the state's registered voters. The thought of lugging around 80 petitions and asking already suspicious homeowners to sign their names to each and every one was enough to daunt even a Jehovah's Witness.

The 1940s, predictably, was not a decade marked by the welcoming of radical dissent.

War has been one of the great centralizing forces in political life. The economy, the culture, social life: central authorities assume greater control over each in time or war or threatened war. Marginal parties have also suffered from the inevitable abridgements of freedom when armies are mobilized and a premium is placed on unanimity of thought.

As Hugh A. Bone of Queens College wrote in the *National Municipal Review* of November 1943, "Minor political parties are on the road to becoming one of the casualties of the home front."[23] Vote totals for the Socialist Party, for instance, had fallen sharply in recent years. A conventional explanation, with some plausibility, might be that President Roosevelt's New Deal had co-opted the Socialists and stolen from them their most salable platform items. But other causes, less obvious, were at work.

"There has been a tendency to associate subversive influences with minor political groups and this in turn has led to agitation to keep their names off the ballot," writes Bone. "State legislatures have resorted to extraordinary devices to make minor party nominations more difficult."[24]

These devices often had all the subtlety of a sledgehammer. Arkansas instituted fees for presidential electors in each of the state's counties, which placed a severe financial burden on underfunded parties. Maryland, Indiana, Maine, New Hampshire, and Vermont required notarized signatures on third-party or independent petitions. Maryland further mandated that the names of those who sign minor-party petitions be published in newspapers – at party expense.

Other states, notably California and Ohio, boosted the number of signatures required to make the ballot so high as to outdistance the efforts of the most Stakhavonite petition-gatherers. Illinois, in requiring at least 200 signatures from each of 50 counties, ensured that rural-based parties and urban-based parties would never make the ballot. Florida's election law made "no provision for independent or new party nominations."[25] In Ohio, a new party could not make the ballot unless its tireless petition-gatherers submitted sheets containing the John Hancocks of fully 15% of the total voters in the previous gubernatorial election. It is doubtful in the extreme whether or not the Republicans or Democrats could meet this test, let alone a rag-tag band of socialists or anti-New Deal right-wingers. The duopoly, it seems, was cast in stone.

California, Pennsylvania, Michigan, Oklahoma, West Virginia, and several other states moved their filing dates up so far as to make it almost impossible for a third-party to attain ballot status. In North Carolina, the attorney general made an additional threat: anyone who signed a Socialist Party petition was guilty of fraud unless he or she joined the Socialist Party.

Rather than monkey around with tightened access laws and constrictive ballots – such niggling was for wimpish lawyers! – some states simply outlawed "subversive" parties. The Communist Party was banned from the 1940 ballot in California, Arkansas, Indiana, Arizona, Georgia, Kentucky, and New Mexico. The next year, nine more states barred the CPUSA from their ballots. Ironic developments as the nation was on the verge of a war against a different totalitarian power.

The Communist Party was simply barred from the ballot in 19 states in the 1940s, and even less revolutionary parties were subjected to far more onerous requirements as a result of the world wars of the teens and the forties. As with most government regulations, they remained in place even after the war had ended. "The hostile and suspicious political climate surrounding the two world wars prompted many restrictions on ballot access," write Rosenstone, Behr, and Lazarus.[26] Dissent equals treason in the eyes of many super-patriots, especially during wartime, and third parties, organized vehicles of dissent, are a prime target.

Professor Bone, writing in 1943, veers somewhat from the libertarian path of advocating freedom of vote and the ballot when he points out that "the Communists today constitute some of the most vigorous workers for all-out war against the Axis." (They became ardent warhawks when Hitler betrayed Stalin by attacking Russia in 1941, thus nullifying the Russo–German non-aggression pact.) Bone quotes CPUSA chieftain Earl Browder, who promised President Roosevelt that his legions would "intensify every effort to weld unbreakable national unity under the Commander-in-Chief for victory in the war."[27] To "weld unbreakable national unity"? Not exactly the language of liberty!

In any event, Bone warned that legislation both pending and already passed "seems to have the object of keeping all but Republican and Democratic tickets off the ballot."[28] Was this really what Americans were fighting for?

Surprisingly, the 1950s, so often caricatured as a decade of dull and crushing conformity, were quiescent on the third-party repression front. As Richard Winger notes, only Missouri put the squeeze on third parties. Where formerly all a party had to do was hold a meeting in order to qualify for a spot on the Show-Me State's ballot, in 1953 the state's solons insisted on being shown 18,710 signatures in order to make the cut. But other than Missouri, the American states generally refrained from clamping down on ballot-box dissent. It was the 1960s — the free and easy, let-it-all-hang-out sixties — when a truly bad moon rose for those at the political margins.

The deluge began in Wyoming, which, steeped in its populist Western past, ought to have welcomed challengers — or at least not tried to outlaw them. But in 1958, according to Winger, the very laxity of Wyoming's ballot access (100 signatures earned a place on the state ballot) permitted "the Economy Party" to siphon votes from the Republican candidate and give the Equality State a Democratic governor. The Republican establishment was not amused. In 1961, the 100-signature requirement skyrocketed to 6,717. Goodbye, Economy Party.

Eleven states "drastically increased their ballot access requirements" in the 1960s. They ranged from Tennessee to New Mexico, and from Hawaii to Maryland.[29] The *annus horribilus* was 1969, which Winger deems "the single worst year in U.S. history for proponents of lenient ballot access."[30]

Six states — Arizona, Montana, Hawaii, New Mexico, Florida, and Virginia — stiffened their laws against dissent in 1969. Montana and New Mexico, which theretofore had simply asked a party to hold a meeting in order to qualify for the ballot, and Hawaii, which asked only that a party be organized, instituted minimum-signature requirements. In New Mexico's case, the cause of the crackdown was the appearance on the 1968 ballot of Ventura Chavez, the People's Constitutional Party candidate for president.

This localized Hispanic party was not welcome in New Mexico, and to ensure its prompt disappearance the legislature decreed that henceforth almost 16,000 signatures would be necessary to put someone like Chavez before New Mexico's voters again.

Virginia raised its signature threshold by 868%; Arizona went off the charts, percentage-wise, boosting what been a moderate 358 signature standard to 9,680, or an incredible 2,700% increase.

Nineteen-sixty-nine. Hmm. Now why might Democratic and Republican legislators across the nation panic over the threat that a third-party candidate might break up that old gang of theirs?

The answer: George Corley Wallace.

The Alabama bantam, the bareknuckled brawler from Clio, the man who was either the ugly face of Southern racism or the voice of the dispossessed, depending on one's point of view – or maybe he was both – had scared the parties into action. The Wallace campaign fought, rallied, and sued its way onto all 50 ballots, even that of the notoriously anti-third-party state of Ohio, which had erected an insuperable barrier to third-party candidates by requiring signatures from 15% of those who had voted in the previous gubernatorial election: a practical impossibility even for the two major parties. Wallace sued, and the Supreme Court, usually deferential to state ballot access laws, however draconian, overturned the Ohio law.

Wallace made his share of strategic mistakes in the campaign, none more glaring than his unwise choice of a running mate, Air Force General Curtis LeMay, who had once called for bombing North Vietnam back to the Stone Age. He'd have been better advised to run with Colonel Sanders, the kindly fried chicken salesman, whom Wallace asked to serve as his veep. (The Colonel, perhaps mindful that a hostile press would fry his public image till it was extra crispy, said no.)

Wallace did win almost 10 million votes, or 13.5% of the national total (34.3% of the old Confederacy), and 46 electoral votes in the face of perhaps the most negative press any serious candidate has ever received. Yet his populist campaign was not hailed for breaking down doors. Instead, it was maligned. American voters, it was implied by many establishment voices, were better off not having the choice to vote for George Wallace.

Too much democracy, it seems, was a danger. Better to keep the Wallaces who lurk at the fringes of American life off the ballot, or at least make them deplete their treasuries on petition-gathering. As Richard Winger writes, "The history of these changes demonstrates that the United States has restrictive ballot access laws in many states, not because of common-sense concerns about the ballot being overly crowded, but because state legislators simply did not like certain third parties, and found it too tempting to resist revising the election laws to keep them off future ballots."[31]

Four more states – Wallace's Alabama (of all ironies!), Arkansas, Kansas, and Pennsylvania –raised the hurdles in 1971, in time to impede whatever menacing Wallace-types (or left-wing troublemakers) might rise from the vasty deep in time in the 1972 campaign cycle. Arkansas took the 1971 escalation prize for steepening the requirement from "just hold a meeting" to 42,644 signatures. Outside of soliciting names on an anti-Darryl Royal petition at a Razorbacks-Texas Longhorns game, that was a nearly unmeetable task. Whether aimed at Communists or the American Independent Party of Wallace, "any time some third party irritated state legislators," writes Winger, "state legislators were tempted to strike back, by revising the ballot access laws."[32]

The 1970s were almost as bad as the 1960s. Eleven states, according to Richard Winger, "drastically" tightened ballot laws, and while Ohio and Florida eased theirs somewhat, this was due not to the civic-minded magnanimity of Buckeye and Sunshine State legislators but because the U.S. Supreme Court hacked away at those states' outrageous obstacles to third-party ballot access.[33]

The legal war on third parties lessened in the 1980s and especially in the 1990s, thanks largely to the spirited (and litigious) campaigns of John Anderson in 1980 and Ross Perot in 1992, as well as earlier legal struggles by Wallace, People's Party candidate Benjamin Spock in 1972, and Eugene McCarthy in 1976. McCarthy's "eighteen lawsuits not only helped him secure spots on twenty-nine state ballots, but were also instrumental in making it easier for future third-party candidates" to achieve the ballot, say Rosenstone, Behr, and Lazarus.[34]

The McCarthy campaign won a series of notable victories in court, including the overturning of a Michigan law that essentially forbade independent candidacies. The Michigan court affirmed McCarthy's right to run in these words: "The restriction of the rights of independents to equal political expression and association serves no legitimate governmental interest and cannot be sustained."[35]

Third parties of radically different complexions sometimes worked together on these court challenges: for instance, in 1973, William Shearer, a founder of the Wallaceite American Independent Party, "willingly submitted a very helpful affidavit in the lawsuit *Socialist Workers Party v. Eu*, which challenged California's procedures for qualifying new parties."[36] But the "maze of broad stringent requirements that must be met differs in every state," as attorneys Elizabeth Rada, David Cardwell, and Alan Friedman argued in *The Urban Lawyer*.[37] Navigating through the maze is an undertaking arduous enough to sap the will of even the most devout true believer. And the cruel twist is that once you have triumphed — made it through the maze — all you have really done is made the ballot. The race is yet to be run.

Clearing 51 ballot-access hurdles often takes the bulk of a third party's campaign assets. A campaign spends its war chest qualifying for the ballot in Oklahoma, Georgia, and West Virginia and has nothing left with which to reach the voters. But that, wink the Republican and Democratic Party hacks who write these laws, is precisely the point. In the words of Diane Dwyre, assistant professor of political science at California State University, Chico, and Robin Kolodny, assistant professor of political science at Temple University: "Some states have structured their conception of guaranteed ballot position to mean that only Democrats and Republicans will get on the ballot automatically each election year."[38] For the rest it is a long, hard climb.

The whole grueling process of collecting signatures just to earn a place at the table is fatiguing. It can exhaust even the most energetic volunteers. It's damned discouraging, too. And it empties the meager bank accounts of third parties: the Libertarians, for instance, routinely spend upwards of two-thirds of their budget on ballot-access drives. They're beat before they even arrive at the game.

In 1996, a third party needed 1.6 million valid signatures nationwide to put its presidential candidate on the ballot in every state. (An independent would have to get 750,000.) To qualify a slate in all 435 congressional districts, the 33 or 34 U.S. Senate seats that are up, and statewide offices across the nation, the requisite would be an ungettable 3.5 million-plus. This is beyond onerous: it is impossible. The Brennan Center at the New York University School of Law estimated in 1996 that obtaining ballot access in all 50 states would cost a candidate $2.4 million.[39]

In North Carolina, to take one egregious example, an independent wishing to make the presidential ballot must file approximately 70,000 signatures of registered voters — a task so daunting that one wonders if even a run-of-the-mill Republican or Democrat could meet the requirement. (And don't even think about trying to collect any of those signatures on walkways leading into the post office. In *Longo v. United States Postal Service* (1992), the U.S. Court of Appeals for the Second Circuit overturned a lower court ruling and upheld a prohibition on collecting signatures on a "postal walkway." It seems that the court worried that such activity might thrust the "postal workers" into a "political entanglement."[40] Heaven forbid that an unsuspecting patron walking into the post office to buy a roll of stamps might think that the pro-privatization Libertarian asking him to sign a petition is the favored candidate of a politicized U.S. Postal Service!)

Amusingly, one justification for strict access laws is to keep frivolous candidates off the ballot, or to keep it from becoming cluttered, crowded, confusing. As if having a choice of, say, eight presidential candidates rather than two is going to induce headaches, nausea, disorientation. Oh, the curse of too many choices!

This is not merely a matter of isolated injustices at the state level keeping a few kooks off the election ballot. Not that kooks don't have rights, too: they do. The Communists, the Socialist Workers, the UFO party: each deserves the chance to make its views heard. We need more debate, more discussion, not less.

But third parties can also speak to the very real concerns of ordinary Americans – which is, perhaps, one reason why the two major parties have done their damndest to keep alternative voices and alternative choices from having a place in the public square and a place on the ballot. Richard Winger, editor of *Ballot Access News* and probably the most knowledgeable maven on the subject, has written that "if the United States *did* have lenient ballot access laws, there would be one or two substantial third parties in existence most of the time, if not all the time. By 'substantial third party,' I mean a party which, although not competitive with the two major parties, is able to win seats in Congress on occasion, commonly wins seats in state legislatures, fields candidates for Congress in a majority of congressional districts, and regularly polls at least 2% or 3% of the presidential vote."[41]

Our political discussion would be enriched under such a scenario. But we'll never see it without substantial changes in some of the most unjust laws on the American books.

Ballot access is not mentioned in the U.S. Constitution. Article I, Section 4 of the Constitution provides that "The times, places and manner of holding elections for senators and representatives, shall be prescribed in each state by the legislature thereof; but the Congress may at any time by law make or alter such regulations, except as to the places of choosing Senators."

As Rada, Caldwell, and Friedman explain, states have historically based their defense of strict ballot-access laws on four grounds:

1. Preservation of a two-party system
2. Assuring a majority winner
3. Preventing voter confusion and apathy
4. Greater administrative feasibility[42]

More on the first justification in a moment. The second justification – that restricting access to the ballot to two candidates ensures that the winner has a majority of the votes and is somehow more "legitimate" – was seriously advanced by the state of Ohio in *Williams v. Rhodes* (1968), but the Court looked askance at such feeble reasoning. If this is true, why not just rule every candidate but one off the ballot? Wouldn't a unanimous vote confer even more legitimacy? Perhaps East Germany and Ceaucescu's Romania had the right idea after all. Certainly those totalitarian hellholes looked no more favorably on dissident candidacies than did, and does, the state of Ohio.

Williams v. Rhodes was hailed at the time as the judicial battering ram that was going to knock down the barred doors of the duopoly. In *Williams*, the Court, by a vote of 6–3, struck down the absurdly harsh laws by which Ohio kept third parties off the ballot. George Wallace and others were required in 1968 to submit a whopping 433,100 signatures by February, or fully half a year before the Republicans and Democrats held the conventions to determine their nominees. (According to Richard Winger, the most signatures ever collected in a successful ballot-access effort by a third party was 275,975 by Henry Wallace's Progressives in California in 1948.) The Ohio law was manifestly unjust. But Richard Winger has argued that *Williams v. Rhodes* was of limited use as precedent because while the Court declared Ohio's restrictions to be impermissibly draconian, it did rule that by themselves, there was not anything wrong with petition requirements and filing deadlines. They just couldn't be too stringent. This left the other states in a kind of Goldilocks condition: Ohio was too hot, but that is not to say that another combination – say, 100,000 and June? – could not pass muster as just right.

The U.S. Supreme Court has generally looked favorably on the latter two assertions of the Rada–Caldwell–Friedman quartet. The prospect of unwieldy ballots filled with frivolous candidates is an effective, if somewhat fanciful, weapon. Why, the argument goes, if we don't establish certain standards, the ballot will be surfeited with de-institutionalized mental patients! In *Bullock v. Carter* (1972), the specter haunting the state of Texas was that "without restrictions, there would be more potential candidates for office than a voting machine has handles."[43]

This has a surface plausibility, though it was not an issue when private parties supplied their own ballots. Moreover, the increased use of touch-screens and computerized voting will make it an anachronistic concern. The more basic problem, however, is that even without restrictions, the specter has never materialized. Even in states with the most lax filing rules, Senate and

U.S. House races never feature more than a handful of candidates; nor are there plentiful presidential hopefuls who can recruit the necessary presidential electors to stand for them in the 50 states. Warding off the mental cases would be a simple matter of establishing a very low petition-signature threshold – as low as one hundred in a given state. But then that is not the real aim of the Democratic and Republican politicos who set the rules. When they target "laundry list" ballots, what they really mean is a ballot that has room for candidates outside the duopoly. Moreover, the Court has specified (in *Munro v. Socialist Workers Party*, 1986) that states need not "make a particularized showing of the existence of voter confusion, ballot overcrowding, or the presence of frivolous candidacies prior to the imposition of reasonable restrictions on ballot access."[44] In other words, there is no need to prove actual overcrowding or frivolity – the excuse is valid whether or not a hanging chad of evidence even exists in its support.

"Ballot access regulations," write Rada, Caldwell, and Friedman, " . . . effectively preserve and promote a two-party system."[45] In some cases, that is not only a subsurface motive but the stated intention of their sponsors. These people really can be shameless.

Consider the case of *Lippitt v. Cipollene* (1972), in which a sharply divided U.S. Supreme Court upheld an Ohio law which, in that heavy-handed way which Ohio historically has had of snuffing out third parties, barred a man from running on the American Independent Party line.

Briefly, the case involved Mr. Thomas Lippitt, who as a registered Republican voted in the 1970 Ohio Republican primary and unsuccessfully sought the party's nomination for a seat in the U.S. House of Representatives that same year. Souring on the Republicans, Lippitt announced his intention to seek nomination to a House seat in 1972 from the American Independent Party. But there was a catch. In Ohio, there is always a catch. (In Cleveland Browns Stadium there are too few catches, but that is another story.) An Ohio statute stated that "[n]o person shall be a candidate for nomination or election at a party primary if he voted as a member of a different political party at any primary election within the next preceding four calendar years." Lippitt was out of luck.

Attorneys for the state of Ohio defended this statute as necessary to "the formation of recognizable, relatively stable political parties with their own leadership, goals and philosophies. . . . The protection of these purposes is a legitimate State concern." In upholding the law, the federal District Court cited the "compelling State interests" in guaranteeing "the integrity of all political parties and membership therein."

By "all political parties," the court, and the state of Ohio, meant Republicans and Democrats. An inherent state interest in maintaining the two-party system was being asserted. Whence this interest came from no one quite knows. It certainly has no constitutional basis. The U.S. Supreme Court, never a slave to the Constitution, upheld the Ohio statute by a vote of 5–4, though the majority issued no written opinion. For what could they say?

The minority was not so reticent. In a stinging dissent, Justice William O. Douglas wrote, "Not only does the denial of the appellant's right to seek the nomination of the American Independence [sic] Party seriously impair his right of political expression, but the 'compelling state interest' advanced by the appellees and accepted by the court below seems alien to our political and constitutional heritage. The right to run for public office seems a fundamental one."

Douglas challenged the legal basis for the duopoly. "I doubt that any state interest can be so compelling as to justify an impairment of associational freedoms in the area of philosophy – political or otherwise." To essentially bar party-switching to protect the major parties from instability is to lock in a two-headed system. Nowhere is "eternal life for the Democratic and Republican parties" enshrined in a constitution, federal or state. Douglas continues in his dissent: "The District Court and the appellees see a compelling state interest in the need to preserve the status quo and to preserve political stability. This interest, it is argued, is secured by creating impediments to changes in party allegiance. Our history is replete with instances in which politicians – having become disenchanted with their previous parties or perhaps only for the 'opportunistic' reasons condemned by the court below – have changed from one party to another. This list includes Teddy Roosevelt, Strom Thurmond, Wayne Morse, John Lindsay, George Wallace, and a host of others. Though these breaks from past political ties add vitality to our political process, Ohio makes it very difficult."[46]

That, of course, was Ohio's intent. The two parties must be protected at all costs. As the song goes, "Way to go, O-Hi-O." (Ohio, by the way, has also been notorious for burdensomely early filing deadlines. Its deadline for general election presidential candidates was struck down in 1980 in *Anderson v. Celebreeze*.)

The Supreme Court seemed to echo Justice Douglas's paean to the vitalizing role of third parties in *Illinois State Board of Elections v. Socialist Workers Party* (1979), in which the Court came down on the side of "the least restrictive means" of ensuring an orderly and not unwieldy ballot. The decision stated: "The State's interest in screening out frivolous candidates must be considered in light of the significant role that third parties have played in the political development of the Nation. Abolitionist, Progressives, and Populists have undeniably had influence, if not always electoral success. As the records of such parties demonstrate, an election campaign is a means of disseminating ideas as well as attaining political office. . . . Overbroad restrictions on ballot access jeopardize this form of political expression."[47] (The Socialist Workers had other forms of repression to worry about as well. It was sometimes said that half the members at any meeting of the Socialist Workers Party were FBI plants. J. Edgar Hoover's Counterintelligence Program, or COINTELPRO, sought to disrupt radical parties through the use of spying, wiretapping, agents provocateurs, planted evidence, and a bag of dirty tricks that would be the envy of Dick Nixon, Bill Clinton, and every other cutthroat politician who ever smeared an opponent.)

Since parties exist outside the Constitution, the courts have treated them in a hodge-podge fashion, sometimes intervening to protect the party against state intervention, other times permitting such intervention.

There is an unfortunate, if understandable, tendency among some supporters of dissident parties and movements to hope for a federal judge on a white knight to ride in and save them from the clutches of the dastardly duopoly. And it is true that courts, up to and including the U.S. Supreme Court, have on occasion overturned onerous laws and regulations. But at the end of all this litigating, this filing of briefs and entreaties for fair treatment, third parties and independents have probably lost ground to the Republican–Democratic monolith. Richard Winger, who knows as much about this subject as any man alive, has written, "If the Supreme Court had never heard a ballot access case, or if it had simply ruled that nothing in the US Constitution pertains to ballot access, third parties would probably be better off than they are now. Such a ruling would have forced State Supreme Courts to examine ballot access laws under State Constitutions, many of which provide that elections must be 'free and equal.'"[48]

As is so often the case, federalism – leaving state matters to the states – is the wiser course. Yet it is also the course less traveled. And so despite the best efforts of insurgents to use the legal system to carve out a little more space for dissent, third parties actually lost ground in the twentieth century. The two-party system had not only triumphed but sought to uproot, to extirpate, to virtually eliminate even the possibility of opposition. The Democrats and Republicans were poor winners – and we, the people, were the poor losers.

In 1997, Katharine Q. Seelye of the *New York Times* captured for posterity a particularly glaring case of the two major parties ganging up on dissenters.

Or in the unusually blunt language of the reporter, "the Pennsylvania Legislature essentially wants to codify that public office in the state belongs exclusively to Republicans and Democrats."

Both Democrats and Republicans in Pennsylvania had been sorely vexed by Peg Luksik, a feisty prolife populist who in 1994 had startled observers by winning 13% of the vote as the Constitution Party's candidate for governor. Luksik was threatening to run again in 1998, when incumbent Republican Tom Ridge, who was later to be the bumbling first secretary of the new Department of Homeland Security, was up for re-election.

In the dead of night near the end of another legislative session, the State Senate voted 47–1 and the House approved by a vote of 140–55 a bill that, among other things, more than tripled (from 23,000 to 71,000) the number of signatures a third-party candidate needed to make a statewide ballot. It also shortened the petitioning season from 14 to 6 weeks.

The general counsel for the legislature's Republicans, Stephen C. MacNett, soberly lectured the *Times* reporter that the bill "is designed to bounce some of the more frivolous candidates off the ballot, the people who really aren't bringing a choice to Pennsylvanians." Another GOP operative, one Joe Carduff, was franker: "It's to perpetuate the two-party system as we know it." An aide to U.S. Senator Arlen Specter, the Pennsylvania Republican, admitted that Specter's staff helped father the measure. The flunky told Seelye that Specter believes that "democracy is not well-served by factionalism posed by nonviable third-party candidates who cloud the field and have no chance of winning."

The only state senator to vote no, freshman Jane M. Earll, explained her courageous vote: "It's just a mechanism by which incumbents are protecting themselves. In this day and age, when people are so apathetic and hesitant to get involved, we shouldn't be making it tougher."

And Peg Luksik, target of this late-night skullduggery, framed the matter perfectly:

"This amendment is the big guys telling the little guys to get in line and shut up. This is supposed to be a participatory democracy. But they don't want you to participate."[49]

Shamed by Seelye's exposé, Gov. Ridge vetoed the bill. Yet Pennsylvania remains an unfriendly state to third-party and independent candidates.

Ballot access attracts scant attention from the establishment get-out-the-vote organizations. These feckless do-gooders hector non-voters, they plead with the rest of us to do our patriotic duty by trudging to the polls, where we are faced with unappetizing choices, but they are blind, whether willfully or through ignorance, to the ways in which the powers-that-be keep those who are not with the program well away from the playing field.

The Brennan Center for Justice is an exception. The Brennan Center, a nonprofit organization associated with the New York University School of Law, is generally pegged as a left-leaning group. Named after the late U.S. Supreme Court Justice William J. Brennan and founded by the justice's friends, family, and admirers, the Brennan Center has as one of its missions the opening up, the expansion, of democracy. And while there are manifestations of such a desire that might lead to a more intrusive regulatory state, the Brennan Center has also spoken out for a democratization of the ballot, and an end to the two-party control over who gets to challenge Tweedledum and Tweedledee. As center founder E. Joshua Rosenkranz writes, "Burdensome ballot access laws are impeding minor party formation and weakening the democratic process in America. By imposing onerous rules for how candidates may qualify for each state's general election ballot, Democratic and Republican legislators have kept minor parties from effectively competing in elections."[50]

The most common paths to the ballot are a party's performance in a previous election (48 states) and via petition (48 states). The former is essentially a free pass to the major parties. These states automatically place the Republicans and Democrats on the ballot. How? Well, since access is tied to a party's vote total in the previous election, that vote threshold is finely calibrated to easily qualify the two major parties while barring most if not all others. The state with the highest threshold – Alabama – set its at 20%, which is low enough to guarantee that even an anemic Democrat or Republican will hit the mark. As a Texas Republican Party official joked during the 1990s, "The one thing Democrats and Republicans agree on – they don't want more parties. . . . [T]hey would rather continue to fight with one another." Yes, the spirit of bipartisanship lives.

So minor parties must run a gauntlet. Or perhaps it is more accurately termed a maze. For as the Perot advisor Russell Verney said of the task of making the ballot across the country, "This is so complex, it would give an aspirin a headache."[51]

The pettiness of petition challenges is legendary. Minor misspellings, writing "Street" instead of "Avenue," using nicknames, mistaken election districts – any trivial error can be used to disqualify a signature, or sometimes an entire sheet of signatures. The major parties employ law firms whose specialty is the petition challenge: lawyer-drones whose billable hours consist of tracking down tiny mistakes and using those honest mistakes (or differing interpretations of law) to bar candidates from the ballot. Candidates who have faced such challenges – John Anderson in 1980, Ralph Nader in 2004 – use up enormous portions of their limited treasuries employing their own lawyers to defend their petitions. So that even if successful, their campaign cash on hand is much depleted.

There are less common ways for a party or a candidate to make the ballot. A party that has registered a set number of voters qualifies in 14 states. Setting the threshold cynically high, as Pennsylvania does at 15%, can be an effective bar, for outside Alaska, "no third party in history has ever gotten on the ballot through party registration where the registration requirement was more than 1% of the total state registration."[52]

Six states open the ballot to any party that has met in convention or caucus: these states are regarded as the friendliest to political outliers, and they range from Mississippi to Vermont. Three states let you buy your way on with a filing fee.

The Brennan Center undertook in 1996 to compile the first comprehensive report card on state ballot access – or what the Center, with an eye toward marketable political language, called "voter choice." Its finding: "Devised by the major parties, ballot rules are almost invariably tilted to eliminate competition from outside the political mainstream."[53]

The "most difficult" states to achieve ballot access, according to the most recent (2000) Brennan Center report, were Wyoming and California. For his part, Richard Winger lists Georgia, Oklahoma, West Virginia, and Wyoming as the worst states.

The easiest states for a hopeful to land on the presidential ballot are, from the top, Colorado, Arkansas, Ohio, Nevada, and Florida – again, a quintet notable for its diversity. Colorado permits parties or independents to qualify by (1) tallying 1% of the statewide vote in either of the two prior general elections; (2) registering 1,000 members by June of the election year; or (3) paying a $500 filing fee. It's not quite as open as the old paper ballot system, but it's not far off.

Arkansas, too, requires 1,000 signatures on a petition. Florida, whose tight and constricting laws harassed Ross Perot, greatly liberalized its rules in 1998. Now any party that holds a national convention makes the ballot.

The hoops through which a minor party must jump are narrower and higher than those through which the donkey and elephant tumble. For instance, the Brennan Center's comprehensive report found that while the average number of signatures required for a major party candidate to make the primary ballot is 5,177, the average for an independent running in the general election is 16,438, and the average for a third party is 33,320. This is almost beyond mere discrimination; it approaches a kind of oppression, an official burdening of dissent that ill becomes the land of the free. It is also a repeatable oppression, for states almost always require the minor parties to do it all over again at each new election.

And woe unto the major party candidate who, having lost the nomination he sought, wishes to go the third-party or independent route. Four states – Mississippi, Ohio, South Dakota, and Texas – have "sore loser" laws that bar persons from running for president on another line if they have lost a primary election. (Other states punish "sore losers" who seek lower offices but permit White House aspirants greater latitude.) Many of these restrictions were enacted after Theodore Roosevelt's 1912 Progressive Party candidacy cost Republican William Howard Taft the election – though it may as well have been said that Taft's weak candidacy cost TR the election. Related to these "sore loser" bans are disaffiliation laws which mandate that a candidate cannot pursue an independent course unless he has been separated from a party for a set time – that time, coincidentally enough, being long enough to keep a losing primary candidate from bolting for an independent run. These laws have "the practical effect of compelling party allegiance and continuing the dominance of the two major parties," charges E. Joshua Rosenkranz of the Brennan Center.[54] By their very name – "sore loser laws" – they presume to judge the motive of a candidate. But is this not for the voters to do? Why should the government be given the power to assess motives for a candidacy and to declare some motives improper? (The craving for power, or the desire to tell other people what to do and how to live their lives, is apparently *not* an illegitimate motive for office-seeking in the eyes of the ballot-law writers.)

The Brennan Center's Rosenkranz estimated that a third-party candidate for president using the petition route would have to spend more than $1.6 million (in 1996 dollars) in order to appear on the ballot in all 50 states. (That's $1.6 million minus the cost of printing paper ballots *more* than he would have had to spend in 1888.) An independent candidate would have to spend $1.1 million to make each state's ballot. And what of a Democrat or Republican who went the petition route? About $300,000. The 50 state solons, in their finite wisdom, have made it more than five times more expensive for a Green or a Libertarian or a Mad as Hell Party candidate to make it even as far as the starting line – by which time, of course, the Green or Libertarian or Mad as Hell standard bearer has depleted her treasury and exhausted her door-to-door petition-holding supporters. Even if candidates do get on every ballot, as independent John Anderson did in 1980, they are crippled, for "While the major parties prepare media ads, buy television time, and plan campaign strategy, third-party candidates devote their scarce resources to getting on the ballot."[55] The system is rigged. And outside those most immediately affected, no one really seems to give a damn.

Among the weapons in the great two-party onslaught against upstarts was the antifusion law. Fusion is the practice by which a candidate is endorsed by multiple parties. It was, says historian Peter H. Argersinger, "a significant feature of late nineteenth-century politics, particularly in the Midwest and West, where full or partial fusion occurred in nearly every election." Typically, a smaller party – the Greenbackers or the Grangers or the Populists – would team up with the second party in a region – often the Democrats in the Republican-dominated West – and cross-endorse a candidate or candidates. In some cases, a minor party would link up with whatever the local "out" party was. Now, this may seem like the small party is trying to hitch a ride on a bandwagon, or any passing dog, as it were, but then there are times when the tail wags the dog. The danger to third parties is that in fusion they will lose their identities, become subsumed by the senior partner, but fusion also "helped maintain a significant third-party tradition by guaranteeing that dissenters' votes could be more than symbolic protest, that their leaders could gain office, and that their demands might be heard."[56]

However, fusion threatened the two-party hegemony. It had to be dispatched, with dispatch. The story is a direct contradiction, says Argersinger, to the establishment myth that alterations to the American electoral system are "essentially apolitical or nonpartisan" and do not "ste[m] from an 'antidemocratic conspiracy' to control the political system." For the spate of antifusion laws were "a conscious effort to shape the political arena by disrupting opposition parties, revising traditional campaign and voting practices, and ensuring Republican hegemony – all under the mild cover of procedural reform."[57]

In the wake of the Australian ballot, and the removal of the ballot from the private party sphere and into the government's hands, antifusion laws spread like an Australian virus. They were so easy to write that even the most incompetent party lawyer could do it. No more would winning candidates be indebted to third parties; no longer could minor parties of the future, whether Socialist or American Independent or Libertarian, cross-endorse candidates in most states. Combined with the Australian ballot and its empowerment of the state to determine who could and could not run candidates, antifusion laws simply wiped out vital third parties.

The antifusionists made no bones about their goal. A Michigan Republican legislator explained in 1893, "We don't propose to allow the Democrats to make allies of the Populists, Prohibitionists, or any other party, and get up combination tickets against us. We can whip them single-handed, but don't intend to fight all creation."[58] Praise the honesty of the candid hack! (The Republicans were hardly the only villain in this story. The GOP made use of fusion in states and cities – e.g., the New York City of the Tammany Hall era – where Democrats ruled. And even the Populists, who were often the immediate target of fusion laws, were not immune to the temptation to outlaw dissent. In 1897, the influential Kansas Populist Party, piqued by a separate group of radical Kansas Populists who had run their own slate in 1896, helped the legislature "to quintuple the number of signatures required to gain a ballot position through petition and thereby keep 'small bodies of reformers out of politics.'"[59] The temptation of power snares even the insurgent!)

In 1893, South Dakota became the first state to ban fusion with a model law that read: "the name of no candidate shall appear more than once on the ballot for the same office."[60] Simple, clean, and effective. Others soon followed: by 1897, Oregon, Washington, Michigan, Ohio, Illinois, Iowa, North Dakota, Pennsylvania, Wisconsin, Wyoming (which barred linguistic fusion, too, by banning parties whose names were more than one word long), and Indiana had joined the exclusivist club.

There were court battles, of course. Antifusion laws were a "scheme to put the voters in a straightjacket," according to the Nebraska Supreme Court.[61] One straightjacket leg was marked Republican, the other Democratic. But it worked. As a Michigan Populist writer explained, that state's antifusion law "practically disfranchises every citizen who does not happen to be a member of the party in power. . . . They are thus compelled to either lose their vote . . . or else unite in one organization. It would mean that there could be only two parties at one time."[62] What more, asked the party bosses, could one want? In the eyes of some, even two parties were one too many.

"Ending the effective cooperation of Democrats and third-party groups was both the primary goal and the major result of these efforts," writes Peter H. Argersinger. The Populists, the primary (but not sole) target of antifusion laws, disappeared. Similar parties on the "right," or the classical liberal side, such as the Gold Democrats, never had a chance to really cohere. As a North Dakota Populist cracked, the legislature ought to have gone "a little further and say there shall be but one ticket allowed on the ballot, and that must be the Republican ticket."[63]

Between 1890 and 1920, there were fusion candidates for governor in 56 races in 19 states. Between 1920 and 1950, by stark contrast, there were just 12 fusion nominees in but six states.[64] By 1960, the year after California abolished fusion, only New York, Connecticut, and Vermont permitted cross-endorsements. The practice – as well as the party, in many cases – was over.

(Today, New York, with its semi-potent Conservative Party and its barely alive Working Families and Independence Parties, is the only state in which fusion remains a real going concern. New York's minor parties veer between principle and opportunism, patronage and idealism, but they do provide an outlet, a means of political expression, for a not insubstantial minority of citizens and serve to influence the major parties. Conservative James Buckley won the U.S. Senate election in 1970, when the Democrats and Republicans nominated the liberals Richard Ottinger and Charles Goodell, respectively. That victory has not been repeated, although in 1990 the Conservative Party's candidate, Dean Herbert London of New York University, almost overtook the lame Republican nominee Pierre Rinfret, losing to him by only 22 to 21% in a race won by incumbent Democrat Mario Cuomo.)

The U.S. Supreme Court upheld antifusion laws in the closely watched *Timmons v. Twin Cities Area New Party* (1997). The majority decision, and a cogent dissent by Justice John Paul Stevens, makes for a revealing read.

The New Party was a failed attempt at launching a largely urban liberal-leftist challenge to what its members viewed as the Democratic Party's creeping moderation. In 1994, its Minnesota manifestation, the Twin Cities Area New Party, cross-endorsed Andy Hawkins, a Democratic (or, in its Minnesota form, the Democratic-Farmer-Labor Party) candidate for the state House of Representatives. Hawkins accepted the endorsement. Election officials rejected the New Party's nomination, since a Minnesota statute forbade fusion candidacies. The Twin Cities Area New Party filed suit; a district court found for the government; and the Court of Appeals reversed the decision, "finding that the fusion ban was unconstitutional because it severely burdened the Party's associational rights and was not narrowly tailored to advance Minnesota's valid interests in avoiding intra-party discord and party splintering, maintaining a stable political system, and avoiding voter confusion." Finally, the U.S. Supreme Court reversed the Court of Appeals and by a vote of 6–3 (Stevens, Ginsburg, and Souter in dissent) upheld the ban.

Even in the summary of the Court majority, Minnesota's justification of the fusion ban is almost embarrassingly flimsy. "Minnesota fears that a candidate or party could easily exploit fusion," harrumphs the Court, "as a way of associating his or its name with popular slogans and catchphrases, transforming the ballot from a means of choosing candidates to a billboard for political advertising." This is a novel reason for suppressing third parties: that they might choose names like the "Vote For Me and Get Laid Party" or the "Party of the Eternal Bliss"!

Rather than laughing the Minnesotans' claims out of court, the justices took the opportunity to affirm the state's interest in "the stability of its political systems," which is a euphemism for the two-party system. Seemingly unmindful of the ways in which the duopoly has sought to outlaw potential challengers, the Court's majority worries that "fusion might enable minor parties, by nominating a major party's candidate, to bootstrap their way to major party status in the next election and circumvent the State's nominating petition requirements for minor parties, which is designed to ensure that only bona fide minor and third parties are granted access to the ballot." This is an ahistorical description of ballot access laws, but it leads inexorably to an antifusion conclusion.

Note that the Court does not simply decide the case on the constitutionally legitimate grounds that states may set the rules for elections. It goes well beyond states' rights and into the rights of the major parties. While they may not be "completely insulate[d] . . . from minor parties' or independent candidates' competition and influence" – don't you just love that "completely"? – major parties enjoy a privileged position. States can "enact reasonable election regulations that may, in practice, favor the traditional two-party system." In fact, the "Constitution permits the Minnesota legislature to decide that political stability is best served through a healthy two-party system." Just how "healthy" is a system anyway, if its survival depends on the repression of competitors?

As for fusion, while the New Party "has the right to select the New Party's 'standard bearer,'" the party is not "absolutely entitled to have its nominee appear on the ballot as that party's candidate." Barriers to third parties are permitted under the Constitution, ruled the Court in *Timmons*, even though nowhere in that Constitution are such barriers mentioned.

Justice Stevens was not buying it. In his *Timmons* dissent, Stevens held that the New "Party and its members had a constitutional right to have their candidate's name appear on the ballot despite the fact that he was also the nominee of another party."

The Minnesota law, argued Stevens, imposed a significant burden on the New Party and abridged its members' First Amendment rights. While Minnesota did not explicitly argue for its ban on the grounds that it wished to preserve a two-party system, Stevens emphasized that in his view "it is impermissible for the Court to consider this rationale" in any event. The Minnesota antifusion law "was both intended to disadvantage minor parties and has had that effect," an important fact, "that should weigh against, rather than in favor of, its constitutionality."

Justice Stevens distinguished the fusion ban from other arrangements that may favor a two-party system, for instance single-member districts. These latter do not "imping[e] on the associational rights of those third parties; minor parties remain free to nominate candidates of their choice; and to rally support for those candidates." Single-member districts and the like may strengthen and stabilize a two-party system, but they do not do so by hampering the rights of those who do not pledge allegiance to the two parties.

Stevens concluded with a sharply worded protest: "It demeans the strength of the two-party system to assume that the major parties need to rely on laws that discriminate against independent voters and minor parties in order to preserve their positions of power."[65]

The eulogy for fusion was written by historian Peter H. Argersinger, who traces the cause of death all the way back to the 1880s: "the Australian system opened to Republicans, given their dominance in state governments, the opportunity to use the power of the state to eliminate fusion politics and thereby alter political behavior."[66] He who controls the ballot controls the outcome, or at least has a disproportionate say in that outcome.

Political scientists often wring their hands over the suboptimal voter turnout in the United States. While most other Western democracies see turnouts in the 80% range, only about half of Americans 18 and over vote in presidential elections, and far fewer bother going to the polls in off-year elections. This is said to be a most distressing dereliction of democratic duty.

How to boost voter turnout?

"Giving voters a greater choice of candidates" never seems to be the answer of the blue-ribbon panels and convocations of experts that explore that question. Instead, the wise men of our age have suggested everything from moving Election Day to the weekend to paying people to cast votes. It seems as if every expedient short of putting a gun to the heads of nonvoters has been proposed.

One secondary remedy at least recognizes the fact that parties have written laws to manipulate turnout. The bureaucratization of elections, after all, did not end with transferring control over the ballot to the state. Voter registration, now taken for granted, was another means by which the state narrowed in this case not the choices but those who do the choosing. As political scientist G. Bingham Powell Jr. of the University of Rochester has written, "registration laws make voting more difficult in the United States than in almost any other democracy."[67]

A confusing panoply of poll taxes, literacy taxes, registration deadlines, and requirements for periodic registration depressed voter turnout throughout the United States, but especially in the Jim Crow South, during the twentieth century. Even after the racist poll tax and literacy test were abolished during the civil rights era of the 1960s, potential voters, both white and black, still faced hurdles on their way to the polls: specifically, the seemingly odd demand that they pre-register during an electorally quiescent period in order to vote come Election Day.

In the standard study of "The Effect of Registration Laws on Voter Turnout" (1978), political scientists Steven J. Rosenstone and Raymond E. Wolfinger estimated that "State registration laws reduced turnout in the 1972 presidential election by about nine percentage points."[68] Early registration deadlines were the single largest contributor (6% of the 9%) to the reduction. In recent years, the Democrats, seeking to boost registration of their target constituencies, have overridden traditional state prerogatives via such measures as the Motor Voter Act. The Republicans have not responded with a Country Club Voter Act – at least not yet.

What to do about voter turnout is a question that has vexed reformers for over a century now, or ever since the government took over the ballot from private parties. (Before that, with turnout often exceeding 90%, the question was moot.) Sooner or later, people casting about for a solution to some alleged problem, however serious or trivial, hit on the notion that "it ought to be a law." Voter turnout is no different. Believe it or not, progressives of the 1890s pursued the most coercive route possible to getting people to the polls: they proposed to make voting *mandatory*. Some of the more fervent reformers proposed that hand in glove, or hand in iron first, as it may be, with the Australian ballot went "compulsory voting," which is just what it sounds like. The government would force you to vote, and if you didn't you were in *big* trouble.

The compulsory voting movement is now almost completely forgotten. In this we may be lucky, for it would no doubt appeal to many of those who haven't any philosophical objection to coercing people to make them *good*. The neo-prohibitionists, for instance, abhor alcohol and tobacco and would ban their neighbors from using the demon rum or the devil weed. Or those misguided civil rights activists and hustlers who want to ban use of the offensive word "nigger," thus licensing Big Brother to police private conversations and streetcorner joshing.

About 30 nations of the world currently have compulsory-voting laws, though many enforce them laxly or not at all. The typical penalty is a monetary fine, and even these are imposed spottily. Jail is threatened in some nations but the threat is very seldom carried out. The countries in which citizens are compelled to do their civic duty – or else! – include Australia, Uruguay, Gabon, Liechtenstein, Fiji, Belgium, and Thailand. Not exactly a libertarian honor roll, but neither is it a catalog of police states. And, in its own coercive way, it works: turnout in Venezuela was over 90% when people were forced to vote, but this dropped to 60% when freedom of choice was introduced in 1993.

In the United States, compulsory voting became an issue, at least at the margins, in the late 1880s. Writing in the *North American Review*, Harris J. Clinton expressed horror that almost "one-fifth of the registered voters neglect to vote in all States," a figure that in our alienated age seems laughably minuscule. Mr. Clinton, not exactly the keenest study of political behavior, proceeds to state that "all the evils in government result from neglecting the exercise of the right of franchise" – a claim so manifestly untrue as to cast doubt on the alertness of the *North American Review*'s editorial staff.[69] All the evils of government – every war, every payoff to a favored interest, every crackdown on personal liberty – are the fault of nonvoters? That would come as news to those subjects of the Soviet bloc who faithfully cast their votes in 100%–0% contests every election day!

The nonvoter was subject to every manner of insult and ridicule. He was a slacker, a deadweight, a moron. "A more deliberate and extensive betrayal of trust would be difficult to find," tut-tutted politicial scientist Frederick W. Halls.

Incredulous Americans might reply that the right to vote carries with it the right not to vote – that not voting is a political statement, too – but "the independent who remains away from the polls is guilty of passive treason, for if everyone followed his example the result would be anarchy."[70] To avoid anarchy – the lack of government – we need total government.

The argument from personal liberty carried little weight with the compulsion crowd of the late nineteenth century. After all, jury duty was mandatory; why shouldn't voting be as well? Moreover, politics was passing from the art of politics into a "science," with testable hypotheses and immutable laws. If it could be "proved" that mandatory voting improved the operation of government, what possibly could be the objection? It is a matter, really, of "the inculcation of the idea of Duty toward the State." The idea that Americans are freeborn citizens and that the State should be strictly limited in powers and a servant of the people was an anachronism. This was the age just preceding the idea of the State triumphant, the State exalted, the State deified.

Americans were subjects now, and "since the scope of governmental action is daily becoming wider," the duties owed by those subjects to their master were becoming greater.[71]

Opponents might throw such tired epithets as "un-American," "oppressive," "tyrannous," and "interference with individual liberty" at the compulsory-voting prophets, sighed Frederick W. Halls, but "such opposition is, in the present case, hardly worthy of serious attention."[72]

Brilliant! Halls's strategy is to simply ignore the most basic objections to his plan and to mock those who stand on the old American principles. His strategy would be borrowed many times by statists in the years to come.

The legislative campaign for mandatory voting never really got rolling, though it picked up more steam than one might imagine. Its partisans liked to point out that Colonial Virginia had a law on the books since 1705 that held that "Every freeholder actually resident in each county, shall appear and vote at such election, or shall forfeit Two hundred pounds of Tobacco to the Informer, recoverable as before."[73] This seems not to have been enforced with much vigor, but when you have as little precedent as the compulsory-voting crowd had, you grab on to what you can.

The ideal statute, according to political scientist Halls, would fine delinquents between two and five dollars for their "crime." Anything more – for instance, the $25 fine for which county district attorneys were to sue nonvoters in an 1889 proposal considered by the New York legislature at the request of Governor David Bennett Hill – would inhibit passage. There would have to be exceptions for things like illness or travel, but these exceptions should be narrow and precisely defined, else treasonous nonvoters would slip through the cracks and full-scale anarchy would be loosed on the land.

Massachusetts, which has so often led the nation in the enactment of far-reachingly wise and disastrously wrongheaded statutes, very nearly imposed on its citizens the nation's first compulsory-voting law in 1886. It failed by a vote of 48–43.

The Massachusetts bill stated that "It is and shall be the duty of all persons having qualifications of voters . . . to cause themselves to be registered as voters, and to cast their ballots at the polls at each National, State, county, town, and municipal election."[74] Failure to do so would result in the levying of a fine between five and twenty dollars. The duty of arresting these miscreants fell to the local police and constables. Thus did the new "science" of politics imply sending cops door to door to arrest those who failed to choose between Tweedledum and Tweedledee.

Compulsory voting has virtually fallen off the radar screen – at least for now. One suspects that if the idea is revived, it will wear a name less suggestive of coercion: say, a tax on nonvoting.

I say "virtually" because the idea re-emerges, like a long dormant dermatological disease, every now and then, usually in scholarly articles by the usual suspects. In 1996, for instance, Arend Lijphart of the University of California, San Diego, delivered a presidential address to the American Political Science Association in which the learned professor praised compulsory voting as "an egalitarian instrument." The goal, said Professor Lijphart, should be "near-universal turnout," and while there are other, less certain paths to that goal – including "relatively infrequent elections," which would seem on its face to be a denial of democratic principles; and, as an adjunct, "complete and exclusive public financing of political parties and campaigns" – Lijphart is nothing if not ardent in his ardor for total state control of our civic lives.[75] Compulsion is the way to go. It's clean, it's neat, it gets the job done. Threaten people with jail or fines if they refuse to vote and they will vote.

Lijphart brushes aside the argument of W.H. Morris-Jones in 1954 that compulsory voting belongs "to the totalitarian camp and [is] out of place in the vocabulary of liberal democracy" with the assertion that "compulsory voting entails a very small decrease in freedom," really. It's not like conscription. Or if it is like conscription, it only lasts for a little while. You get to go home after you vote. Objections to compulsion, he says, are "selfish and immoral."

It may be unconstitutional, admits Lijphart, who cites an 1896 decision of the Missouri Supreme Court that stated that "voting is not such a duty as may be enforced by compulsory legislation, that it is distinctly not within the power of any legislative authority . . . to compel the citizen to exercise it."[76] But constitutions don't carry quite the weight they used to. Especially when the greater good is at stake.

Of course voting exacts its own costs, particularly in terms of time spent reading about and considering the candidates and then making one's way to the voting booth to cast the sacred ballot. Who is to say that these costs are not excessive?

Indeed, in 1976 the economists Burton A. Abrams and Russell F. Settle, writing in the journal *Public Choice* and borrowing part of a title from Jonathan Swift, offered "A Modest Proposal for Election Reform." Abrams and Settle estimated the "voting costs" incurred by those who cast ballots in the 1972 presidential election at $270 million in 1972 dollars. They used conservative estimates in coming up with this figure: the scholars assumed that each voter expended one hour in thinking about and voting in the election – a number that may well be an understatement. They then multiplied the hours devoted to voting by the average hourly wage to come up with the "opportunity cost of a voter's time."[77]

Abrams and Settle made similar calculations for presidential elections going back to 1872. They found that since 1940, the voting costs have been from five to ten times higher than total campaign expenditures. "[E]conomic efficiency considerations," they write, "suggest that lower turnouts are preferred to higher ones."[78]

With tongues planted (perhaps not all that firmly) in cheek, Abrams and Settle outline a proposal seemingly intended to give heart attacks to the board of directors of Common Cause: random voting. Or, rather, randomly selected voters. If too small a sample of Americans cast ballots, the results have a significant probability of varying from the results had all Americans cast ballots. But if, say, one million Americans, selected randomly, cast ballots in a presidential election, the probability that these million will select a different winner than would have been selected by the entire voting population is just 2.3%. Is this an acceptable level of error? Maybe not. But consider this: the savings in voters' opportunity costs in 1972 would have been $267.03 million. And "if we assume that all previous savings from 1872 to the present had been invested in infinitely-lived capital assets offering a real return of 10% (which is reinvested), the present value of the savings [as of 1976] exceeds $200 billion!"[79]

Does that alter the equation?

Abrams and Settle go on to note that with a limited voting population, candidates would focus more on personal contacts and less on the quadrennial televised assault on our senses. And voters might become more conscientious. "Participation in a limited-voting election would presumably be viewed as a greater honor and entailing more responsibility than does voting under present circumstances," write the authors.[80] They concede the drawbacks of this Swiftian proposal. The psychic benefits of voting would be lost to all but the lucky million. The random sample might make a "mistake" – that is, select a candidate who was not the plurality choice of the entire, unsifted electorate. (Though given the fairly minor differences between the Republican and Democrat in most elections, this wouldn't matter all that much.) And as for the electoral college . . . well, once embedded in the cheek, a tongue can only do so much.

Abrams and Settle perform the useful function of making us look at a seemingly "settled" issue – in this case, the desirability of high voter turnout – from a new, fresh, and somewhat startling angle. The science-fiction writer Isaac Asimov, in his short story "Franchise" (1955), spins his fancy — or nightmare — even farther down the line. You've heard of the much-derided slogan of the U.S. Army: "An Army of One"? Asimov's tale imagines an Electorate of One.

In Asimov's tale, a computer called Multivac selects one male between the ages of 20 and 60 to cast the sole vote in determining the next president of the United States. The univoter is not the result of some totalitarian experiment. Instead, it is the product of bright-eyed reformers. As a grandfather in the story explains, Multivac "would end partisan politics, they said. No more voters' money wasted on campaigns. No more grinning nobodies high-pressured and advertising-campaigned into Congress or the White House."[81]

So rather than dirty themselves in the muck and mire of democracy, Americans have delegated the franchise to a single man, in this case a Bloomington, Indiana, schlub named Norman Muller, who is chosen Voter of the Year by computer and visited in mid-autumn by a severe-looking secret service agent, who tells Norman that "it is necessary for me to inform you on behalf of the President of the United States that you have been chosen to represent the American electorate on Tuesday, November 4, 2008."[82] The honor, if honor it is, is compulsory.

It turns out that poor Norman doesn't even get to choose a candidate. He merely answers a series of questions from Multivac, which uses his answers to create a psychological portrait of the electorate, from which the computer selects winners in every race from comptroller of Phoenix, Arizona, to President of the United States. This is far from an ideal setup, our reformers would admit, though the compulsion and the cleanliness of the process would probably attract more than a few admirers. And besides, most of the voting reforms enacted at the behest of good government advocates have had the practical effect of shrinking our choices anyway. Isn't Multivac just a ballot-access law taken to its ultimate conclusion?

Notes

1. James Madison, Alexander Hamilton, and John Jay, *The Federalist Papers*, Federalist 10, p. 78.
2. Mark Lawrence Kornbluh, *Why America Stopped Voting: The Decline of Participatory Democracy and the Emergence of Modern American Politics* (New York: New York University Press, 2000), pp. xi–xii.
3. Ibid., pp. 12–13.
4. Ibid., p. 15.

5. Ibid., p. 21.
6. Ibid., pp. 69–71.
7. Ibid., p. 52.
8. Erik Falk Petersen, "The Struggle for the Australian Ballot in California," *California Historical Quarterly* (Vol. 51, Fall 1972), p. 228.
9. Jerrold G. Rusk, "The Effect of the Australian Ballot Reform on Split Ticket Voting: 1876–1908," *American Political Science Review* (Vol. 64, No. 4, December 1970), p. 1221.
10. Lionel E. Fredman, *The Australian Ballot: The Story of an American Reform* (Lansing: Michigan State University Press, 1968), pp. 72–73.
11. Mark Lawrence Kornbluh, *Why America Stopped Voting*, p. 37.
12. Jerrold G. Rusk, "The Effect of the Australian Ballot Reform on Split Ticket Voting," p. 1221.
13. Herbert J. Bass, *"I am a Democrat": The Political Career of David Bennett Hill* (Syracuse: Syracuse University Press, 1961), pp. 99–100.
14. Frederick W. Halls, "Compulsory Voting," *Annals of the American Academy of Political and Social Science* (Vol. 1, April 1891), p. 587.
15. Lionel E. Fredman, *The Australian Ballot*, p. 85.
16. Mark Lawrence Kornbluh, *Why America Stopped Voting*, p. 89.
17. Ibid., p. 112.
18. Lionel E. Fredman, *The Australian Ballot*, p. 129.
19. Quoted in Elizabeth Rada, David Cardwell, and Alan Friedman, "Access to the Ballot," *The Urban Lawyer* (Vol. 13, No. 4, Fall 1981), p. 799.
20. Richard Winger, "How Ballot Access Laws Affect the U.S. Party System," *American Review of Politics* (Vol. 16, Winter 1995), p. 323.
21. Ibid., p. 328.
22. Ibid., p. 331.
23. Hugh A. Bone, "Small Political Parties – Casualties of War?" *National Municipal Review* (Vol. 32, November 1943), p. 524.
24. Ibid., p. 525.
25. Ibid., p. 526.
26. Steven J. Rosenstone, Roy L. Behr, and Edward H. Lazarus, *Third Parties in America*, p. 22.
27. Hugh A. Bone, "Small Political Parties – Casualties of War?," p. 527.
28. Ibid., p. 565.
29. Richard Winger, "How Ballot Access Laws Affect the U.S. Party System," p. 327. For the details of state laws, see Winger passim, pp. 321–50.
30. Ibid., p. 340.
31. Ibid., p. 338.
32. Ibid., p. 333.
33. Ibid., p. 327.
34. Steven J. Rosenstone, Roy L. Behr, and Edward H. Lazarus, *Third Parties in America*, p. 115.
35. Quoted in Elizabeth Rada, David Cardwell, and Alan Friedman, "Access to the Ballot," p. 807.

36. Richard Winger, "William Shearer Dies," *Ballot Access News*, March 5, 2007, http://ballot-access.org/2007/03/05/william-shearer-dies.

37. Elizabeth Rada, David Cardwell, and Alan Friedman, "Access to the Ballot," p. 793.

38. Diana Dwyre and Robin Kolodny, "Barriers to Minor Party Success and Prospects for Change," in *Multiparty Politics in America*, edited by Paul S. Herrnson and John C. Green (Lanham, MD: Rowman & Littlefield, 1997), p. 176.

39. E. Joshua Rosenkranz, *Voter Choice '96: A 50-State Report Card on the Presidential Elections* (New York: Brennan Center for Justice, 1996), p. 14.

40. *Longo v. U.S. Postal Service*, 983 F.2d 9 (2nd Cir. 1992), p. 9.

41. Richard Winger, "How Ballot Access Laws Affect the U.S. Party System," p. 321.

42. Elizabeth Rada, David Cardwell, and Alan Friedman, "Access to the Ballot," p. 795.

43. Ibid., p. 797.

44. Quoted in Richard Winger, "How Ballot Access Laws Affect the U.S. Party System," p. 341.

45. Elizabeth Rada, David Cardwell, and Alan Friedman, "Access to the Ballot," p. 795.

46. *Lippitt v. Cipollone, 404 U.S. 1032* (1972), Mr. Justice Douglas dissenting.

47. Quoted in Elizabeth Rada, David Cardwell, and Alan Friedman, "Access to the Ballot," p. 810.

48. Richard Winger, "How Ballot Access Laws Affect the U.S. Party System," pp. 343–44.

49. Katharine Q. Seelye, "Parties Team Up to Protect Their Turf," *New York Times*, June 24, 1997.

50. E. Joshua Rosenkranz, *Voter Choice 2000: A 50-State Report Card on the Presidential Elections* (New York: Brennan Center for Justice, 2000), p. 2.

51. Quoted in E. Joshua Rosenkranz, *Voter Choice '96*, pp. 11–12.

52. Ibid., p. 58. The statistics following may be found in Rosenkranz, *passim*, pp. 5–85.

53. Ibid., p. 74.

54. Ibid., p. 64.

55. Steven J. Rosenstone, Roy L. Behr, and Edward H. Lazarus, *Third Parties in America*, p. 24.

56. Peter H. Argersinger, "'A Place on the Ballot'," pp. 288–289.

57. Ibid., pp. 287–88.

58. Ibid., p. 296.

59. Ibid., p. 300.

60. Ibid., p. 297.

61. Quoted in Theodore J. Lowi, "Toward a More Responsible Three-Party System: Deregulating American Democracy," p. 366.

62. Peter H. Argersinger, "'A Place on the Ballot'," p. 304.

63. Ibid., pp. 303–304.

64. Howard A. Scarrow, "Cross-Endorsement and Cross-Filing in Plurality Partisan Elections," in *Electoral Laws and their Political Consequences*, edited by Bernard Grofman and Arend Lijphart (New York: Agathon Press, 1994 [1986]), p. 248.

65. *Timmons v. Twin Cities Area New Party* (1997), U.S. Supreme Court Syllabus, No. 95–1608, unpaginated.

66. Peter H. Argersinger, "'A Place on the Ballot'," p. 291.

67. G. Bingham Powell, Jr., "American Voter Turnout in Comparative Perspective," *American Political Science Review* (Vol. 80, No. 1, March 1986), pp. 20–21.

68. Steven J. Rosenstone and Raymond E. Wolfinger, "The Effect of Registration Laws on Voter Turnout," *American Political Science Review* (Vol. 72, No. 1, March 1978), p. 22.

69. Harris J. Clinton, "Compulsory Voting Demanded," *North American Review* (Vol. 145, December 1887), p. 685.

70. Frederick W. Halls, "Compulsory Voting," p. 602.

71. Ibid., pp. 600–601.

72. Ibid., pp. 602–603.

73. Quoted in ibid., p. 591.

74. Quoted in ibid., p. 613.

75. Arend Lijphart, "Unequal Participation: Democracy's Unresolved Dilemma," *American Political Science Review* (Vol. 91, No. 1, March 1997), p. 2.

76. Ibid., p. 11.

77. Burton A. Abrams and Russell F. Settle, "A Modest Proposal for Election Reform," *Public Choice* (Vol. 28, Winter 1976), p. 39.

78. Ibid., p. 45.

79. Ibid., p. 47.

80. Ibid., p. 50.

81. Isaac Asimov, "Franchise," in *Earth Is Room Enough* (New York: Fawcett Crest, 1957), p. 60.

82. Ibid., p. 63.

.

Chapter 4

Then Along Came FECA

There were no campaign finance laws to speak of from the founding of the republic through the end of the nineteenth century. This laissez-faire circumstance burdened the nation with such prominent political figures as George Washington, Thomas Jefferson, Andrew Jackson, Abraham Lincoln, and Grover Cleveland – certainly a far cry from such products of the campaign finance reform era as Michael Dukakis, Bill Clinton, and George W. Bush.

Government employees, who as agents of the state had a vested interest in its expansion, were the first organized contributors to campaigns, though in many cases their "donations" were as voluntary as that of the cornered pedestrian handing over his wallet to a pistol-wielding mugger. The Jacksonian Democrats of the 1830s, founders of the spoils system, imposed a levy on New York US customs employees. As Robert E. Mutch notes in *Campaigns, Congress, and Courts* (1988), his history of campaign finance, the result of this shakedown was an 1839 bill by the Whigs to ban federal officers from paying "any money toward the election of any public functionary, whether of the General or State Government."

The bill failed, of course. Politicians were not about to cut off the most reliable source of campaign revenue. But, the Democrats were not alone in this practice. Soon they were to be joined by the party that succeeded the Whigs. In the post-Civil War era, the Republicans milked federal employees just as vigorously as the Jacksonian Democrats had, if not more so: in 1876, for instance, federal employees paid 2% of their salaries to the GOP.[1]

If this sounds outrageous, it is because it was outrageous. Press coverage of such abuses fueled the civil service reform movement and the passage of legislation prohibiting such assessments. The burden of funding the parties

J. T. Bennett, *Not Invited to the Party*, DOI 10.1007/978-1-4419-0366-2_4,
© Springer Science+Business Media, LLC 2009

then shifted to the corporations, many of which, anyway, were busy lobbying for tariffs, land grants, and special subsidies. Political contributions became merely a cost of doing business.

For instance, close to half of the Grand Old Party (GOP)'s national war chest in the 1888 campaign, won by protectionist Benjamin Harrison against the free-trade Democrat Grover Cleveland, came from Pennsylvania corporate and manufacturing interests with a direct stake in trade and industrial policy. Department store muckamuck John Wanamaker staked Harrison $50,000 – which is about half a million dollars in current value.[2] It is no coincidence that the rise of the lavishly contributing tycoon coincided with the swelling of the national government and its increasing involvement in the national economy.

The states were first to regulate campaign contributions. Four states banned corporate contributions during the 1890s, as the populist movement blew in from the West. The critics of corporate subsidies of the parties had a point, but they missed the larger point: if the problem is government dispensing favors to large contributors, rather than institute a series of difficult-to-enforce and possibly unconstitutional restrictions on those contributors, why not just bar government from dispensing the favors? Why not sharply reduce the goodies government has to hand out? Corporate contributions, in such a world, would dry up with a Saharan completeness.

Corporations were barred from contributing to federal campaigns by the Tillman Act in 1907; similar restrictions were placed on labor unions in 1943. In 1925, the Federal Corrupt Practices Act reinforced the ban on corporate or bank contributions and also mandated the reporting of contributions. This act was about as effective as a jaywalking statute in midtown Manhattan: no one was ever prosecuted under it. The Hatch Act of 1940, which limited individual donations to candidates for federal office to $5,000, was similarly limp: because an individual could donate to as many campaign committees as he wished, well-heeled candidates simply set up an array of committees, effectively gutting the contribution limit.

The first major American politician to propose that government foot the bill for campaigns seems to have been the irrepressible President Theodore Roosevelt in 1907. His intention was to drive out corruption with the massive infusion of tax monies. This was something of an irony, given that Roosevelt's presidential campaigns were largely subsidized by Wall Street, or at least those Wall Street interests his trust-busting policies had not harmed. But then scourging corruption is, along with "leveling" the playing field by barring large donations, one of the two basic arguments advanced even now for public financing.

The Rooseveltian big stick may have been fine for diplomacy, but the begging cup, it seems, was better suited for the candidate. TR's public subsidy proposal went nowhere. The next president to endorse public financing was another enthusiast of activist government, Harry Truman, who also failed to convince Congress of his nostrum's wisdom.

Meanwhile, in the laboratories of democracy, the first state to directly subsidize its political parties was Colorado, which in 1909 enacted a law by which parties were given 25 cents for each vote received in the most recent election for governor. The funds were split 50–50 between the state party and its local affiliates. Private contributions, except that from the candidate (and those were capped), were banned. This would have amounted to a rich-get-richer scheme, as the party in power subsidized itself to the comparative disadvantage of its rivals. The Colorado Supreme Court struck down the law in 1910.[3]

Agitation for a national public finance law was sporadic. Its most prominent congressional promoter was Senator Richard L. Neuberger, an Oregon Democrat who in 1956 introduced legislation to subsidize the Republican and Democratic National Committees from the public treasury. Neuberger's bill failed to gain traction: it was burdened by a complicated allocation formula tying the subsidy to votes received for president and Congress, and besides, the whole thing smacked of socialism, which then was still a potent word. Senator Neuberger had been a *New York Times* correspondent before embarking on his political career, and this was precisely the sort of big-spending, regulation-happy measure that was made for the *Times* but not the times.

The advocates had succeeded, however, in attaching a blandly vanilla name to their scheme. Yet "Public funding," as the dissident Federal Election Commission (FEC) commissioner and law professor Bradley A. Smith has written, "is a misnomer. Campaigns are funded by the public now — by hundreds of thousands, even millions of citizens who make voluntary contributions to various candidates and organizations. What is euphemistically called 'public' funding actually means 'government' funded campaigns, or 'tax' funding of campaigns."[4] Senator Neuberger declined to call his plan "tax funding" and the press went along with him and his successors.

Dipping into the treasury to pay for politicians' campaigns was excused on the grounds of (1) equality, or leveling the playing field; and (2) removing corruption from the messy process of campaign fundraising. As we shall see, neither goal was achieved, though an unstated goal — securing a tax-funded entitlement for the two major parties and giving them a greater leg up on challengers — was achieved quite nicely, thank you.

In 1966, Senator Russell Long (D-LA), son of the legendary populist Huey Long and mainstay of the Senate Finance Committee, sponsored legislation for public financing of presidential campaigns through a taxpayer checkoff. Long sold his plan with populist language directed at the fat cats, but underneath the veneer was a raw power-grab: the Long bill proposed to give the two parties one dollar for each vote received in the previous presidential election. What splendid timing the senator had! For the previous election had been a Democratic blowout in the popular as well as the electoral vote. Democrat Lyndon B. Johnson won 43,167,895 votes to Republican Barry Goldwater's 27,146,969. Thus the Democrats would receive $16 million more than the Republicans under Senator Long's plan. And as for third parties, well, they were out of luck. As chance had it, 1964 was the worst year for third parties in American history. The best showing by a candidate other than Johnson or Goldwater was the measly 42,642 votes tallied by the Socialist Labor Party's Eric Hass. The SLP's take under the Long bill would have been $42,642, or not even enough to pay LBJ's bourbon bill. As for other third-party or independent candidates who might rise to challenge the status quo – as George Wallace would in the very next election – well, the Socialist Laborites were getting 42,000. Wasn't that enough choice for you?

The Long bill passed, in modified form. The Senate Finance Committee altered it to more equitably distribute funds among those parties that tallied more than 10 million votes – which effectively limited the subsidy to two parties. The committee also created the Presidential Election Campaign Fund (PECF), which was to be primed with money from an income-tax checkoff. As one observer noted, this was "the lone historical example of Congress determining the size of an appropriation not by the needs of a program, but by what in essence is a yearly public referendum."[5] Not a bad idea – certainly such a referendum would effectively starve much of the federal government and greatly shrink the size of the national state. As one PECF supporter asked, "Given the same choice for other government programs, how many would receive the support of even a quarter of eligible taxpayers?"[6] An excellent question – but of course the questioner is not proposing to extend this principle to other programs but rather to deprive taxpayers of even this one limited choice.

Long's bill was signed by that impeccable paragon of clean elections and Common Cause-like virtue, President Lyndon Baines Johnson. Much of the act was repealed or suspended the next year, so no funds were distributed in 1968 or 1972. Remember that 1966, the year when public financing was born, albeit in a stillbirth, was the last year of the Democratic Goldwater-landslide Congress, so the Democrats pretty much had their way. Republicans staged a comeback in 1966; unlimited federal spending was passing from fashion. The Republican Party, which at that time had a faction skeptical of huge new government programs, acted as a semi-brake on the ambitions of the public financing crowd.

The first congressional proposal for public financing of presidential elections had been advanced early in the twentieth century by Bourke Cockran (D-NY), a Tammany Hall Democrat, famed orator, and stalwart of the laissez-faire wing of the Democratic Party. Cockran, somewhat incongruously given his libertarian views, proposed that all parties that receive above 15% of the vote would receive equal monies; those below 15% – that is, everyone other than the Republicans and Democrats – would get none.

Government funding of political campaigns became lodged within the Democratic Party, not as an official plank but as a "new idea" that reformers occasionally dug out and dusted off. Public finance was to "purify" politics, to remove from it the dirty money of the corporations. What the Democrats never seemed to realize is that the best way to remove corporate influence from elections is to greatly reduce the scope of what the government does. If there are no subsidies to dole out to favored corporations, corporations won't much care which candidate is elected to public office.

Opponents of public financing of parties, as Senator Long's bill called for – that is, financing of the *two major* parties; independents and new third parties were out of luck – ranged from conservative Republicans to independent-minded liberal Democrats. North Carolina Democratic Senator Sam Ervin said that it "could . . . lead to monolithic party structure with rigid, stifling party discipline." Perhaps surprisingly, Senator Bobby Kennedy (D-NY) also criticized it, saying that he feared "its potential for centralization of political power."[7]

More philosophically, critics of public financing and spending caps have asked why inequalities in wealth demand legislative correction but why other inequalities – just as glaring – in such campaign-related talents as oratory, the ability to think on one's feet, comeliness or the lack thereof, and charisma, do not. Was it fair that Walter Mondale had all the magnetism of, um, Walter Mondale? Ought not there have been a remedial program to bring him up to the charisma level of Ronald Reagan? Or, conversely, to bring Reagan down to the charm line of Walter Mondale?

Treating money differently than other contributions or campaign assets advantages those well-educated elites who are able to give substantially to political candidates in ways not measurable by the system. Bradley A. Smith offers the example of "a politically talented, twenty-five-year-old Harvard law student from a privileged background, who chooses to volunteer on a presidential campaign during summer break, passing up a law firm clerkship paying $15,000 for the summer. Consider, at the same time, a West Virginia high school dropout who goes to work in a body shop at the age of 17, scrapes together some money to launch his own shop at age 22, opens a second shop 2 years later, and then at age 25, angered over government policies affecting his business, seeks to promote political change by contributing $15,000 to a political campaign. Each individual seeks to forego $15,000 in consumption to promote his political beliefs, but only the activities of the Harvard law student are legal."[8]

Where, one wonders, is the fairness or justness in that?

Of course, as it is the Harvard law graduates who write the laws, not the West Virginia garage owners, the question would never even occur to the reformers.

"Politicians generally hate the process"[9] of fund-raising, says Richard C. Leone, president of the Twentieth Century Fund and a former Democratic aspirant for a US Senate seat from New Jersey. Well, many of us hate the process of paying our utility bills, or taking out a second mortgage to send our children to college, or shelling out a hundred bucks for tickets to a premier sporting event. But does that mean that we have the right to pass the bill along to the American taxpayer?

Democratic campaign finance enthusiasts thought so. And so Russell Long's dream of public financing was resurrected in 1971.

The 1971 Federal Election Campaign Act (FECA) provided the bare bones on which the FECA amendments of 1974 would build. Among other things, it limited a candidate's contributions to his own campaign and toughened fund-raising reporting requirements. Meanwhile, the Revenue Act of 1971 put into place the income tax-checkoff-financed system of campaign financing that would take effect in the 1976 presidential election.

As amended in 1974, FECA sought to revolutionize – or stifle – the way Americans paid for federal political campaigns. A heretofore private system was partially nationalized. Taxpayers, motivated by patriotic duty or Mugwump zeal or just a "what the hell" impulse, could direct a dollar ($2 for joint filers) toward the PECF, the exchequer of the FECA. Out of the PECF came payments to primary hopefuls, to the parties for their conventions, and to general election candidates. The checkoff was supposed to permit the taxpayer to choose which political party gets his dollar, but the IRS commissioner told the Senate in 1973 that this option would take up too much space on the tax return. (Which is not exactly a model of concision, as you may have noticed.)

FECA limited individual or group contributions to a candidate for federal elective office to $1,000 per campaign (the limit for political action committees was $5,000). Individuals were forbidden from contributing more than $25,000 annually. (The self-described liberal fat cat Stewart Mott was bewildered by this provision: "I'm allowed to give one thousand dollars directly to any one of twenty-five different candidates but why would a twenty-sixth gift of one thousand dollars be corrupting if the first twenty-five such gifts are not?"[10] An unanswerable question.) With the contribution limit, FECA squelched the possibility of an insurgent candidate, whether working within or without the two-party system, making waves with the backing of one or a handful of well-off supporters. As the chairman of the Libertarian Party, Edward Crane, observed, FECA is "the only law that ever did exactly what it was intended to do: cement the two-party system in an impregnable fortress of cash from which no challenger could ever evict them."[11]

The limits applied also to candidates expending personal funds. Various record-keeping and clerical responsibilities were mandated by FECA, as was the creation of an eight-member FEC to administer the law. The FEC would have eight members: two appointed by the President (subject to congressional confirmation), two by the President Pro Tempore of the Senate, two by the Speaker of the House, and the other two were ex officio, being the Secretary of the Senate and Clerk of the House.

The 1974 FECA amendments clamped spending limits of $75,000 on races for the US House of Representatives and $250,000 (and up, depending on a state's population) for US Senate campaigns – "amounts wholly inadequate for modern campaigning,"[12] as Bradley A. Smith noted.

For the first time, the federal government had entered the business of paying for partisan political campaigns. The FECA amended the Internal Revenue Code to establish a system of public financing for presidential primary and general election campaigns. Primary candidates who received at least $5,000 in private contributions from at least twenty states – that is, $100,000 – were eligible for government matching funds on the first $250 of each donation. Only that $250 was counted toward the $5,000 threshold. (The 1974 act did *not* include public funding of congressional elections, as the Senate had wanted.)

In return for the quick cash – for there is always a catch – those who accepted federal monies were bound by spending limits. There were and are also state-by-state ceilings, which are determined by an absurdly intricate formula which begins by multiplying a state's voting-age population by 16 cents and goes from there. What this really does is simply to apply the gloss of science to an act of sheer arbitrariness. But don't worry: candidates routinely ignore or circumvent the state-by-state ceilings through bookkeeping legerdemain or the manipulation of loopholes.

In the general election for president, the FECA created a three-tier party system: "major" parties, or those that received at least 25% of the vote in the last election – read: Democrats and Republicans – are blessed with the fullest funding. "Minor" parties, or those whose presidential candidates received more than 5% but less than 25% of the vote in the last election, were eligible for a fraction of the pie. And "new" parties may receive a limited subsidy after Election Day in the event their candidate receives at least 5% of the nationwide popular vote.

The FECA also provided for the subsidization of the parties' quadrennial nominating conventions, those stage-managed bacchanals which H.L. Mencken, back in the day that conventions still had a smidgen of spontaneity and authenticity, described thusly: "One sits through long sessions, wishing heartily that all the delegates and alternates were dead and in hell – and then suddenly there comes a show so gaudy and hilarious, so melodramatic and obscene, so unimaginably exhilarating and preposterous that one lives a gorgeous year in an hour."[13] The theory behind the FECA provision was that conventions, freed from the fetor and grime of dirty private money and liberated by the beneficence of public money, would cease to be wild and wooly affairs directed by cigar-chomping backroom bosses. Well, they certainly ceased to be that. But what they became, instead, were antiseptic and soulless advertisements for the Republican and Democratic Parties, paid for by the federal government.

The political atmosphere in which FECA was conceived was not exactly fecal, but it wasn't far from it. Richard M. Nixon was in the White House, with all the corruption (and, from his opponents, the feverish overreaction) that the name Nixon implies. Reform was in the air, and when that happens, defenders of the Constitution and liberty had best duck. Or at least put on hardhats. A semi-hysterical *Time* cover story, "The Disgrace of Campaign Financing," which appeared in the heat of the '72 campaign, is illustrative.

This was before the days of bylined *Time* dispatches, so the author or authors speak with pompous, almost magisterial anonymity. They are, they want us to know, disgusted. Are they disgusted by an undeclared war that has claimed 50,000 Americans lives and hundreds of thousands, if not millions, of Vietnamese lives? Well, no. What had excited their disgust in October of 1972 was "the venerable US political practice of making every candidate for public office, from President down to town clerk, depend upon voluntary contributions to get elected." (Public financing of elections for town clerk? This is certainly a new frontier in campaign finance reform!)

The verb choice in that passage is revealing. The "US" is "making" those who run for office collect funds by "voluntary" means. Just how voluntarism has become compulsory is a confusion the author passes by. For he is (or they are) in high dudgeon. It seems that "the system embarrasses and compromises both donor and candidate, openly invites corruption, and suggests to an increasingly cynical public that favors can be bought." True, though the best way to defuse this system – seriously reduce the power of those elected to office so that in turn special interests have little if any incentive to offer bribes, even if politicians are eager to accept them – never enters the *Time* writer's mind. Democratic US Senator and losing 1968 presidential candidate Hubert Humphrey (MN) may whine that "Raising campaign funds is the most distasteful, demeaning and embarrassing aspect of elective politics," but leaving aside the hypocrisy – few candidates in memory were better at sweet-talking rich men out of their money than Humphrey was – what he is saying is that it would be much more pleasant for him if he could unload this burden onto the taxpayer.

But now here comes the kicker: the current system "undermines the premise that all individuals, regardless of wealth, are equal under the law."[14] In this formulation, sending a check to a favored candidate (or cause) is an unacceptable exhibit of inequality. Any contribution greater than that made by the poorest (or most indifferent) member of society is an affront to equality. Presumably it should be banned. And so the entire responsibility for funding campaigns should fall on – or be seized by – the government.

Democrats' embrace of public financing was not necessarily motivated by purity and good intentions. As Robert E. Mutch points out, "Hubert Humphrey's 1968 presidential campaign had plunged the party $9 million into debt." New incumbent Richard Nixon had a formidable fund-raising team; the Republicans were far more unified than the war-riven Democrats. The Nixon war chest was fortified by illegal six-digit corporate contributions as well as enormous subventions from such men as Clement Stone ($2.1 million) and Richard Scaife ($1 million).

The self-proclaimed party of the people needed to even the playing field, and how better to do that than by coercing the people into funding its campaigns through taxes? (As with Humphrey, many of the leading Democrats were eager shakers-down of rich men for money. Senator Albert Gore (D-TN), father of the future vice president and global-warming Cassandra, was a prominent public financing advocate – even though Armand Hammer's

Occidental Petroleum had proven very helpful to Senator Gore, both personally and professionally, through the years.)

"The Democrats' revival of government election subsidies had been
planned in the summer of 1971 at a meeting of presidential primary con-
tenders and congressional party leaders in the apartment of national chairman Lawrence F. O'Brien," writes Robert E. Mutch.[15] The bill introduced in
1971 was similar to the earlier Russell Long measure, though rather than
directly subsidize the parties it subsidized the candidates. (Mischievously,
Wyoming Republican Clifford Hansen offered an amendment providing that
no taxpayer money could fund a candidate if his party had not paid off a
previous campaign debt. Take that, Democrats!)

Those hunting for a partisan twist to the story need go no further than the
1976 presidential election, the first in which FECA's public financing was in
effect. Writing in 1978 in the *Journal of Political Economy*, the economists Burton
A. Abrams and Russell F. Settle of the University of Delaware examine the first
FECA-controlled election from the vantage point of the economic theory of
regulation, which holds that "rational, self-interested individuals, groups, or
industries seek regulation as a means of serving their own private interests."[16]
Regulations, in this view, do not advance some theoretical public interest but
rather the interests of those who write the regulations. In the case of FECA, that
would be the Democrats who wrote and passed the legislation establishing the
public financing and spending limit provisions.

As Abrams and Settle point out, the alarmist hysteria over "skyrocketing
campaign costs" was unsupported by facts. Before the admittedly expensive
1972 race, spending on presidential campaigns had been relatively flat for
years. Indeed, it had declined sharply since the 1928 and 1936 elections,
which were, prior to 1972, the most expensive of the century. In 1928, the
candidates spent an average of 38.3 cents per adult (in 1972 dollars); in
1936, the spending surged to 49.4 cents, or far greater than the expenditure per adult in such elections as 1948 (7.2 cents), 1952 (15.8), and 1960
(23.1). The most noticeable development in the elections just prior to the
passage of FECA was the growth in Republican campaign spending. The
gap between the parties "widened dramatically in the 1964, 1968, and
1972 campaigns," as the GOP established itself as the party with the largest (and still growing) war chest. While in 1960 the Republicans barely
outspent the Democrats in the presidential campaign ($10.1 million vs.
$9.8 million), the difference opened to canyonesque proportions in subse-
quent elections: $7.3 million in 1964, $11.8 million in 1968, and $22
million in 1972.[17]

So it should not surprise anyone aside from the most terminally naïve officer of the League of Women Voters that Democrats, able to tell which way the campaign winds were blowing, took a bold stand for reform. Not just for any reform: for a reform that would cap campaign spending and nullify the Republican advantage. Abrams and Settle note that in the Senate, the 1974 FECA amendments were supported by 80% of Democrats and 42% of Republicans, while in the House, an overwhelming 99% of Democrats and 75% of Republicans cast their ayes on it.

Surely the Republicans who voted for FECA – and the Republican president who signed it into law, knowing that he had run his last race anyway – basked in the glow of media praise. But they may also have shot themselves in the foot. Or rather in the head. For as Abrams and Settle write, "empirical evidence . . . strongly suggests that the public financing and expenditure limitation provisions of FECA cost Gerald Ford the [1976] election."[18]

The Ford and Jimmy Carter campaigns were given $21.8 million apiece for the general election. Using a spending-share variable to capture the expected party expenditures absent federal financing and the expected vote gain per increase in spending, the economists present models in which Ford's share of the popular vote would have increased from the 48% he received to 52% – presumably enough to have tipped the vote in enough states so that he would have defeated Carter in the electoral college as well as the popular vote. Conclude Abrams and Settle, "These findings suggest that the Federal Election Campaign Act was instrumental in determining the outcome of the 1976 presidential election."[19]

(The trends described above continue. As Vice Dean of the Columbia University School of Law Richard Briffault notes, "[l]arge donors" – that is, those who give $200 or more to congressional candidates – are "more conservative in political orientation and more Republican in party affiliation than the general population."[20] It is therefore in the interest of the Democratic Party to cap their donations.)

The Ford-Carter race, especially the presence of the relatively unknown Georgia peanut farmer, was part of the unknowable future when on January 2, 1975, a seemingly motley but in some ways perfectly congruent set of individuals and organizations filed suit against the FECA of 1971, as amended in 1974.

The plaintiffs included ex-Senator Eugene McCarthy, who would launch an independent run for the presidency in 1976; US Senator James Buckley (Conservative-NY), who had been elected on a third-party line in 1970 and would run (unsuccessfully, as it turned out) for reelection in 1976; liberal moneybags donor Stewart Mott, who was a major financial backer of McCarthy in 1968 and later John Anderson in 1980; McCarthy's campaign organization, the Committee for a Constitutional Presidency; the Conservative Party of New York State; the Mississippi Republican Party; the national Libertarian Party; the New York Civil Liberties Union (NYCLU); the American Conservative Union; the Conservative Victory Fund; and the right-wing newsletter *Human Events*. All in all, a curious gathering unlikely to be duplicated at any Georgetown cocktail party, but a set of people and organizations who at least shared, at some level, a commitment to more speech, not less speech; and freer speech, not more restricted speech.

The plaintiffs had kicked off their suit contesting the constitutionality of FECA with a December 1974 press conference featuring Senators Buckley and McCarthy and NYCLU executive director Ira Glasser. Senator McCarthy, who had bid farewell to the two-party system and was exploring alternative ways to mount a national campaign, said of FECA that "It is the same as saying the country is going to have two established religions."[21]

(Buckley, significantly, was elected to the Senate in 1970 as the candidate of the New York Conservative Party, a party that is the product of the Empire State's fusion law, though he won without benefit of fusion: the Republican incumbent, the appointed US Senator Charles Goodell, seemed too much like the Democratic liberal candidate, Rep. Richard Ottinger, and so the field was clear for a right-wing alternative. The mild-mannered and genial Buckley took the three-way race with 38% of the vote. Next time around, in 1976, he ran as the Republican-Conservative fusion nominee and lost to the Democrat-Liberal, Daniel Patrick Moynihan.)

The D.C. Circuit Court of Appeals upheld the constitutionality of the FECA, though it did strike down the limits on campaign expenditures, individual expenditures, and a candidate's personal expenditures as violating the First Amendment. The Court of Appeals rejected the plaintiffs' assertion that FECA invidiously discriminated against new and third parties in violation of the due process clause of the Fifth Amendment; in fact, it stated, in revealing language, that it furthered "vital governmental interests in relieving major-party candidates from the *rigors* of soliciting private contributions" and by "not funding candidates who lack significant public support."[22]

That "relieving" nominees of the Republican and Democratic parties (but not other parties) of the "rigors" of paying for their own campaigns is a "vital governmental interest" would have come as news to the Framers of the Constitution. They purposely omitted any reference to parties in the document; they certainly never dreamed that the federal government would fund the parties whose development they dreaded. The case went on to the US Supreme Court.

The resulting US Supreme Court decision, *Buckley v. Valeo* (1976), is probably second only to *Roe v. Wade* (1973) on any list of famous or infamous Supreme Court rulings of the latter half of the twentieth century. And like *Roe*, the titular figures were not cardboard cutouts. The Valeo who gave his name to history was Francis R. "Frank" Valeo, Secretary of the US Senate from 1966 to 1977. As usual in history, veins of irony run through his story. Frank Valeo was the Brooklyn-born son of a shoe-factory foreman who hooked up with Senator Mike Mansfield (D-MT), the softspoken Montana Democrat who succeeded the un-softspoken Lyndon Baines Johnson as Senate Majority Leader. Mansfield placed his highly regarded aide in the Senate's top administrative slot. Valeo was a shrewd mixture of streetcorner politics and intellect, and he counseled against the reformist spasm with which the Democratic Congress greeted Watergate. He was said to be against several provisions of the FECA, which, among other things, placed Secretary of the Senate Valeo on the FEC as an ex officio member – as a kind of counter-watchdog, to make sure the FEC didn't bother incumbents *too* much. So while Valeo's name was on the lawsuit and was thereby incised into the pages of judicial history, the man behind the Valeo name was ambivalent about the lawsuit. According to the *Washington Post*, he and Senator Buckley jokingly exchanged autographed copies of the Supreme Court decision, which Senator Buckley inscribed "to a good loser." After retirement, Valeo went on to an elective political career of his own on the Friendship Heights (Maryland) Village Council. He didn't need to accept matching funds or have a limit imposed on his expenditures by the all-wise muckamucks of the FEC. Instead, Councilman Valeo "walked around town with his French bulldog, Buddy, to whom he had attached a sandwich board announcing his candidacy."[23]

The Supreme Court gave Congress half a loaf in *Buckley v. Valeo*. It upheld FECA's public financing provisions and contribution limits but struck down its spending limits. Justice Potter Stewart, in oral arguments, gave a preview of the decision when he said: "We are talking about speech, money is speech and speech is money, whether it is buying television or radio time or newspaper advertising, or even buying pencils and paper and microphones."[24]

The Supreme Court linked political expenditures to the First Amendment: "A restriction on the amount of money a person or group can spend on political communication during a campaign necessarily reduces the quantity of expression by restricting the number of issues discussed, the depth of their exploration, and the size of the audience reached. This is because virtu-ally every means of communicating ideas in today's mass society requires the expenditure of money. The distribution of the humblest handbill or leaflet entails printing, paper, and circulation costs. Speeches and rallies generally necessitate hiring a hall and publicizing the event. The electorate's increasing dependence on television, radio, and other mass media for news and informa-tion has made these expensive modes of communication indispensable instruments of effective political speech."

The FECA's limits on campaign expenditures, therefore, "represent substantial rather than merely theoretical restraints on the quantity and diversity of political speech." Yet the cap on an *individual*'s donations "entails only a marginal restriction upon the contributor's ability to engage in free communication." It "permits the symbolic expression of support evidenced by a contribution but does not in any way infringe the contributor's freedom to discuss candidates and issues."[25] If this seems like a contradiction of the principle laid down in the previous paragraph, that's because it is. And it contained the seeds of further mischief in this strange decision, which is by parts lucid and obscure, liberty-friendly, and regulatory-happy.

For instance, the appellants charged that the $1,000 contribution ceiling violated the First Amendment by restricting political speech and that it also "discriminates against candidates opposing incumbent officeholders and against minor-party candidates in violation of the Fifth Amendment."[26] It becomes exponentially more difficult for an outsider candidate to raise money when such a low ceiling is placed on donations. Long-shots and radi-cals, lacking large bases of upper-middle-class donors, need sugar daddies. Clamping down on big-money contributors amounts to an incumbent-pro-tection and minor-party suppression scheme. Contribution limits, argues Bradley A. Smith, "insulate the political system from challenge by outsiders, and hinder the ability of challengers to compete on equal terms with those already in power."[27]

No one knew this better than Stewart Mott. Heir to an industrial fortune, Mott became involved in liberal politics as a young man in the 1960s. His youth was no handicap, though, rather in the way that the boy who brings the football to the sandlot always gets to play in the game, no matter his skill level. Mott was rich, and his riches bought him access. He played a major role in financing Eugene McCarthy's 1968 primary campaign, dipping into his fortune to the tune of $210,000; he was also a significant supporter of George McGovern in 1972 and John Anderson in 1980.

The FECA cramped Mott's style. More fundamentally, he believed, it violated his rights. In 1980, as the Anderson campaign sputtered to a disappointing close, Stewart Mott unloaded on the law he called not only an incumbent protection act but "an employment act for attorneys."

"I am not a lawyer," declared Mott. "I am a fat cat." He struck directly at the philosophical premise of limiting expenditures, saying that "there are always going to be imbalances in campaigns. Some candidates are going to have the good looks of a Robert Redford and others are not. I question whether it is in the public interest to start regulating all the aspects of campaign activity." Exhibiting a praiseworthy respect for those on the other side of the partisan divide, he continued, "I would hate to see, for example, a law which in the interest of preventing corruption, would say that Frank Sinatra can only make so many appearances on behalf of his favorite candidate. Or that Jerry Falwell can speak only so many times or that Richard Viguerie can only use so many pieces of direct mail in his mail operation."[28]

Mott argues that in restricting individual expenditures, the law chokes off grassroots activity. He points to the dearth of campaign buttons in post-FECA elections. Contributing money is a direct and personal entree into politics; shutting off that route is going to deprive politics of invigorating participants as well as the dreaded fat cats. The law also dampens "spontaneity and fluidity." Once upon a time, says Mott, the engaged or outraged (and well-heeled) citizen could buy an ad in a newspaper or form an ad hoc committee on the spur of the moment. But now one must check first with a lawyer, or request an opinion from the FEC, if one's action touches, even slightly, on a candidate for federal office.

The Supreme Court, in *Buckley v. Valeo*, left individual expenditures unrelated to political campaigns protected but subjected expenditures related to campaigns to a dizzying array of regulations. This was not the law's only inconsistency, of course: it also created "a fine distinction between giving money and spending money which is very hard for me, as a layman, to understand." Says Mott: "I find it very, very hazardous to create a body of law which says just how much money a person may spend on behalf of a cause."[29]

Because Mott was an ideologue, not a party hack, and had just come off a frustrating experience with the independent campaign for president of the somewhat dithering suburban liberal John Anderson, he was especially sensitive to the ways in which the FECA discriminates against third parties and independents. (Parenthetically, he castigated Anderson for his Beltway mentality in leaping the ballot-access hurdles. The candidate retained the Washington establishment law firm of Arnold & Porter, which plodded heavily — and no doubt expensively — through the obstacle course. Anderson ought to have taken a lesson from the Libertarians, George Wallace, and Eugene McCarthy in 1976, who although "very short on both troops and money . . . had broken down the door to the ballot in many states."[30] He should have waged a guerrilla campaign — but then if he had done that, he would not have been John Anderson.)

Anderson had insisted early on that his was an independent candidacy, and that he was not creating a third party. But to qualify for federal subvention, he needed to pretend that he was the standard bearer of the somewhat imaginary National Unity Party. Independents — being independent, one supposes — were kept from the trough by FECA. Parties were not. As Mott writes, "the candidates of national parties beginning with capital 'D' and capital 'R' and now John Anderson, are the beneficiaries" of federal campaign funding. "But the independent candidate or third-party candidate who has not qualified for presidential funding is stuck with the old one-thousand dollar ceiling on contributions from individuals. That ceiling does not rise with inflation and is an inequity which will continue to dampen the effectiveness of third-party activities."[31] (As it happens, Anderson let the National Unity Party die, failing to run a candidate in 1984. But then the party was always a fiction anyway, for Anderson's was an independent run.)

"I'm in favor of repealing the whole damn law," concludes Mott of FECA, "except for the disclosure provisions — the American public should know where the money is coming from and base its decisions on the merits and demerits of the candidate."[32]

Mott, based on personal experience, had broken with liberal orthodoxy. He had seen that campaign finance reform is just another way of privileging elites over outsiders, the status quo over possibilities for change. And he had seen just how debilitating FECA, and those sections of *Buckley v. Valeo* that upheld it, were to American dissent.

Back to the decision. The Court's opinion in *Buckley v. Valeo* is alternately incisive and confusing. For instance, in one footnote, it handily rejects an analogy used by some advocates of regulation: specifically, the Court in *Kovacs v. Cooper* (1949) had ruled that just as the government has the right to regulate the decibel level of a sound truck blaring a political message, so may it regulate the volume of money in a political campaign. The "fundamental misconception" of the regulators, stated the Court in *Buckley v. Valeo*, is that the local ordinance upheld in *Kovacs*, while it banned "loud and raucous" political speech emanating from the soundtruck, imposed "no restriction upon the communication of ideas or discussion of issues by the human voice, by newspapers, by pamphlets, by dodgers," or even by soundtrucks, as long as their sound systems didn't blow out an auditor's eardrum.[33] Government could regulate decibels, but it could not silence the voice that is measured in decibels. (To carry the analogy into the general attitude of the duopoly toward challengers, third parties not only can't set up sound systems, they aren't even given drivers' licenses to operate the trucks!)

So the Court held high the banner of political speech – at times. Yet at the same time, in the Court's opinion, as Stanford Law Professor Kathleen M. Sullivan has summarized, "the government interest in preventing 'corruption' or the appearance of corruption justified limits aimed at preventing any single donor from gaining disproportionate influence relative to others."[34] And in subsequent cases, this asserted governmental interest in preventing corruption has been the peg on which legal limitations on political speech have been hung. Once you concede that the government may keep the candidate or his backers from playing their campaign theme at deafening volume, the argument switches to just what constitutes deafening volume. To sensitive ears, it may be set at a very low pitch.

The Court did throw one life jacket to independents, though it fit only the wealthiest. FECA had limited a candidate's expenditures on his own campaign to $50,000 in a calendar year for presidential or vice presidential races, $35,000 for US Senate candidacies, and $25,000 for US House candidates. These ceilings "impose a substantial restraint on the ability of persons to engage in protected First Amendment expression," found the Court. "The candidate, no less than any other person, has a First Amendment right to engage in the discussion of public issues and vigorously and tirelessly to advocate his own election and the election of other candidates."[35] (Presidential candidates who accept public funds are still bound by limits on self-financing.)

Actually, the candidate would seem to have not only "no less" a First Amendment right than other persons, but somewhat larger a right, for those "other persons" were subjected to donation ceilings that the Court upheld. This Jesuitical distinction would enable oil heir and vice presidential candidate David Koch to finance an energetic Libertarian Party run in 1980 and Ross Perot to wage his billionaire populist crusade in 1992, but it prevented Stewart Mott from endowing John Anderson with the millions that might have given him a fighting chance as the liberal Republican hope of suburbia in 1980. *Buckley* helped make possible Perot's astonishingly successful 1992 bid – but who can tell how many other third-party or independent challenges it stifled by retaining the cap on individual contributions, thus preventing men and women of Perot-like wealth from donating sums sufficient to launch challenges to the status quo?

In its decision, the Court smugly asserted, contrary to entire shelves full of political science studies, that "There is no evidence to support the claim that contribution limitations in themselves discriminate against major-party challengers to incumbents. Challengers can and often do defeat incumbents in federal elections."[36]

Oh, really? And in what country does *that* happen, Mr. Justices? In the United States? Well, yes — if you're talking about the first century or so of Congress (1790–1898), when the turnover rate was within the 30–76% range.[37] But by the time the Supreme Court heard arguments in *Buckley v. Valeo*, congressional reelection was a surer thing than the Cubs falling short of the World Series. Congressional reelection rates reached 96.8% in 1968, 94.5% in 1970, and 93.6% in 1972. The blip came in 1974, in the Watergate election, when they slipped to a still ridiculously high 87.7%, but they rebounded nicely in 1976 to 95.8%. (Naturally, in its footnotes, the Court evidenced 1974 in support of its contention that close races were still possible. Thus atypicality becomes a rationale for law.)[38]

In 1974, political scientist David R. Mayhew had coined the term "vanishing marginals."[39] *Marginals* were US House of Representatives districts in which the margin between the winning and losing candidate was less than 10% — in other words, competitive districts. Not only were reelection rates approaching obscenely high levels (soon they would hit 98% in some elections), but even *close* elections were becoming a thing of the past. But to the Court, laboring under the delusion that challengers can and often do defeat incumbents in federal elections, all was hunky-dory, and surely those vanishing marginals would turn up somewhere. (They never did: in fact, the gap between spending by congressional incumbents and spending by challengers *rose* after FECA.)

The Court addressed the matter of discrimination against minor parties most directly in upholding the establishment of the PECF, the income-tax checkoff through which tax filers might designate one dollar (two for joint returns) to be placed in a fund that subsidizes primary campaigns, general election campaigns, and party nominating conventions. The appellants protested that this vast public financing scheme was "contrary to the general welfare" and not a legitimate function of the federal government.

Take it up with John Marshall, replied the Court. The "General Welfare Clause" is not "a limitation upon congressional power," lectured the jurists. "It is rather a grant of power, the scope of which is quite expansive, particularly in view of the enlargement of power by the Necessary and Proper Clause."[40] The argument that the federal government had exceeded its powers was treated as a quaint anachronism. Besides, FECA was not censorious but rather an attempt to use "public money to facilitate and enlarge public discussion and participation in the electoral process," according to the Court. Only in modern Washington is the mulcting of the citizenry by taxation judged equivalent to "discussion and participation in the electoral process."

The prominence of such plaintiffs and appellants as Eugene McCarty and the Libertarian Party suggests the extent to which *Buckley v. Valeo* was about the rights not only of political donors but also of challengers to the two-party system. The plaintiffs pointed to Wallace's 1968 campaign, which under FECA would have been unfunded while Humphrey and Nixon were larded with government cash, as evidence that the act "irrationally overcompensates declining parties and undercompensates those on the rise."[41]

Their claim was that the PECF, in boosting the major parties at the expense of other parties or potential parties, invidiously discriminated against those other parties. A divided Court rejected this claim. The majority, surveying the twin towers of American politics, the Democrats and Republicans, noted that since the GOP replaced the Whigs in 1856 "no third party has posed a credible threat to the two major parties in Presidential elections." Not quite true – certainly Teddy Roosevelt's Progressive "Bull Moose" Party, which outpolled incumbent Republican President William Howard Taft by 4,119,507–3,484,956, was "credible." As were, to a lesser extent, the 1924 Progressive Party candidacy of Senator Robert LaFollette and the 1968 American Independent Party run of Governor George Corley Wallace, not to mention the post-*Buckley* runs of Ross Perot. But the Court majority insisted that this supposed third-party irrelevancy "justified" the Congress "in providing both major parties full funding and all other parties only a percentage of the major-party entitlement."[42] The duopoly had achieved that apex feat of all governmental dependents: it had an entitlement. And as any once-intrepid but now older-and-wiser free market advocate who has taken on the welfare state can tell you, the only way to remove entitlements from dependents, whether corporate, bureaucratic, or individual, is to pry them from their cold, dead fingers. No one, nothing, gives up a government entitlement voluntarily.

As if reading from the feeble roster of excuses that states have used to erect Matterhorn-style ballot access laws, the Court's majority asserted "governmental interests against the use of public money to foster frivolous candidacies [unlike, say, the PECF-funded ethically challenged California

Democratic Senator Alan Cranston in 1980 or the Beltway Christian-Republican operative Gary Bauer in 2004 – no, these were not frivolous in the least, were they?], create a system of splintered parties, and encourage unrestrained factionalism."[43]

What were most interesting about *Buckley v. Valeo* were the dissents. Chief Justice Burger called public financing of presidential campaigns "an impermissible intrusion by the Government into the traditionally private political process."[44] The requirement that small contributions be publicly disclosed he thought jeopardized the First Amendment association rights of citizens. A rank-and-file union member, for instance, might fear retribution if he donated to a candidate disfavored by the union; so too with a junior executive, or a businessman who wishes to give money to a David-like challenger to a powerful incumbent.

Public financing itself the Chief Justice regarded as unconstitutional – a position that the libertarian critics of FECA, who seem to include current Justice Clarence Thomas, continue to push. Moreover, "the use of funds from the public treasury to subsidize political activity of private individuals would produce substantial and profound questions about the nature of our democratic society." Is it right that the central state be responsible for financing political parties and their candidates? Senator Howard Baker (R-TN), no one's radical libertarian, raised much the same point in 1967 when he told the Senate, "I think it is extraordinarily important that the Government not control the machinery by which the public expresses the range of its desires, demands, and dissent." Burger teases out the implications of Baker's remark. Government, he writes, does not give grants without strings. If you take the cash, you accept the strings. Except that the conditions are stronger, more binding, than simple strings. A whole panoply of regulations, "varying measures of control and surveillance," accompany government assistance. Is it really wise to subject the political parties to such monitoring? Is this not a kind of J. Edgar Hoover-like power? Certainly the lawsuits surrounding delegate selection to the Democratic convention in 1972 and earlier portended new interventions by the feds in party matters.[45]

Not that the parties worried about this. Their hands were in the till, their bellies were full, and they would prove quite adept at finding ingenious ways to raise banks full of campaign cash while at the same time allowing Uncle Sam to pay for part of their primary campaigns, their national conventions, and their entire general election campaigns.

Minor parties were a different story. New York's Conservatives, the national Libertarians, and the independent-minded Eugene McCarthy were central figures in the suit against the FECA. It is fitting and proper that the Supreme Court case bears the surname of the only US Senator elected from a minor party since Robert M. LaFollette Jr. of the Progressive Party represented Wisconsin from 1935 to 1947.

Justices Burger and William Rehnquist, the latter a future Chief Justice, dissented from the Court's decision in their contention that "the scheme approved by the Court today invidiously discriminates against minor parties."

Burger and Rehnquist conceded the obvious: the American system has been dominated by Republicans and Democrats since long before any member of the Court had been born. But that fact alone does not sanction a law, "enacted by incumbents of the major political parties," as Burger notes, that would hobble the minor parties as it boosts the majors. "The fact that there have been few drastic realignments in our basic two-party structure in 200 years is no constitutional justification for freezing the status quo of the present major parties at the expense of such future political movements," protested Burger.[46]

Rehnquist concurred with the Court's opinion in all of *Buckley v. Valeo* except that part dealing with minor parties and independent candidates. In discriminating against these and in favor of Democrats and Republicans, FECA had run afoul of the First and Fifth Amendments to the Constitution, he asserted.

This act was not a matter of keeping frivolous candidates off the ballot, said Justice Rehnquist, or limiting the list of names on a ballot to a manageable size. (Although, as we have seen, this latter excuse is as flimsy and believable as a debtor's promise that the check is in the mail.) Rather, Congress "has enshrined the Republican and Democratic Parties in a permanently preferred position, and has established requirements for funding minor-party and independent candidates to which the two major parties are not subject." By legislation, and not at the ballot box, the parties have attempted to freeze for now and forever the current arrangement of political parties. Justice Rehnquist wasn't buying it: "I find it impossible to subscribe to the Court's reasoning that because no third party has posed a credible threat to the two major parties in Presidential elections since 1860, Congress may by law attempt to assure that this pattern will endure forever."[47]

The ineligibility of new parties for campaign funds until after the campaign is as invidious an act of discrimination as one can find in election law. It amounts to a vast subsidy to the existing parties, a subsidy so large that only a new party riding a wave of *Poseidon Adventure*-like proportions could overcome. One way — the spendthrift way, the conventional liberal way, the co-opting the dissenter way — to remedy this inequity would be to make independents and new parties eligible for funding during the campaign. The other way — the Jeffersonian way, which upholds frugality and the principle that "to compel a man to furnish contributions of money for the propagation of opinions which he disbelieves and abhors, is sinful and tyrannical"[48] — would be to repeal the FECA and abolish the PECF. To put the parties — all the parties — back on an equal footing. You can imagine which of these two alternatives is never discussed in congressional committee hearing rooms or in the plush dens of the establishment Washington think tanks.

One more secondary point about *Buckley v. Valeo*: as mentioned earlier, the FECA created a FEC consisting of six members, plus two ex officio members. The six were divided by party: three Democrats, three Republicans, and were to be appointed — two each — by the White House, the Speaker of the House, and the Senate Majority Leader, subject to confirmation by both houses. This was a bizarrely devised body, clearly a creature of the government without an ounce of independence, and, importantly, it enshrined the two-party duopoly. The commissioners were party men — party hacks, as it worked out, and as we will see later. The six FEC members represent the two parties. There is no provision for an independent on the board, or, God forbid, a representative of a minor party.

Just how independent commissioners who were appointed by Congress to oversee the behavior of congressmen and women were going to be was a question that observers didn't really bother to ask. After all, the commission was cloaked in the mantle of reform, of good government, of purity. It may have been designed to be ineffectual — it may have been cursed from birth — but why spoil the orgy of self-congratulation with tough questions?

In any event, the Supreme Court, in *Buckley v. Valeo*, struck down the congressional appointments as an intrusion on the power of the executive. All six FEC members must be appointed by the President, though they remain equally divided by party, which would lead to the odd spectacle of presidents appointing nominees whom they disdained. But it should not be assumed that the Court's minor tweaking of the FEC created a body of the highest integrity: the executive appointments were not going to be of a higher caliber than those of the legislative branch would have been.

FECA and its bureaucratic offshoot did not usher in an era of clean campaigns, robust competition, and respect for dissident voices. But then who really — *really* — thought it would? The real purpose of the FECA, as

Xandra Kayden and Eddie Mahe wrote in *The Party Goes On: The Persistence of the Two-Party System in the United States* (1985), was that it "paved the way for the renaissance of the major political parties." And in that it succeeded – oh, did it succeed.[49]

Notes

1. Robert E. Mutch, *Campaigns, Congress, and the Courts: The Making of Federal Campaign Finance Law* (Westport, CT: Praeger, 1988), p. xvi.
2. Bradley A. Smith, *Unfree Speech: The Folly of Campaign Reform* (Princeton, NJ: Princeton University Press, 2001), p. 21.
3. Alexander Heard, *The Costs of Democracy* (Chapel Hill: University of North Carolina Press, 1960), pp. 431–32.
4. Bradley A. Smith, "Some Problems with Taxpayer-Funded Political Campaigns," *University of Pennsylvania Law Review* (Vol. 148, No. 2, December 1999), p. 592.
5. Quoted in Anthony Corrado, *Paying for Presidents: Public Financing in National Elections* (New York: Twentieth Century Fund, 1993), p. 8.
6. Ibid., p. 34.
7. Quoted in Robert E. Mutch, *Campaigns, Congress, and the Courts: The Making of Federal Campaign Finance Law*, p. 40.
8. Bradley A. Smith, "Faulty Assumptions and Undemocratic Consequences of Campaign Finance Reform," *Yale Law Journal* (Vol. 105, January 1996), n.p.
9. Richard C. Leone, Foreword to Anthony Corrado, *Paying for Presidents: Public Financing in National Elections*, p. v.
10. Stewart Mott, "Independent Fundraising for an Independent Candidate," *New York University Review of Law and Social Change* (Vol. 10, 1980–1981), p. 137.
11. Brian Doherty, *Radicals for Capitalism: A Freewheeling History of the Modern American Libertarian Movement* (New York: Public Affairs, 2007), p. 398.
12. Bradley A. Smith, *Unfree Speech: The Folly of Campaign Reform*, p. 33.
13. Quoted in James Boylan, "A Raucous Century of Covering Politics," *Columbia Journalism Review*, July 1, 1999, p. 1.
14. "The Disgrace of Campaign Financing," *Time*, October 23, 1972, p. 24.
15. Robert E. Mutch, *Campaigns, Congress, and the Courts*, p. 119.
16. Burton A. Abrams and Russell F. Settle, "The Economic Theory of Regulation and Public Financing of Presidential Elections," *Journal of Political Economy* (Vol. 86, No. 2, 1978), p. 247.
17. Ibid., pp. 248–49.
18. Ibid., p. 252.
19. Ibid., p. 256.
20. Richard Briffault, "Public Funding and Democratic Elections," *University of Pennsylvania Law Review* (Vol. 148, No. 2, December 1999), p. 575.
21. Quoted in Mutch, *Campaigns, Congress, and Courts*, p. 50.
22. *Buckley v. Valeo*, 424 U.S. 1 (1976), 4c, http://caselaw.lp.findlaw.com.

23. Adam Bernstein, "Francis R. 'Frank' Valeo; Player in Campaign Finance Debate," *Washington Post*, April 11, 2006.
24. Quoted in Mutch, *Campaigns, Congress, and Courts*, p. 55.
25. *Buckley v. Valeo*, "Contribution and Expenditure Limitations," IA.
26. Ibid., IBI.
27. Bradley A. Smith, "Faulty Assumptions and Undemocratic Consequences of Campaign Finance Reform," *Yale Law Journal* (Vol. 105, January 1996), n.p.
28. Stewart Mott, "Independent Fundraising for an Independent Candidate," *New York University Review of Law and Social Change* (Vol. 10, 1980–1981), p. 135.
29. Ibid., p. 136.
30. Ibid., p. 139.
31. Ibid., pp. 139–40.
32. Ibid., p. 135.
33. *Buckley v. Valeo*, footnote 17.
34. Kathleen M. Sullivan, "Against Campaign Finance Reform," *Utah Law Review* (1998), n.p.
35. *Buckley v. Valeo*, "Expenditure Limitations," C.2.
36. Ibid., "Contribution and Expenditure Limitations," I.B.I.b.
37. Eric O'Keefe, *Who Rules America* (Spring Green, WI: Citizen Government Foundation, 1999), p. 11.
38. David C. Huckabee, "Reelection Rates of House Incumbents, 1790–1994," Congressional Research Service, March 8, 1995, p. 11.
39. David Mayhew, "Congressional Elections: The Case of the Vanishing Marginals," *Polity* (Vol. 6, Spring 1974), pp. 295–317.
40. *Buckley v. Valeo*, "Public Financing of Presidential Election Campaigns," III.B.
41. Robert E. Mutch, *Campaigns, Congress, and Courts*, p. 143.
42. *Buckley v. Valeo*, "Public Financing of Presidential Election Campaigns," III.B.1.
43. Ibid.
44. *Buckley v. Valeo*, Mr. Chief Justice Burger, concurring in part and dissenting in part.
45. Ibid., Burger dissent, "Public Financing." For a survey of the warning signs Burger espied on the horizon, see John G. Kester, "Constitutional Restrictions on Political Parties," *Virginia Law Review* (Vol. 60, No. 5, May 1974), pp. 735–84.
46. Ibid.
47. Ibid., Mr. Justice Rehnquist, concurring in part and dissenting in part.
48. *The Jefferson Cyclopedia*, edited by John P. Foley (New York: Funk & Wagnalls, 1900), pp. 141–42.
49. Xandra Kayden and Eddie Mahe, Jr., *The Party Goes On: The Persistence of the Two-Party System in the United States* (New York: Basic Books, 1985), p. 212.

Chapter 5

FECA: The Demopublicans' Best Friend

So how did the Federal Election Campaign Act (FECA) work out in practice?

Like a dream – if you are a major party candidate who prefers to have the feds pay your bills for you. For the rest of us, if FECA has not quite been a nightmare then it has been an awfully expensive dream that has narrowed our choices and made our politics even blander.

FECA was ushered into existence on a red carpet of good publicity and seemingly noble intentions. It was going to return politics to the little guy – as if the "little guy" had ever really been in charge. It was going to democratize the system, to spread out the donor base for candidacies. Yet, irony of ironies, it has failed even in this task. In 1972, the last presidential election before federal financing kicked in, both Richard M. Nixon and George McGovern attracted approximately 600,000 contributors in the general election. By 2000, after a quarter century of the allegedly democratizing federal election campaign law, the *total* number of contributors for all candidates, primary and general election, totaling more than a dozen, was 774,000. Not only had FECA failed to bring the financing of political campaigns back "to the people," it had actually shrunken the donor base and further centralized the core group of contributors to presidential campaigns. FECA has coincided with a decline in the number of contributors. It has achieved exactly the opposite of its intent!

FECA was, or at least was sold as, a good government response to the Watergate mess. Politicians were going to clean up politics. Dirty money would be cleaned (not laundered), sleazy characters would be banished, and the disproportionate influence on federal elections exercised by crafty rich

J.T. Bennett, *Not Invited to the Party*, DOI 10.1007/978-1-4419-0366-2_5,
© Springer Science+Business Media, LLC 2009

men would be purged. None of this really happened, of course, but then only the most hopelessly credulous would think that electoral reform devised by incumbent politicians would ever benefit anyone other than those very same politicians. Still, there are always those like League of Woman Voters President Susan Lederman, who said that public funding "is the cleanest money in American politics today."[1]

The 1972 campaign, conducted during that limbo period after the passage of the 1971 act, which tightened disclosure regulations, but before FECA's critical 1974 amendments, was noteworthy for its squalor, unsavoriness, and general filth. The malefactions of Richard Nixon's re-election campaign are well-known and amply documented. This was the Watergate election, after all. But the Democrats, especially those Establishment Democrats who ran in the primaries, were hardly models of electoral rectitude. Wilbur Mills, the Arkansas Democrat and chairman of the House Ways and Means Committee, is today remembered for his dalliances with a buxom stripper named Fannie Foxx, but in his 1972 campaign for the Democratic nomination he was sold as the sober voice of fiscal responsibility – which he may have been, compared to his freespending liberal colleagues, at least as long as he didn't have a fistful of dollar bills and a front-row seat at a palace of ecdysiasm.

Hubert Humphrey, the Minnesota chatterbox who had been defeated by Nixon in 1968, ran a nasty campaign against his old friend George McGovern (D-SD). Humphrey, despite his sunny image, was a bare-knuckled political brawler of dubious principles. Jack L. Chestnut, who managed Humphrey's 1970 US Senate comeback campaign, was later convicted in federal court of accepting illegal payments for that campaign from Associated Milk Producers, Inc. If money is the mother's milk of politics, Humphrey was well-fed in 1968, 1970, and the 1972 primaries by the milk lobby, which appreciated his no doubt highly principled support of dairy price supports. (Of course in the narrative provided by the reformers, the dirtiness of the 1972 presidential campaign, unaffected as it seemed to be by the 1971 FECA disclosure laws, only proved the need for a tougher, more stringent federal law.)

Perhaps not coincidentally, 1968, the last race before the passage of the 1971 act, was also the last time a third-party candidate won electoral votes. (In 1972, John Hospers, the Libertarian, was awarded one electoral vote when a Virginia elector bolted from Nixon, who had won the state.) George Wallace, the Alabama Democrat, won 5 states and 46 electoral votes on the American Independent Party ticket. Whatever one thinks of Wallace, he added a populist voice to the campaign that has not been audible (with the significant exception of 1992) since the feds took over regulation of presidential campaigns. And he did it the populist way: 75% of his 750,000 individual contributions came in amounts of under $100.

Prior to FECA, the sky had been the limit for individual contributors. The candidacies of men like McGovern and Wallace attracted many smaller donations, but the Nixon juggernaut of 1972, which raised $62 million to ensure a sure thing, picked up fully one-third of that total ($21.3 million) from just 154 donors. That averages out to about $138,000 per donor. Enter public financing and contribution limits: exit the big donor. Enter the small donor? Not quite.

Under FECA, the first $250 a presidential candidate raised from individual donors was matched by a federal grant of the same size – if the candidate agreed to limits on his or her campaign spending. Thus public funding was tied to a cap on spending, and the person of modest means would see his $250 donation matched by the feds, presumably doubling the sound of his voice. The matching grant was in effect only for the primaries.

The theory was that this would somehow promote giving by small or less-well-heeled contributors. It has not. Such persons already gave to candidates of their choice: witness the presidential campaigns of George C. Wallace in 1968 and 1972. By contrast to Wallace, after a quarter-century of FECA's allegedly purifying influence, more than two-thirds of the contributions in 2000 to Republican front-runner George W. Bush and the two candidates for the Democratic presidential nomination, Albert Gore and Bill Bradley, came in amounts of $750 or more. (Since 1976, it has been Ronald Reagan who raised the greatest percentage of his funds from donations of less than $200: fully 47% in 1980 and 46% in 1984. Reagan, incidentally, never checked the Presidential Election Campaign Fund (PECF) box in his life – though he did accept a total of $22.5 million in matching funds over his 1976, 1980, and 1984 campaigns.[2] Reagan's Vice President, George H.W. Bush, set the mark for the smallest percentage of his war chest raised in donations under $200, with a mere 6%.)

Proponents of public financing exhibit a naïvetè that might be charming were it not so expensive for the rest of us. As late as 1999, an advocate of government-financed elections argued that the "more campaign funds come from the public fisc, the less elected officials need to be sensitive to the views of large private donors, and the more they can act on their view of what the public interest requires."[3] Take private money out of the equation and we'll have a Congress of Platonic philosopher-kings, brilliant and honorable, learned men and women who ruminate over the great questions of the day and decide them on their merits. Ah, the kingdom of Heaven on earth – and all we need do is to pay the bills of politicians' campaigns.

Those bills have added up. The monies expended due to FECA have been substantial, at least in the old Everett Dirksen sense of a million here and a million there and pretty soon we're talking of real money. Over $1.3 billion was transferred to candidates and the parties between 1976 and 2004: $342 million to primary candidates, $152 million to the party committees, and $839 million to the general election candidates. True, the sum would pay for only about a week of the US occupation of Iraq, but in the days before Big Government Bush Republicanism, conservatives would have regarded $1.3 billion as real money.

That $1.3 billion has gone almost entirely to Republicans and Democrats. The Reform Party claimed $42 million in 1996 and 2000, and other third parties laid claim to crumbs equaling about 1% of the total. The rich have gotten richer, and the poor poorer, thanks to this government transfer.

This was expected; indeed, it was planned. "[T]he Federal Election Campaign Act functions in a manner that benefits the two major parties at the expense of minor parties," write political scientists John F. Bibby and L. Sandy Maisel. By guaranteeing Republicans and Democrats full funding if their nominees reach 25% of the vote in the previous election – and the ballot access laws have made sure *that* will happen – "the FECA, in effect, seems to guarantee the two major parties a government-subsidized existence in perpetuity."[4]

In 1972, the last pre-public-financing year, former California Rep. John Schmitz ran a feisty campaign on the remnants of Wallace's American Independent Party (AIP), gaining over one million votes nationally. Leftist pediatrician Benjamin Spock, running on the People's Party ticket, attracted about 80,000 votes. It was not a great year for third-party candidates: the Democrat, George McGovern, was considerably to the left of previous Democratic candidates, the Cold War liberals John F. Kennedy, Lyndon Baines Johnson, and Hubert Horatio Humphrey. The McGovern campaign co-opted the left and prevented the emergence of an antiwar candidate from a minor party. On the right, the shooting of Wallace silenced a potent voice of right-wing populism. Still, third parties won 1.8% of the vote in the last presidential campaign conducted pre-1974 FECA. By contrast, in 2004, when the major parties put up widely reviled candidates – one a dim incumbent presiding over an unpopular war (George W. Bush), the other an arrogant Massachusetts limousine liberal who failed to tap the large antiwar vote

(John Kerry) – third parties tallied 1.01% of the popular vote. The independent Ralph Nader led the pack with 463,000 votes.

These were two elections – 1972 and 2004 – in which prospects for a vigorous third-party campaign were less than robust. Yet in the former, third parties gained almost double the percentage of the vote. FECA had done nothing to encourage challenges to the status quo. Third parties were in no better shape due to the law than they had been in 1972. The duopoly was stronger than ever. It should not surprise us. Economists understand, and understood then, that incumbents, much like firms that seek the regulation of their markets, desire to limit entry into their field of business. They want to make it harder for potential competitors to arise. And if they can cripple these potential competitors while using the perfumed language of goody-goody reform, so much the better.

No wonder that J. David Gillespie, author of *Politics at the Periphery: Third Parties in Two Party America* (1993), says that FECA was "the most substantial [burden for third parties] ever coming from the US Congress."[5]

The magnitude of the major-party subsidies is almost blindingly huge. For instance, in 1976, the first election year in which monies were disbursed from the PECF, a total of $70.9 million was sent out to candidates and parties for their conventions. Of that sum, $38.5 million went to Democrats, $32.4 million to Republicans (who had only two primary candidates, Ford and Reagan, while the Democrats had a passel), and a grand total of $0 went to all third-party candidates combined.

Former Senator Eugene McCarthy (D-MN), running as an independent, offered himself as a kind of constitutionalist liberal, very much concerned with the rights of the individual in an era of big government, big business, and big labor. It was an intriguing platform for a man who had electrified his youthful followers in 1968, when his insurgent Democratic presidential primary campaign forced incumbent Lyndon B. Johnson out of the race after a much closer than expected vote in New Hampshire. But McCarthy – who was among the plaintiffs in *Buckley v. Valeo* – looked to the Federal Election Commission for help. Lotsa luck, Clean Gene!

McCarthy petitioned the Federal Election Commission (FEC) for a ruling that a 5% showing by a party-less independent candidate would entitle that candidate to retroactive funding by the PECF. This would later become policy – but too late for McCarthy, whose hope it was to leverage the prospect of retroactive funding into a large loan which would greatly enhance his campaign's visibility.

The matter went to the FEC. Its six commissioners deliberated. Or, rather, they looked to their inner hacks. For in a typically disgusting display of unprincipledness, the FEC split three to three on McCarthy's request. The three commissioners who voted for McCarthy were Republicans; the trio that denied his request were Democrats. Might this have anything to do with the assumption that McCarthy would draw more votes from Democratic candidate Jimmy Carter than he would have from incumbent Republican Gerald Ford? Perish the thought!

In any event, the FEC draw doomed McCarthy, who never was able to raise substantial private monies anyway: Jimmy Carter looked like a winner, and liberals were not about to throw their donations away on a quixotic long-shot campaign. Conservatives such as Russell Kirk saw much to admire in McCarthy – but no one really heard the call, and the independent attracted 740,000 votes nationwide, or less than 1% of the total popular vote.

The next presidential election year, 1980, saw the most serious centrist third-party campaign in many decades – that of the moderate-liberal Illinois Republican Congressman John Anderson, who ran on a National Unity ticket with liberal Wisconsin Governor Patrick Lucey. In springtime, national opinion polls showed Anderson running as high as 25% nationally. Unlike George Wallace in 1968, he was not a regional candidate. Realistically, Wallace's best case scenario had been to win a few Southern states and throw the race into the House. By contrast, John Anderson, like Perot in 1992, had the potential to run well across the country (except in the South) and, in a best-case scenario, win the race by sweeping New England, winning several large Eastern and Midwestern states, and taking the liberal states of the West Coast. In April–May 1980, it seemed doable.

Anderson didn't do it, for many reasons. Voters tired of his sanctimony. Republicans sensed nominee Ronald Reagan, once considered too old and too right-wing to mount a serious candidacy, might win (as he did, in a landslide). But also contributing to Anderson's decline was the artificial boost FECA and the PECF gave to the Republicans and Democrats and their strangulating effect on third parties. Of the $100.5 million disbursed under the PECF in the 1980 campaign cycle, $96.3 million went to Republican and Democratic candidates and the party conventions. "Others" – the Anderson-Lucey ticket – were awarded just $4.2 million.[6]

Anderson, taking note of the FEC's hack rejection of McCarthy's 1976 petition, ignored the FEC and went straight to the US District Court in Washington. Like McCarthy, his "National Unity" ticket was not a party in any real sense of the word: it ran no candidates for other offices, and it had no independent existence outside the Anderson-Lucey campaign. But he won retroactive funding, which helped – a bit – in raising campaign cash. Reimbursement after the election has its limits, however: As one poll watcher noted, "money that arrives in December doesn't buy much television time in October."[7]

Repealing FECA would have helped him a good deal more, as Stewart Mott has noted. If Anderson had had a sugar daddy funding his campaign during the late summer and early fall, when Reagan and Carter received public relations jolts in the form of the (federally subsidized) party conventions, he might have remained competitive. Or maybe not. We'll never know. Stewart Mott was forbidden by law to give Anderson the money he needed. Tax dollars, Mott predicted and Anderson discovered, were a very poor substitute.

Nineteen-eighty also had a candidate who demonstrated an alternative fund-raising style: choose a rich running mate. Ed Clark, a California attorney running as the Libertarian candidate for president, selected the extremely wealthy oil and gas heir David Koch as his vice presidential partner. Koch pledged to spend at least half a million dollars on the campaign, since under the *Buckley v. Valeo* ruling the FECA could not limit the amount a candidate spends on his own campaign.

Consistent with his libertarian philosophy, Ed Clark eschewed federal subsidy. He didn't need it. Running primarily on the $3 million donated by Koch, Clark won 920,000 votes, an impressive showing for a new party. (In Alaska, the Clark–Koch ticket exceeded 11%.)

The Libertarians faltered after 1980; and 1984, perhaps fittingly in recognition of George Orwell, was an even worse year for third parties. A grand total of $131.8 million was disbursed from the PECF, and of this a mere $200,000 – or less than two-tenths of 1% of the total – went to third parties, in this case to the Citizens Party primary campaign of ex-Mormon feminist Sonia Johnson. If dissent had not exactly been smothered in the literarily fateful year of 1984, it had been outspent – heavily, and by the government.

The next two elections were much the same story. In the 1988 cycle, the PECF disgorged $176.5 million, of which a princely sum of $900,000 – about half of 1% of the total – did not feed the major parties. In 1992, the year that featured the liveliest and most serious third-party candidacy since Theodore Roosevelt's Bull Moose Party effort in 1912, just $2.4 million of a PECF total of $173.3 million was spent on other than the Democratic and Republican Parties. (Teddy Roosevelt, by the way, raised

$675,000, a substantial sum, for that 1912 race. More than three-quarters of it came from just 18 persons in those pre-FECA days.)

Ross Perot, of course, disdained public financing, at least for his first shot at the gold ring in 1992. Perot's race was extraordinary in so many ways. For one, he showed just how large a market there existed for an alternative to the duopoly. In a 1984 study of *Third Parties in America*, authors Steven J. Rosenstone, Roy L. Behr, and Edward H. Lazarus had written that people vote third party because of "major party deterioration, attractive third-party candidates who present a viable alternative to the major party nominees, and an influx of voters with weak allegiance to the two major parties" but that these factors are usually overcome by counterfactors: "Working against these forces are a set of formidable constitutional, legal, and political constraints that make it difficult for people to cast a third-party ballot."[8]

Perot surmounted these obstacles, broke these constraints, because he had the fortune (he spent an estimated $73 million on his own campaign), he commanded media attention – which was rather favorable at first, at least until the smear-artists of the Clinton campaign took aim – and he participated in the presidential debates, by all accounts winning them. He was the worst nightmare of the FECA crowd: an outsider who disdained taxpayer financing and spent a bit of his own fortune mounting a challenge to the cozy two-party duopoly. You can well believe that if not for the certainty that the Supreme Court would strike down such a measure on First Amendment grounds, the Republican–Democrat campaign reformers would place strict limits on self-financers, thus ending the ominous threat of a future Perot-type bid.

By 1996, however, Perot had had a change of heart, or perhaps he merely wondered why he ought to write out tens of millions of dollars worth of checks when Uncle Sam would do it for him. In any event, third-parties consumed $29.6 million of the $234 disbursed from the PECF in 1996 – 12.6%, a peak that has not been matched since. (The Perot campaign accounted for almost whole of the 1996 handout: $29.1 million. The rest went to Natural Law Party perennial John Hagelin. Perot was allowed to raise funds privately up to the spending limit imposed on the major parties, though his out-of-pocket contribution was capped at $50,000.)

In 2000, the fractured post-Perot Reform Party, riven by a split between the right-wing populist Patrick J. Buchanan and John Hagelin of the Natural Law Party, whose campaign was based on the mellow joys of transcendental meditation and the promise of human levitation, ate up nearly $5.8 million in primary subsidies. A good-sized chunk of $2.5 million went to pay for the

Reform Party convention, which was wild and wooly and utterly unpredictable – the way Republican and Democratic conventions never are. And $12.6 million was spent by Reform in the general election, for a total of $20.8 million. (Green Ralph Nader also received PECF monies, to the everlasting sputtering anger of the Al Gore forces.)

In 2004, a quiet year for third parties, the presence of Ralph Nader as an independent – harassed at every turn by Democrats challenging his petitions – was barely enough to push the total third-party vote above 1%. Nader received about $900,000 in government monies. He made nary a splash.

Changes in the shape and timing of campaigns have also tested FECA and found it wanting. (Wanting more of our money, that is.) In 1976, the nominations for both major parties were still in doubt as of June; Democrats and Republicans enjoyed competitive races, and in fact the Grand Old Party nomination was not really decided until Gerald Ford narrowly defeated Ronald Reagan at the August convention.

Over time, however, the parties have "frontloaded" their primary schedules. Instead of the almost leisurely primary schedule of 1976, which stretched from February to June, the parties – or more accurately, the state parties – have jammed their primaries and caucuses into the earliest possible date, not wishing to be afterthoughts. In 2008, the majority of delegates had been chosen before the snow had even melted. As a result, hopefuls must raise and spend big early if they are to have any chance to prevail. If they have accepted matching funds, they may well graze the spending limit by early spring, as Senator Bob Dole (R-KS) did in 1996, while the virtually unopposed incumbent President Bill Clinton had an untapped war chest from which he spent liberally in the spring months, without the Republicans returning fire.

FECA was supposed to expand primary fields and encourage a broader range of candidates. Yet any fantasy that matching funds would lead to greater choice has been dashed on the rocks of experience. As John Samples of the Cato Institute has pointed out, an average of 7.8 candidates received at least 1% of a party's primary votes in the seven presidential elections after the enactment of FECA. By contrast, the seven elections *prior* to FECA averaged 10.7 candidates who met such a standard. Thus FECA has coincided with a shrinkage of the field. It has, perhaps, even contributed to the shrinkage of the field, as longshots determine that the draconian limit on individual contributions makes it that much harder to catch lightning in a bottle. The much-maligned 1972 campaign that inspired the FECA amendments of 1974 included 12 candidates who picked up at least 1% of the primary vote – a higher total than in any election year since.[9]

General-election major-party candidates who chose to partake of the PECF were limited to $20 million in the 1976 election, an amount adjusted for inflation thereafter. (It reached $81.8 million in 2008.) A participating candidate must pledge not to accept private financing for the general election, unless the fund is incapable of providing the full amount. His or her donations to his or her own cause may not exceed $50,000. Minor-party candidates are eligible for a fraction of the major-party subsidy; the amount is tied to the party's previous performance as long as that performance garnered more than 5% of the nationwide popular vote. Parties can receive a post-election grant if they tallied over 5% of the vote. (Vice presidential candidate expenditures are lumped in with those of the head of the ticket.)

In recent years, deep-pocketed candidates and those with awesome fund-raising machines have begun to opt out of the system. Why accept an artificial limit on your campaign treasury when you can raise (or write your own checks for) far more? The first major party primary hopeful to reject public funds was former Texas Governor John Connally, the Democrat turned Republican horse-trader whose 1980 campaign was premised on the unlikely pair of assumptions that (1) Ronald Reagan was too old to win the hearts and minds of Republican voters; and (2) those hearts and minds would open to a turncoat Texan who was best known for riding in the JFK Dallas motorcade and later being acquitted in a high-profile bribery case. Connally assumed wrong. He raised $11 million and for his efforts won a grand total of one delegate, Mrs. Ada Mills of Arkansas, forever immortalized as the "$11 Million Delegate."

Publishing heir Steve Forbes chose to forego public funding in the 1996 and 2000 GOP primaries, spending a whopping $76 million of his own money in the latter election. George W. Bush followed Forbes's lead in 2000 and 2004. So did eventual Democratic nominee John Kerry in 2004, thanks to his marriage to the widow of ketchup heir John Heinz. The system's administrators breathed a sigh of relief: Had Bush not opted out in 2000, "the Treasury might well not have met its financial obligations" under the program. Bush's decision "saved the system from financial collapse."[10]

In 2008, the leading Democratic candidates (Senators Hillary Clinton of New York and Barack Obama of Illinois) ignored the primary public financing program and raised their money from private sources. When another contender, former Senator John Edwards (NC), announced that he was accepting matching funds, it was widely taken as an admission that his campaign was in trouble. Who but an anemic failure would participate in this system?

The opters-out have bought the system time but nothing else. It is collapsing of its own weight and inconsistencies. And as leading candidates pull out, it is sinking into irrelevance.

While the spending limit for candidates has increased with inflation, the matching grant limit of $250 has remained constant. Yet the spending limit was an arbitrary number in 1974; its upward adjustments since that time have the patina of rationality, since they are tied to the Consumer Price Index (CPI), but there is no reason to think that an arbitrary number tied to a government statistic somehow evolves into a sacred and time-tested figure. In fact, the limit has proved insufficient, which is why increasingly candidates are bypassing the matching-funds system.

Similarly, the maximum on contributions per person per election was set arbitrarily at $1,000 in 1974. It was not tied to the CPI: if it had been, it would be about $4,000 today. But it was bumped up to $2,000 in 2002 and indexed for inflation, so that today it is $2,300. This is still a rather cramped ceiling, and the unintended consequence of pegging the upper limit so low was to encourage the proliferation of political action committees (PACs) and soft money. Moreover, even after indexing, the participation rate of taxpayers in the PECF is so low as to threaten solvency of the system. People just do not like paying for politicans' campaigns.

Speaking of PACs and soft money, words which have the same effect on the tender ears of reformers as the sight of a bare midriff used to have on the ladies of the Legion of Decency, they are the offspring of good intentions. FECA's limits on individual donations spawned the dramatic growth of PACs. The number of these much-lamented committees, with their deceptively peaceful acronyms, exploded from 608 federal PACs in 1974 to 2,551 in 1980 and 4,009 in 1984. It has since leveled off, sitting at 4,168 at last count in July 2007.[11]

Necessity was the mother of the political action committee; influence-seeking the father. If the amount of free speech via monetary contribution a person may exercise is strictly regulated by the FECA, that person will, inevitably, seek other outlets through which to exercise that speech. Enter the PAC. Whether ideological (right-to-life, right-to-choose, pro-Second Amendment, pro-gun control) or rent-seeking (pro-corporate welfare, pro-welfare state), PACs spend monies promoting political causes but skirting the edge of candidate advocacy. Contributors are not bound (and gagged) by niggling limits, though PACs are subject to boundaries that have been drawn such that Kathleen M. Sullivan, a critic of FECA, calls their emergence "the closeting of frank electoral speech."[12]

It is PACs through which corporations and unions funnel their campaign contributions, though it should be noted that corporate PACs raise their money from corporation managers, and union PACs raise their treasury from union members, so "individuals," as professors Stephen Ansolabehere, John M. De Figueiredo, and James M. Snyder Jr. of Massachusetts Institute of Technology note, "are the ultimate source of all PAC contributions."[13]

PACs have proliferated like poison mushrooms after a monsoon. Of the 4,168 on the current FEC list, 1,586 are corporate-tied; 926 are related to a membership group (for instance trade or health); 273 are the creatures of labor unions; and most of the rest are "non-connected" or driven by ideology or political philosophy.[14]

There is a school of thought that PACs are a sign of civic health, of public engagement with the process of governing. After all, aren't they organizations of individuals banding together voluntarily to further some favored cause? Isn't that what democracy and the right to petition the government are all about? True – to a point.

Yet the number of PACs may also be seen as an index of state power. Under a government with strictly limited powers and few favors to dispense, the number of PACs would be tiny. If subsidies, tariffs, taxes, and government contracts were not available in the first place, there would be no mad scramble to secure them. Only where they exist will organized entities compete for them.

FECA limits on individual campaign expenditures drove would-be givers to another outlet, and one that the Republican and Democratic parties found most congenial: the parties themselves.

"Soft money," whose very name whispers illicit activity, à la soft porn or softcore, flows through a FECA loophole. Under FECA, the national parties could raise unlimited funds from persons, PACs, unions, and corporations to be spent on "nonfederal" activities such as gubernatorial or state legislative elections. In practice, this was an accounting subterfuge, a kind of sleight-of-hand by which the parties acted as conduits for donations greatly exceeding the nominal $1,000 FECA limit. It was a way of flushing FECA, of ignoring putative ceilings. The national party sent much of the money to the states, which in turn used it to support the campaigns of candidates for federal office. Soft money was passed along to candidates for such activities as polling, travel, and other obviously campaign-related expenses, as long as they did not "expressly advocate" a candidate's election or defeat. That phrase – "expressly advocate" – was drawn so narrowly that even the most hamfisted, last-in-his-class-at-Dimwit U lawyer could maneuver around it. The Supreme

Court, in its very brief footnote 52 to *Buckley v. Valeo*, had listed eight "express words of advocacy," which subsequently became a kind of sacred octet: by avoiding these eight phrases – "vote for," "elect," "support," "cast your ballot for," "Smith for Congress," "vote against," "defeat," and "reject" – soft-money interests could spend to their heart's delight.[15] The soft-money explosion reached its acme, or nadir, when during 1995–1996 various committees associated with the Democratic Party ran $34 million worth of pro-Bill Clinton ads that evaded expenditure limits by their avoidance of the "express words." Four years later, the Democrats used soft money "to demonize the Greens," as a Green Party candidate in Michigan complained to a researcher.[16] The two parties spawned grouplets, not subject to FECA contribution limits or disclosure requirements, "for the express purpose of raising and spending unlimited sums on issue advocacy," as election consultant Anthony Corrado writes.[17]

Soft-money contributions routinely ran into the hundreds of thousands of dollars, giving the lie to the claim that FECA had purged politics of big money. And once the parties learned how to exploit this loophole, they drove virtual convoys of cash-laden trucks through it: between the 1991 and 1992 cycle and that of a decade later, soft money contributions zoomed from $86.1 million to $459.9 million.[18] In restricting individual contributions and creating the pool of soft money, FECA had artificially strengthened the political parties. Candidates were more, not less, beholden to the central party apparatus: they were restricted in how much they could raise from real live flesh and blood persons, but the parties, through the soft-money loophole, had millions to dispense – especially to pliable candidates who would subordinate their own consciences and intelligence to the demands of the party machine. FECA was about as reformist – in practice if not in theory – as Boss Tweed or Mayor Richard Daley. We shall consider the congressional response to soft money later – a response, as you might guess, that did not place liberty and robust speech at the center of its concerns.

Those who wrote FECA and its amendments misestimated – by a truly ridiculous order of magnitude – the public support for the program. That is why its health is a perennial source of fretting for the public financing crowd.

The original idea was that the millions collected by the income-tax check-off would be funneled into the PECF within the US Treasury Department. (Presumably within an Al Gore-quality lockbox.) Come the presidential election, the sums accumulated in the previous four years would finance the new "clean" elections. Corruption would be banished from presidential elections, "influence-buying" would be a thing of the past, billionaire and denizen of skid row alike would be on an equal footing, and never again would a

Nixonian crook haunt the American polity. Or at least that was the theory. As for the fact, the voluntary checkoff has been a crashing failure.

The checkoff amount has risen slowly over the years: what began as $1 ($2 for a joint filer) was trebled to $3/$6 in 1993 – not a daunting number, especially when the taxpayer is assured that his tax burden will be unaffected by his participation in the program. Affirming one's support doesn't cost a red cent. All it takes is a stroke of the pen. But for the vast majority of tax-payers, that is a stroke too far.

It is quaintly amusing to go back and read the high hopes and optimistic projections of the men and women who conceived this strange hybrid known as the "voluntary" federal election checkoff. (The notion that the federal government, the most coercive institution in the United States, is in charge of a "voluntary" activity is in itself cause for an arched eyebrow or two.)

Participation in the federal-income tax presidential election-fund check-off was never exactly robust, even in the heady early years of the program, when a general disgust over Watergate and the Nixonian fund-raising appa-ratus was pervasive. In 1975, the first year that the IRS 1040 forms included the option, 24.2% of filers checked the box. Thus less than one-fourth participated. And "participation" is almost too strong a word. Usually, when we think of a person "participating" in politics, we think of a dedi-cated true-believer stuffing envelopes, licking stamps, ringing doorbells, calling potential voters, writing out a check to a favorite candidate, and the like. Acts that require a certain measure of time and commitment. By con-trast, the "participation" necessary to the federal election income-tax check-off consists of checking a box on a government form. This takes approximately one second. And it doesn't cost the checker a penny or add in any way to his tax bill: the dollar(s) that is directed major-partyward expressly does *not* add to the filer's tax burden. For a full 75% of filers to refuse this simplest of acts – one second in duration, costing nothing – was an overwhelming act of rejection. And that 75% was in the program's first year, when it was bathed in favorable press.

The checkoff brigade inched upward in the late 1970s: 25.5% in 1976, 27.5% in 1977, 28.6% in 1978, down to 25.4% in the Carter malaise year of 1979, but back to 27.4% in 1980 and then peaking, ironically, with Ronald Reagan's first year in office, when in 1981 28.7% of income-tax fil-ers designated a dollar for the presidential campaign fund. Still, even at its 1981 zenith, 71.3% of filers refused to check the box.

The percentage declined throughout the 1980s: 27.0% in 1982, 24.2% in 1983, 23.7% in 1984, until in Reagan's final year, 1988, it stood at

21.0%. Unlike 1981, the presidential transition year of 1989, when George H.W. Bush moved into the White House, did not bring with it a bump in the proportion of income-tax filers who wished their tax dollars to feed the politicians. The percentage declined to 20.1% in that first year of the first Bush. It fell to 17.7% in Bush's final full year, 1992, rebounded slightly (to 18.9%) in Bill Clinton's initial year in office, 1993, and then sunk like a stone throughout Clinton's scandal-plagued two terms. The single sharpest fall came between Clinton's first and second years, when the percentage dipped from 18.9% to 14.5%. By 1995, it was 13.0%; by 2000, it was 11.8%. Like his father, George W. Bush failed to push the percentage upward in his first year, as it fell to an all-time low of 11.0% in 2001. Nor was the checkoff rescued by 9/11: it was just 11.2% in 2002. In 2005, the last year for which figures were available, an incredibly meager 9.1% of taxpayers bothered to check the PECF box.[19]

It would seem clear that the American people have rejected, fully and completely, the presidential election income-tax checkoff. If fully 90% refuse even to make a pencil scratch (or, more likely, press the "enter" button on the computer or tell their accountant to do same) to steer $3 or $6 into this fund *at no additional charge to the taxpayer making the checkoff*, surely the people have spoken, the matter is decided, and the fund should be liquidated.

Surely, alas, this is *not* how the establishment interprets the public's rejection. Consider one sterling example of the establishment viewpoint. Those working to "improve" the system of government financing of presidential candidates usually have pedigrees that cause raised eyebrows of suspicion in all but the hopelessly unsavvy. Such are the authors of one of the major recent studies in the field, "Participation, Competition, Engagement: How to Revive and Improve Public Funding for Presidential Nomination Politics," by the Campaign Finance Institute (CFI). Sponsored by grants from the Joyce Foundation, Open Society Institute, Pew Charitable Trusts, and the Smith Richardson Foundation, the 13-person CFI Task Force on Presidential Nomination Financing included William E. Brock, former chairman of the Republican National Committee; Charles T. Manatt, former chairman of the Democratic National Committee; and 11 more lobbyists, PAC chairs, politically engaged political science professors, campaign managers, and the kind of paralytically cautious people who are always serving on blue-ribbon panels that ratify the status quo. One surprise on the task force: Ross Clayton Mulford, the Texas attorney who managed Ross Perot's insurgent 1992 campaign and was general counsel to Perot in his half-hearted 1996 effort.

Not to spoil the suspense for you, but the task force concluded that "losing the system would be a loss for democracy."[20]

When the assorted Republican–Democrat panjandrums of the CFI's Task Force on Presidential Nominating Financing appraised the checkoff system, they saw two outstanding flaws. The problems were, first, that the checkoff level is too low and ought to be jacked up to $5/$10; and second, and more importantly, that it has been crippled by a "lack of public education about the workings and purposes of the system and electronic filing software that discourages participation."

The solution? "The Federal Election Commission and Internal Revenue Service should institute new educational programs about the checkoff aimed at professional tax preparation services and software providers, as well as at taxpayers."[21]

Aim it at taxpayers, all right. Unwilling to accept that the "public" cares not to pay for politicians' campaigns out of tax dollars, the task forcers recommend a propaganda blitz by the Internal Revenue Service (IRS) as well as government harassment of H&R Block, your local tax preparer, and software providers who are said to be insufficiently supporting the income-tax checkoff.

While the ignorant public and scoundrel tax preparers are chastised, the IRS comes in for praise by the task force. It offers "useful explanatory language" in the instruction section of the form 1040. For "useful" substitute "partisan" or "prejudicial"; the supposedly politically neutral IRS informs taxpayers, "The fund reduces candidates' dependence on large contributions from individuals and groups and places candidates on an equal financial footing in the general election."[22]

Sure it does – in a funhouse-mirror way. As we have seen, the fund has coincided with a decline in the percentage of small contributions to political candidacies. In this way it has actually magnified the importance of large contributors, though of course these contributions are supplemented by government assistance in its nakedest form – cash. And the candidates whom the fund so generously places "on an equal financial footing" are the nominees of the two major parties. In artificially boosting the positions of the Democratic and Republican candidates, the fund acts to diminish third parties and potential independent candidacies. But then those are the sorts of troublemakers who all too often in our turbulent past have shown an insufficient appreciation for the good works and charity of the IRS.

The IRS is further encouraged by the blue-ribbon panel of establishmentarians to take a more active role in dictating the content of tax-return software.

Specifically, the group reasons, "Since the IRS authorizes all e-file providers, it should mandate that participants *not* present a negative default on the checkoff, and use verbatim IRS questions and explanations."

Now we're getting past the boilerplate and into the heart of the matter. When words like *mandate* start appearing, you know you've found the true heart of a proposal. The software industry is, at last report, part of America's vital and prosperous private sector. Those who design its products do so with an eye toward making programs that are both user-friendly and efficient. Neither description has often been applied to the IRS, by the way. When the IRS and software designers meet, there is unlikely to be a good deal of overlap in their approach to the matter at hand. The software designers are liable, in fact, to fashion their handiwork in a way that favors the tax-filer over the revenuers. This might be good and customer-friendly business, but it will not do for the IRS.

Those who prepare taxes, too, are to come under the purview of the IRS, whose surveillance powers are evidently to be increased rather substantially. (Maybe it's a homeland security thing.) As the task force explains, "Tax preparers typically explain the meaning of their clients' choices to them in private conversations. We know little about such discussions, but the IRS should also instruct professional tax preparation services and accountants not to assume a negative response to the checkoff question."[23]

Is this a suggestion or a threat? How is the accountant to take this? If the IRS, which has a kind of life or death power over the accountant, instructs him or her to present the PECF option in a favorable light, how is your average accountant going to respond? By automatically checking the box, one might guess. Better safe than sorry.

What an extraordinary assumption of power this would be by the IRS. And consider that rather plaintive phrase: "We know little about such discussions." Sounds like they wish they knew more, doesn't it? Perhaps accountant-client conversations can somehow be subjected to the same scrutiny now given prison chats between terror suspects and court-appointed lawyers? Maybe accountants can wear wires? Or perhaps on visiting his neighborhood bean-counter or H&R Block preparer, the client can be subjected to a taped recitation of the glories of the Presidential Election Campaign Fund and a dark warning of the consequences of not checking the box. After all, as with so many reforms, this one is for our own good.

The enduring fantasy is that if only taxpayers knew how noble this system was, they'd fill it to bursting. As Anthony Corrado, a political scientist who has acted as a consultant and staffer for Democratic candidates, including

President Bill Clinton, writes, some claim that the ebb in participation does not represent an informed decision by nonparticipants at all. Instead, they claim just the opposite, and attribute the decrease to a lack of public awareness, inadequate understanding of the purposes of the program, and a rise in the number of taxpayers who do not remember the events and abuses that led to the adoption of the campaign finance reforms."[24] Perhaps the appropriate answer is mandatory classes in Watergate Remembrance.

As Corrado admits, an ambitious FEC public-relations program during 1990–1991 – which included television and radio announcements in English and Spanish, flyers, brochures, and government-subsidized travel by commission members to plump for the checkoff – "had little effect."[25] Despite reaching an estimated 200 million Americans at its peak, the campaign did nothing to boost taxpayer checkoffs. You can lead a 1040 filer to the PECF, but you can't make him check the box.

That is why some advocates of public financing, tired of public relations campaigns that don't work and stupid obdurate taxpayers who refuse to check the damned box, advocate abolishing the PECF and financing the program out of general revenues. At least they are honest: Americans, by overwhelming margins, do not like the income-tax checkoff. And the only way the federal government is going to replenish the PECF is by making the checkoff mandatory – like every other federal government program.

(Parenthetically, 12 states also provide a box on state income-tax returns which taxpayers can check to direct funds to political parties. Or at least some parties: Ohio and North Carolina expressly limit the options to Democrat and Republican, the Coke and Pepsi of our system. If you prefer another party, tough. However, in Maine, interestingly, the state Green Party received more money – $4,467 – via the 2007 checkoff than did the Republican Party – $4,349.)

Unlike the checkoff statistics, opinion surveys on public financing of campaigns are notoriously unreliable. As *Washington Post* director of polling Richard Morin concedes, "Questions that suggest majority opposition to public financing typically are brief and to the point." For instance, Hotline offered several succinctly described proposals. "Full campaign financing by the federal government" won the support of just 15% of respondents.[26] In 1999, in the heat of the McCain–Feingold fever, CBS News asked, in neutral language, "Public financing of political campaigns – that is, using tax money to pay for campaigns and prohibiting large donations from individuals and special interest groups – do you favor or oppose that?" The opposers outnumbered the favorers, 58 to 37%.[27]

The people, it would seem, have spoken. The overwhelming majority do not wish Washington to subsidize political candidates. But tendentious pollsters have ways of eliciting more positive responses to public financing. Long, detailed, and obfuscatory questions that slip in loaded words such as "reform" and that use the word "public" instead of "government" usually find a more significant number of respondents in support of government-financed campaigns. The key is hiding the true nature of the plan behind innocuous phrasings. Cynical? Yes. But how else are you going to sell a scheme that critics unkindly label "welfare for politicians"?

Even the CFI's task force concedes that "Some campaign finance rules treat minor parties and Independents unfairly."[28] (One suspects that the presence on the task force of former Perot advisor Ross Clayton Mulford led to that bone being tossed.) This is an understatement, to be sure, but at least the statement has been made. Achieving ballot access in the fifty states, with their hoops and hurdles that range from manageable pains in the necks to impossible dreams, soaks up nearly every dollar the insurgent candidate can raise. He has exhausted his resources just in order to reach the starting gate!

Should the third-party candidates enter the tangle and thicket of federal subsidization, as Ross Perot did not do in 1992 but John Anderson, Patrick J. Buchanan, and Ralph Nader have done, they find themselves still at a distinct disadvantage in the alms line. As the task force authors write, "if a minor party or independent candidate triumphs over all these obstacles [such as ballot-access laws] and amasses enough support to gain widespread ballot access, he or she still cannot get any public general election funding until *after* the election — and then only on receiving 5% of the general election vote."[29]

Such post-campaign funding is about as untimely as it gets. While major party candidates run their campaigns on the fuel of government grants, third-party standard-bearers run on private donations and the half wished-for, half-promised subventions that come to those who exceed 5% in the national popular vote. This is perfectly consistent with the insights of the economic theory of regulation, which holds that "well-entrenched political parties will seek regulations that hinder the entry of new parties."[30]

Proposals have been advanced to level the field somewhat: for instance, by permitting a third party or independent to maintain a separate ballot-access account, contributions to which are unlimited. In this way, a sugar daddy of considerable means might pay the whole shot (or a large portion thereof) for nationwide ballot access. Others have suggested mechanisms by which third-party candidates would be eligible for PECF dollars during the election, not after.

But there is no prospect of any such alterations being made as long as the Republicans and Democrats write the laws. Besides, it is always worth remembering and restating that the two modern third-party candidacies that have had far and away the most success were conducted without a dime of taxpayers' money: George Wallace's pre-FECA AIP campaign of 1968, and Ross Perot's self-financed Reform Party run in 1992. And it is also worth noting that one of the biggest crackpots in American politics, the conspiracy theorist Lyndon LaRouche, "has received more than $5.5 million from the public to underwrite his five attempts at gaining the Democratic nomination for president."[31] There is no filter in the FECA which keeps money from flowing to the disreputable. Nor should there be, for just what government body is capable of – or should be given the power of – deciding which views are "acceptable" and which are not? The way to ensure that the likes of Lyndon LaRouche – who, it must be repeated, received his money as a major-party primary candidate – are not subsidized by the taxpayer is by repealing FECA.

The Federal Election Commission is not entirely without champions. After all, it does its best to defend the parties that appoint its members. It does its best to ensure, as Justice Rehnquist wrote with respect to *Buckley v. Valeo*, that FECA "enshrin[es] the Republican and Democratic Parties in a permanently preferred position." Of course Rehnquist believed that this was patently unconstitutional, for "Congress may not by law attempt to ensure that this pattern will endure forever."

But the FEC tries to do just that.

The commissioners are almost always abject hacks, party loyalists, and time-servers who can be counted on to vote with their party and against the opposition, no matter the merits of any particular case. The historian Robert Mutch writes, "Congress wants more than the statutory balance between Republicans and Democrats on the commission – Congress wants the right kinds of Republicans and Democrats."[32]

In its early years, the FEC was a dumping ground for retired politicians who had not made names in upholding principle over party. More recently, the trend has been to appoint Washington attorneys of measurable political sympathies. In either case, the general makeup of the commission has not been one of distinguished and nonpartisan statesmen and women. These commissioners are placed on the FEC to do the bidding of the major parties. In this role they can be judged successful. There are more party-line votes in FEC deliberations than one can find anywhere this side of the North Korean Supreme People's Assembly.

Despite its manifest failures – and despite the fact that even if it succeeded that success might be counted a failure in the ledger of American liberty – the FEC retains a large cadre of defenders. The love affair between the modern liberal and the bureaucracy is sometimes touching to observe. No amount of faithlessness, no act of treachery, or pattern of scandal is sufficient for the liberal to give up on his true love. It's almost heart-warming. Almost. For as Stuart Taylor of *National Journal* has written, "One thing might be more dangerous than a weak FEC: a strong one."[33]

More interesting, if perhaps more tragic, are those liberals of a self-consciously cynical or realist variety. They are invariably disenchanted with the bureaucracies set up to administer progressive programs. They are often among the sharpest and most incisive critics of those bureaus. They write books, as *Wall Street Journal* Washington reporter Brooks Jackson did, with titles like *Broken Promise: Why the Federal Election Commission Failed* (1990). These are often good books containing lots of useful information. They paint devastating pictures of the agencies involved. But their conclusions are of a piece: As always, the agency needs more/better/stronger enforcement powers and, naturally, a bigger budget and more employees!

Take Brooks Jackson's aforementioned thin volume, which he wrote for the nonpartisan goo-goos of the Twentieth Century Fund. Jackson sees quite clearly that "the FEC is a captive of the members of Congress and the two major political parties, the very ones it was supposed to regulate."[34] This is a phenomenon well-known to students of political economy: regulating agencies are, almost invariably, captured by the very organizations they are charged with regulating.

The FEC is a bureaucratic rara avis: an agency that was created by an act of Congress and a stroke of President Nixon's pen and charged with regulating the electoral behavior – that is to say, the self-preservation and self-perpetuation – of members of Congress and the President. To say that it was born into a kind of servitude and has worn the leash ever since would be an understatement. Brooks Jackson writes of the FEC, "Those it regulates include the members of Congress who wrote its charter, control its budget, and influence selection of its membership. From the start, Congress repeatedly used its power to weaken the commission and to club it into submission whenever it showed signs of independence."[35]

The wonder is that anyone could ever have thought that it could be otherwise. When, pray tell, has the Congress ever created a watchdog that had the teeth to take a bite out of Congress? It would be an act of masochism to do so. And a piece of foolhardiness to expect it to.

FECA is a sham, writes Jackson, a weak-willed joke. The Federal Election Commission "has neither the will nor the means to deter wanton violators."[36] He cites case after case of deep-pocketed influence-peddlers who commit flagrant violations of the law and are let off, after ridiculously belated investigations, with slaps on the wrist. One Beverly Hills commodity trader gave the 1984 presidential campaign of the notoriously ethically challenged US Senator Alan Cranston (D-CA) $45,000, which was $44,000 above the legal limit for contributions. The case was open and shut but the commission seemed never to get around to opening it.

It has, at times, cracked down on actual violations: some astonishingly petty, but others so flagrant that they cast doubt on the very premises of the program. For instance, there have been cases of candidates faking donations in order to qualify for matching funds. The bizarre perennial candidate Lyndon LaRouche did so in 1976, as did the hapless Pennsylvania Governor Milton Shapp, whose 1976 campaign for the Democratic presidential nomination was boosted by $300,000 in fraudulent matching-fund-eligible donations.[37]

Wrangling over campaign finance violations or exposing FECA follies, as the liberal critics of the law do, is to miss the forest for the trees. For there is a more basic answer to the question of campaign finance, an answer that campaign finance reformers do not want to hear. But the provocative political economist John R. Lott Jr. has given it. Why, Lott asks, is campaign spending increasing? Simple. Because "the government is getting bigger."[38]

Lott obtained time-series cross-sectional data on government spending and spending on gubernatorial and state legislature races for 16 states. His findings? "The relationship between state budget expenditures and state house or senate campaign expenditures" is "both statistically and economically significant."[39] In other words, "higher government spending produces significantly higher campaign expenditures."[40] If the pie to be divvied up is big enough, those who are fighting for a plate will invest considerable sums of money to guarantee a seat at the table.

Reformers, concludes Lott, are attacking the symptoms, not the real cause of the spike in campaign spending. Interest groups and donors rationally determine that political donations return to the giver many fold, at least if their favored candidates win. And since incumbent re-election rates in the Congress and in the state legislatures make a mockery of the idea of democratic competition, it hardly takes a Machiavelli to figure out which solons to back. The amount of government loot at stake is staggering, and the more prize money that's available, the more greedy interest groups will spend to get access to it.

If, Lott suggests, "one really wants to reduce the resources society spends on campaigns, the solution is to make government smaller." That silence you hear is the collective membership of Common Cause ignoring Lott's point.

But Lott is not finished. He poses another question to the goo-goos. The "real puzzle," he says, is "why are campaign expenditures so small when there is so much money at stake? Why are federal budget expenditures 2,500 times larger than total federal legislative campaign expenditures and state budget expenditures 1,250 times larger than total state legislative campaign expenditures?"[41]

Don't the pigs understand just how bottomless the trough really is?

Given the stakes, why do Americans spend so little on politics? In 2006, the federal government spent $2.8 trillion. That's a huge jackpot. This sum does not, of course, include the billions that companies must spend to comply with regulations and otherwise dance to the federal tune. Yet total spending by all presidential candidates of all parties in 2004 was less than $700 million – and that was an exceptionally expensive campaign year, as President George W. Bush and Democrat John Kerry bypassed the PECF.

It this too little? Too much? Just right? As Bradley A. Smith points out, "Americans spend more than twice as much money each year on yogurt, and two to three times as much on the purchase of potato chips, as they do on political campaigns."[42] The average American might reply that we get far more satisfaction from yogurt, and pleasure from potato chips, than we do from Hillary Clinton commercials.

Be that as it may, are campaign contributions good investments? Evidence weighs on both sides. A solid body of congressional research suggests a limited, perhaps even nonexistent, link between campaign contributions and a congressman's voting record. Party, ideology, and responsiveness to constituent preferences, and not campaign donations, seem to explain voting patterns. Then again, what the donor is buying may be access and the kind of action that does not show up in a roll-call vote: helping to secure an HHS grant, a federal highway bridge repair grant, a tariff increase on plastic soldiers or toy marbles or whatever foreign imports may compete with businesses in a member's home district.

MIT professors Ansolabehere, de Figueiredo, and Snyder argue that "the evidence that campaign contributions lead to a substantial influence on votes is rather thin." The votes of legislators, they assert, "depend almost entirely on their own beliefs and the preferences of their voters and their party. Contributions explain a minuscule fraction of the variation in voting behavior in the US Congress."[43]

This alternative explanation holds that people donate to candidacies not to receive direct benefits but for more elusive and less crass reasons. They agree with a candidate. They know a candidate. They want to please a boss. They like to throw money around. They believe in a cause.

In a related study, economist Filip Palda of Vancouver, Canada's Fraser Institute, measured the relationship between what he somewhat puckishly calls "the jackpot" – that is, the amount of money that an officeholder has access to – and the amount that is raised and spent in the campaign for that office.

Palda begins with a disarmingly honest premise: "contributors give money to candidates in return for promises of government favors."[44] Now, these are not necessarily as crude as bribes and payoffs. But contributors expect *something*; they are not merely casting dollars to the winds. As Palda writes, "Investor-contributors look at a candidate as they might at an uncertain research and development project yielding large monopoly profits if a success, but nothing if a failure."[45] Thus they must calculate the chance of a candidate winning as well as the size of the potential jackpot.

Using data from state gubernatorial races in 1978 and 1986, Palda found that the "larger the jackpot, the more candidates spend." Specifically, spending by candidates rises by .0004 cents per voter for every dollar increase in the per capita jackpot.[46] Contributors – investors, that is – will shell out according to how rich the available resources are.

Significantly, Palda discovered that state laws requiring balanced budgets or placing constitutional limits on debt *discouraged* campaign spending. So the message, again, is clear: if you really want to do something about the spiraling costs of competitive elections, shrink the government.

Bradley A. Smith, he of the yogurt and potato chips analogy, has been among the most incisive critics of FECA. And lo and behold, on February 9, 2000, he received what had to be every FECA critic's fondest wish and worst nightmare wrapped in one present: he was nominated to serve as a commissioner of the FEC. As this was an election year, Mr. Smith, in going to Washington, became a political football.

Stuart Taylor Jr. of *National Journal* dubbed Smith "the President's least-favorite nominee." The President in question was Bill Clinton, whose vice president, Albert Gore, called Smith "unfit for the office." Gore's opponent in the 2000 Democratic primaries, former Senator Bill Bradley (D-NJ), accused the Clinton–Gore administration of "a betrayal of campaign finance reform" in nominating Smith.[47] Editorialists compared him to ex-Klansman David Duke, *Hustler* publisher Larry Flynt, and the Unabomber – all because he placed First Amendment rights to freedom of speech above the imperatives of the regulatory state. Smith complained that "the bulk of both legal scholarship and popular writing on campaign finance has been a literature of regulation, not freedom."[48] He bucked that trend – and the trendmakers bucked him, and hard.

The strange charter of the FEC is to blame for the spectacle of Clinton nominating a man who was reviled by his own vice president. Each party – that is, the Democrats and Republicans; the Senate independent (socialist Bernie Sanders of Vermont) has no such privilege, nor would any other third-party or independent solon – chooses three members of the FEC. The Republicans, at the behest of Kentucky Senator Mitch McConnell, a determined critic of campaign reform, sent Bradley Smith's name to the White House, which grudgingly nominated Smith to fill an open seat on the FEC. After Gore, Bradley, and those politicians and activists who believe there is such a thing as too much speech kicked up a duststorm, the dust settled, and Smith was confirmed by the Senate in May 2000. He would serve five years on the commission, including a year as chairman of the FEC.

A graduate of Harvard Law School, Smith made his name while a professor at Capital University Law School in Columbus, Ohio. He punctured the clichés and platitudes of the campaign finance set with vigor and intelligence. And in the process he made himself some powerful enemies.

Stuart Taylor contrasted Smith's libertarian bias in favor of more speech and freer speech with the restrictionist proposals of his critics. For instance, John McCain (R-AZ), cofather of the McCain–Feingold Act that sought to clamp down on unregulated political speech, said, "If I could think of a way constitutionally, I would ban negative ads." Of course the only way to do so "constitutionally" would be to repeal the First Amendment, which McCain presumably views as an immovable obstacle on the way to paradise (and eternal re-election). Besides, "negative" ads – the adjective is in the eye of the beholder – may expose a vote, a position, or an unseemly act by a politician that the politician would rather keep hidden. So often our free press, which is seldom shy about declaring its fearlessness, is a lap dog for the establishment, ignoring or playing down potentially troublesome positions held by its favorites. A negative ad may be the only way of revealing those feet of clay. And in any event, such an ad augments the political debate, adds to the sum of knowledge voters have about the candidates, and even if the ad is sleazy or distasteful, hey – freedom of speech doesn't only protect pabulum speeches and banal editorials. It protects rough, uncensored, combative opinions, too.

Bill Bradley, paragon of earnest liberalism, declared in 1999, "Special interest groups that run political advertisements should pay their opponents to respond. . . . When issue ads are on, a 100% tax [should be] given to the other side."[49]

Thankfully, the McCain–Bradley Amendment to repeal the leadoff feature of the Bill of Rights never wended its way to ratification. Nor have nightmarish proposals to parcel out licenses to dissent in the form of government speech vouchers found official favor – yet.

McCain did, however, with Wisconsin Democrat Russell Feingold, lead the assault on free speech that found its legal expression in the smarmily named Bipartisan Campaign Reform Act (BCRA) of 2002. (That first word ought to have been the tipoff: what good has ever come of bipartisanship?) The BCRA, as its harsh acronym went, audaciously curbed access to broadcast media by labor and corporate-backed groups within thirty days of a primary or sixty days of a general election. It clamped unprecedented controls on what had theretofore been the rough and tumble of campaign speech. If the AFL-CIO wants to push candidates who favor bumping up the federal minimum wage, or an evangelical PAC wants to attack candidates it views as pro-abortion, by what right does the federal government prohibit this speech? This "effort to segregate formal electoral debate from ongoing, informal political debate necessitates the use of intrusive bureaucracies that have all the institutional disadvantages of traditionally disfavored licensors," writes Kathleen M. Sullivan. Noting the widespread support of McCain–Feingold by newspaper editorial writers, Sullivan puckishly notes that "the institutional press . . . has not been heard to call for a moratorium on political editorials or candidate endorsements in their pages during the sixty days preceding an election."[50]

Also known as the Incumbent Protection Act, the BCRA did increase the maximum contribution per individual per election from $1,000 to $2,000 and indexed it thereafter. (At this writing, the limit is a still ridiculously low $2,300, although this cramped ceiling does permit those beleaguered wealthy donors who contribute to campaigns more out of a feeling of obligation to friends or associates than any particular ardor for the candidates a foolproof excuse to make what are, by their standards, fairly niggardly donations.)

The BCRA also banned the oft-reviled "soft money" which had flowed through the loophole in the 1974 Federal Election Campaign Act. And in a swipe at the advantage FECA had inadvertently given the Ross Perots of the world, the BCRA permitted candidates facing self-financed opponents to raise more from individual donors than would normally be allowed. Members of Congress had long fretted about the possibility that they might someday face a rich foe who could actually give them a run for their money, and this was the chance to build in a little fund-raising wiggle room. As Common Cause president Scott Harshbarger said, "It is disappointing but not entirely surprising to see that the Senate's first move out of the gate on the campaign finance debate is to put forward an amendment dealing with their own self-interests rather than the public interest." The so-called Millionaires Amendment, he complained, "reveals the preoccupation that incumbents have with preserving their advantage over challengers."[51] (The Supreme Court struck down the amendment in the 2008 case, *Davis v. FEC*.)

As this provision suggests, the BCRA was not necessarily an act of high-minded nobility on the part of Congress. The duo of Burton A. Abrams and Russell F. Settle, applying the economic theory of regulation to BCRA as they had a quarter-century earlier to FECA, found that the Republicans had raised 16% more soft money than the Democrats in the six election cycles prior to the passage of the BCRA of 2002. Things looked grim for the Democrats, especially with the Republican takeover of the White House in the 2000 election. Prospects for a widening of the soft-money gap were good. In stepped the reformers to save the day . . . for the Democrats.

Although the law bears the term "bipartisan," in fact the vote on final passage of BCRA was split along starkly partisan lines. In the House, 94% of Democrats but only 19% of Republicans supported it; in the Senate, 96% of Democrats but just 22% of Republicans voted aye. Most members of both parties voted in the self-interest of their parties. This is to be expected. So is the dressing-up of their causes in pretty phrases and the language of political cant.[52]

The BCRA of 2002 survived the expected legal challenge from a *Buckley*-like gaggle of plaintiffs including the National Rifle Association, the California Democratic Party, the American Civil Liberties Union, and the Republican National Committee. The Supreme Court – in *McConnell v. Federal Election Commission* (2003) – upheld its central features, many of them by 5–4 margins. (It did strike down the act's silly ban on political donations by persons 17 and under.)

The law was "an ineffectual speed bump in the chase of money after politicians," wrote David Harwood in the October 31, 2004 *Denver Post*. It was "a near-total bust."[53]

It should at least be pointed that in this field as in others, contrarian viewpoints exist. Sidney M. Milkis, professor of politics at the University of Virginia, was an expert witness for the Republican National Committee in the case of *McConnell v. FEC*. Milkis praises soft money for its revitalizing effect on the parties. Political action committees, he said, had become "a rival to political parties in support of candidates."[54] (Maybe because, while the parties had come to stand for nothing but their own self-perpetuation, the reviled PACs at least stood for *something?*) Because the parties were flush with soft money, they had reasserted their supremacy over PACs in the hierarchy of campaign funding.

In any event, BCRA showed the lengths to which career-conscious reformers will go to protect the political class against the rabble. In fact, a constitutional amendment to repeal those freedoms protected by *Buckley v. Valeo* (by way of the First Amendment) has been introduced in recent Congresses. It would establish that Congress and the states "shall have power to set reasonable limits on the amount of contributions that may be accepted by, and the amount of expenditures that may be made by, in support of, or in opposition to, a candidate for nomination for election to" federal or state office.[55] It has lain dead in the water, with no immediate threat of revival.

But consider how strange this is: "an election exception to the First Amendment," as Kathleen M. Sullivan terms it.[56] Political speech would be placed in a less privileged position than, say, soft-core pornography. Nudie pictures are protected by the First Amendment, but campaign speech would not be. Flag-burning is protected by the First Amendment, but not an ad saying that Senator Smith is a big spending liberal. Does this not represent an almost total inversion of the Framers' intentions? And if a movement has reached the stage of desperation at which it whips out a constitutional amendment to amend the First Amendment, isn't it time to rip up the talking points, fade the screen to black, and start over again? Is this will-o-the-wisp of "clean elections" – even if they were attainable by way of massive taxpayers' subsidies and a clampdown on free speech, which they are not – worth repealing the cornerstone of the Bill of Rights?

Other proposed reforms also enrich the two major parties, flooding them with taxpayers' cash, while obstructing the avenue to advancement of minor parties. For instance, the "More Speech – More Competition" model, which Andrew C. Geddis lays out in the *Journal of Law & Politics*, would fully fund, from the US Treasury, those House candidates who agree to forego all private fundraising. Admittedly, this would "stem the flow of unregulated private money into the political process," though just how a flow of heavily regulated *public money* purifies the process is unclear. Indeed, the public money, as Justice Burger and Senator Baker warned, is likely to come with even more strings attached – strings of a consistency strong enough to choke off those who defy

the system. Geddis takes pains to carve out a space for non-major party candidates in his scheme, for he concedes, "it would be hard to overcome the
suspicion that any public financing system set up to protect the duopoly
would be motivated more by the parties' self-interest than by any supposed
benefits to the public at large."[57]

Yes, it is hard to overcome that suspicion.

There is an alternative to both the corruption of the system and the anti-free
speech regulatory response of the reformers. It is in equal parts of freedom and
transparency. Permit all donations of whatever size, but require their prompt
and public disclosure. Politicians might still be bought off – but at least we'd
know who's doing the buying. And what the going rate for a legislator is.
(Disclosure, however, is not quite so cut-and-dried an issue as it appears at first.
The public disclosure clause of FECA may operate to discourage third-party
contributions. Rather than helping quietly, behind the scenes, without publicity,
the donor is now publicly identified with the third-party cause, which may have
a radical tincture that is bad for business, or reputation, or what you have. A business executive whose milieu is solidly Republican – or Democratic – may think
twice and put away his checkbook before contributing to Libertarians or Greens
or other challengers of the status quo. There is an exemption in the current
disclosure law if a party can demonstrate that its contributors may face threats
or reprisals if identified, but the burden of proof is with the third party, and in
any event it is hard to "prove" the kind of vague social disapproval that can
attend public support of a minor party.)

The contribution limits have also shackled congressional challengers and
virtually shut out the possibility that a minor-party challenger might make a
serious run for a congressional seat.

In the matter of congressional races, FECA, according to the Supreme
Court, got it exactly wrong: the act imposed spending caps on House and
Senate candidates – an unconstitutional act according to *Buckley v. Valeo* – but
it failed to provide for public financing of the campaigns, which would have
been constitutionally kosher. The spending caps are gone, the limits on individual contributions remain, and Congress, despite the best efforts of liberal
reformers, never did succeed in transferring responsibility for paying for
congressional campaigns to the taxpayers.

At the congressional level, as Paul S. Herrnson writes, "FECA's contribution limits disadvantage minor party candidates for the House and Senate."[58]
Limits on contributions rule out the possibility of a third-party candidate
receiving a boost from one or two backers with deep pockets. A Libertarian
or Green or independent might be able to run a credible, even winning, race

against major party foes if he or she ran on an equal financial footing. Except in those rare instances in which a Perot-ish figure emerges and runs outside the party power structure using one's own dime, this just isn't going to happen under the current setup.

Nor was it meant to. Writing in 1975, before the Supreme Court decision that threw out spending caps on congressional races, political scientist Gary C. Jacobson traced the evolution of what all involved seemed to understand was an "Incumbent Protection Act".

By the early seventies, marginals were vanishing and incumbents were becoming as unbeatable as the Harlem Globetrotters. Between 1960 and the anomalous Watergate election of 1974, notes Jacobson, House incumbents won more than 93% of general-election campaigns. The reasons proposed for this were many: skillful exploitation of such incumbency advantages as the frank, free media, and constituent services; gerrymandered districts; the weakening of party ties and consequent rise of incumbency as a "positive shorthand cue" for voters. Whatever the reason, it was well understood that incumbents, particularly in the House, were nearly invulnerable. The only chance, outside of scandal – especially finding the candidate with a dead girl or a live boy, as Louisiana's rascally Democratic Governor Edwin Edwards once quipped – that a challenger had to defeat an incumbent was to spend enough to neutralize, at least partially, the advantage of incumbency. So what strategy would a canny and cynical incumbent adopt to ward off such a challenge? Why, a ceiling on campaign expenditures! It is exactly what the phony reform movement of the early seventies proposed.

Unlike in the Watergate investigation, smoking guns were not hard to find. As Jacobson writes, "Senate conferees fought for and won higher limits on spending in House campaigns than would have been permitted under the original House-passed version of the bill." In other words, the House knew *exactly* what it was doing.[59] It was imposing a ceiling on campaign spending so low that all but the most corrupt House incumbent would feel free to take out a long-term mortgage on that second home in the Maryland suburbs. There was going to be no way he was going back home, at least involuntarily.

The Senate, less sensitive to concerns about the survival rate of House incumbents, raised the ceiling, but only to $70,000 in the general election (plus a maximum of $20,000 by the party and $20,000 for fundraising), still low enough to ward off all but the most vigorous or lucky challengers.

For as Jacobson explained, the evidence on the matter was overwhelming and irrefutable: Money matters a great deal, especially to challengers. The "more that nonincumbents spend, the more likely they are to be known by voters; the more frequently they are known, the more votes they are likely to win."[60] In fact, as later research demonstrated, the more *incumbents* spend, the less likely they are to win. This is paradoxical, at least on its surface, and the explanations vary, though the usual one is that the incumbents who spend the most are those who are already in the deepest trouble. (Economist John R. Lott Jr. offers a somewhat different reason for this curious finding: he says that the marginal return on campaign expenditures depends on the candidate's "stock of brand name." The greater the brand name, the less return there is on spending. So "more well-known politicians may not have to spend very much to win.")[61]

By capping the amount that a candidate may spend on his or her campaign, Congress had crippled competition. Challengers would be unable to spend enough money to get out their messages, to make known their names. "Reform," concluded Jacobson, "may indeed have generated nothing more than an Incumbent Protection Act, hardly necessary for a species which is anything but vanishing."[62] As FEC commissioner Bradley A. Smith later observed, "a flat spending cap may harm those challengers most likely to actually defeat an incumbent." That is why, perhaps, so many incumbents were eager to impose such a cap. And put it as close to the ground as possible. When in 1997 the US Senate again debated capping spending on congressional elections, Smith notes, "Every challenger spending less than the proposed limit in Senate campaigns had lost in each of the 1994 and 1996 elections, whereas every incumbent spending less than the limit had won. Similarly, only 3% of challengers spending less than the proposed limit for House races had won in 1996, whereas 40% of challengers spending more than that limit had won."[63]

It was as cynical an exploitation of "reform" sentiment as had been seen in some time, and while the Supreme Court nixed spending caps and Congress has not seen fit to try its luck again on the matter, such caps later filtered down to the states.

States, too, began regulating campaign finance in various ways. While Kentucky, for instance, has slapped a spending limit on candidates for governor, public financing has generally been the reform of choice. The idea spread like wildfire, or perhaps measles is more like it, during the 1970s. Fueled by disgust with Watergate, by 1979 23 states had, in some form or other, instituted a subsidy program for candidates for state office. More states clamped limits on contributions, though in 1997 the US Court of Appeals for the Eighth Circuit struck down a Missouri law capping contributions to state campaigns at $100 as an abridgement of free speech.

The hope, or rather the public claim, was that transferring the responsibility for paying for campaigns from the private to the public sector would broaden democracy, remove dirty money from state-level politics, and expand the field of potential candidates. This didn't happen, of course, just as it did not happen at the federal level with FECA, but then programs borne of reformist fever always seem to be judged on their highblown intentions, not their disappointing results.

The schemes vary from state to state. Most states assure the voter that checking the appropriate box will not increase his or her tax liability, though a handful of states do employ an "add-on" system whereby the checked box increases the checkee's tax burden. Predictably, tax filers are considerably more likely to opt into the system if it costs them nothing extra. Participation in the add-on program is "quite low."[64] Actually, "quite low" doesn't begin to describe how few taxpayers agree to be fleeced for the state add-on programs. In their comprehensive study *The Day After Reform: Sobering Campaign Finance Lessons from the American States* (1998), political scientists Michael J. Malbin and Thomas L. Gais survey the taxpayer participation in the eight add-on states at that writing (Alaska, Arizona, California, Maine, Maryland, Massachusetts, Montana, and Virginia). In only one state – Maine – had participation risen between 1980 and 1996, and that rise – from 0.5 to 0.6% – was not exactly staggering. Barely one in two hundred taxpayers in progressive Maine bothered to check off the public funding box on their state income-tax return. The rates in other states were just as pathetic, ranging from a high of 1.1% in Massachusetts to such microscopic lows as 0.3% in Virginia and 0.2% – that is, one in five hundred – in Arizona and California. The voters had spoken, and even the deafest advocates of government financing must have heard their message – not that they heeded it.

By contrast, participation rates for the 13 "checkoff" states in which checking the box added nothing to a taxpayer's bill ranged from a high of 24% in Hawaii to a low of 6.6% in Idaho. In the majority of states (nine), the rate was below 10%. As Malbin and Gais conclude, "some of these programs are not much more popular on tax return day than are taxes in general."[65]

At this writing, 22 states have adopted full or partial public financing of state legislative races. The most comprehensive programs belong to Arizona, Maine, and Massachusetts, each of which provides participating candidates with full funding up to the spending ceiling imposed by the law.[66] The latter two fund their programs via checkoffs, à la the federal PECF, but also by tax revenues, since the fits of good government giddiness that move citizens to check boxes that steer money toward politicians tend to strike only a select portion of the populace.

The righteously named Citizens Clean Elections Act of 1998 gave Arizona a system under which candidates for state offices who renounce private funding may receive public funding for their campaigns. Funded by a multiplicity of sources – a fee on lobbyists for trade associations and for-profits, a surcharge on civil and criminal penalties (including traffic tickets), a state income tax checkoff, and a tax credit for donations to the Clean Elections Fund – the act "is notorious for being burdensome and confusing," according to Robert J. Franciosi, director of Urban Growth and Development Studies for Arizona's Goldwater Institute.[67] Nettlesome regulations and fine print so fine that Superman couldn't read it have led to momentous disputes over such questions as "Can candidates serve snacks at parties given in their home to gather signatures?" and, in a matter that would be of special interest to John Edwards, "Are haircuts campaign expenditures?"[68]

The act has been something less than a resounding success. Far more Democrats than Republicans have partaken of the fund, yet a study by the Goldwater Institute found that "publicly funded legislators voted no differently from legislators who accepted private donations."[69] The whole thing has been a wash, really, leaving Arizona's political culture – but not the wallets of taxpayers and those who drive 42 in a 30 miles per hour zone – untouched. (Electoral corruption, or the lack thereof, has also remained essentially unchanged in Maine and Massachusetts, where incumbents are winning as frequently, if not more so, than in days of yore, and competition is just as sclerotic as ever.)

There is a more basic objection to the Arizona act, however. As Robert J. Franciosi has charged, "Taken to its intended limit, the act will make political campaigns, for office at least, a wholly owned subsidiary of the state government, giving the government significant power over political speech in the state."[70] Is that really what anyone wants?

The experience in Wisconsin, which since the heyday of the LaFollette family has been in the vanguard of progressive reform, demonstrates just how radical and cleansing public funding is not. Writing in *Legislative Studies Quarterly*, Kenneth R. Mayer of the University of Wisconsin-Madison and John M. Wood of Hamline University demolish, in stark and overwhelming detail, the claims of campaign finance activists.

Wisconsin, as they note, is an ideal state for this study. It entered the public-funding arena in 1977 in a big way as "the only state that provides [as of their writing in 1995] nontrivial direct public subsidies to legislative candidates who are elected from single-member districts."[71] Candidates for state assembly, senate, and statewide offices who agree to "voluntary" spending limits are eligible for grants from the Wisconsin Elections Campaign Fund (WECF), which is modeled after the PECF. Like the PECF, the WECF was launched with high hopes but soon lapsed into a kind of apathy-induced anemia. The percentage of Wisconsin taxpayers who check the WECF box never exceeded 19.7% (1979) and sunk to a pathetic 5% in 2006. You could probably get a higher participation rate if the state promised to spend the money raised on subsidizing the purchase of skateboards for surly adolescents.

As with the PECF, those who reject involvement with the WECF are not bound by spending limits, so only those challengers incapable of raising non-meager amounts of campaign cash are advised to opt in. In fact, a common thread connecting victorious challengers in the Wood–Mayer study was that they spent far more than the limit imposed by the WECF on those who accept public funding. As the authors write, their "results suggest that the spending limits constrain competition, since incumbents can rely on other forms of advertising and coalition building – such as casework, distributive programs, and district visits – that challengers cannot match."[72] ("Distributive programs" may be translated as *pork*.)

Comparing state legislative elections in Wisconsin from before and after the advent of public financing, Wood and Mayer actually found that "public financing has ironically coincided with less competitive legislative elections: victory margins are larger, incumbent reelection rates are higher, and more incumbents are running unopposed since Wisconsin's public finance system began in 1978."[73] This describes not the fresh and invigorating breath of air that Common Cause-ish advocates promised but a putrid and rotting Incumbent Protection Act covered in a veneer of sanctimony.

"Our conclusion," write Mayer and Wood, "is that public financing has had no effect at all on the level of electoral competition and has not eased the fundraising burden on challengers seeking to launch credible campaigns. Most important, the availability of public money does not appear to have encouraged challengers to emerge when they otherwise might not have."[74]

In other words, public financing in Wisconsin has been an utter failure that delivered on none of its promises, despite substantial funding and a huge reservoir of good will in a liberal state.

The evidence from these "laboratories of democracy" shows that although dressed in the finery of reform, public financing of state campaigns is just another way to ratify the status quo. Ruth S. Jones of the University of

Missouri, St. Louis, writing in the *American Journal of Political Science*, concluded after her study of 17 states that had adopted some level of public financing between 1972 and 1980 that "the majority party is generally advantaged in absolute dollar amounts regardless of policy variations."[75]

John Samples, director of the Cato Institute's Center for Representative Government and a sharp critic of public financing, notes studies showing that Democrats are more likely to participate in such state-level schemes than are Republicans. This pattern holds constant across time and states, ranging from Arizona to Maine to the Upper Midwest progressive redoubts of Minnesota and Wisconsin. Referring to the claim of Michael Malbin and Thomas Gais that, in Samples' words, the "libertarianism of Republicans" makes them less likely to accept government financing, Samples charges that "government financing in practice provides an advantage to nonlibertarian candidates."[76]

It is also true that partisans of the "out" party often believe, with ample justification, that in order to flip the game board and become the "in" party, they need to spend more money – which runs counter to the philosophy and practice of public-funding schemes, which tamp down spending and tend to ratify the status quo.

Political scientists Malbin and Gais pronounce what ought to have been the last word on public financing of state campaigns. Noting that there is virtually no difference in the percentage of the vote achieved by challengers in public financing states and in those without, they write that "one would be hard-pressed to conclude that public funding is doing a great deal to enhance competition. . . . [T]here is no compelling case for believing that elections in states with public funding are more competitive than in states without public funding."[77] Playing fields are just as unlevel as they were before, incumbents remain prohibitive favorites for re-election, and the only chance that a challenger really has is to raise substantial sums of money – the one thing he or she cannot do when accepting public funding that is tied to spending caps. As for minor party candidates . . . dream on.

"[C]hallengers' money, whatever the source, is more important to ensuring competition than incumbents' money," say Malbin and Gais.[78] This is the same lesson that political scientists have drawn from races for the US Congress. And it is a lesson that incumbents have taken to heart and will continue to take to heart, for every time campaign finance is on the tapis, listeners will have to endure pious speeches about the nefarious influence of big money – which means money that feeds a challenger's bank account.

No matter the evidence, there remains an enormously influential interest group with a direct and substantial stake in taxpayer financing of political campaigns: incumbent legislators. Shifting the fund-raising burden to the chumps scratching out their 1040s would be godsend to the solons. As Senator Barbara Boxer (D-CA) explains, having to raise their own campaign treasury means that members of Congress spend "too much time away from work, too much time away from doing the kinds of things that we want to do [in Congress], making life better for people."[79]

Making life better for people. Isn't that what Congress does for you?

Notes

1. Quoted in Anthony Corrado, *Paying for Presidents: Public Financing in National Elections* (New York: Twentieth Century Fund, 1993), p. 10.
2. Ibid., p. 37. For the donor percentages, see Campaign Finance Institute, "Participation, Competition, Engagement: How to Revive and Improve Public Funding for Presidential Nomination Politics," (Washington, DC: Campaign Finance Institute, September 2003), pp. xiv, 29.
3. Richard Briffault, "Public Funding and Democratic Elections," *University of Pennsylvania Law Review* (Vol. 148, No. 2, December 1999), pp. 582–83.
4. John F. Bibby and L. Sandy Maisel, *Two Parties. Or More?*, p. 64. For the breakdown of public funds, see Anthony Corrado, "Public Funding of Presidential Campaigns," in *The New Campaign Finance Sourcebook*, edited by Anthony Corrado, Thomas E. Mann, Daniel Ortiz, and Trevor Potter (Washington, DC: Brookings Institution, 2005), p. 182.
5. J. David Gillespie, *Politics at the Periphery: Third Parties in Two-Party America* (Columbia: University of South Carolina Press, 1993), p. 32.
6. See Campaign Finance Institute, "Participation, Competition, Engagement," p. 49, for PECF disbursements by party.
7. Steven J. Rosenstone, Roy L. Behr, and Edward H. Lazarus, *Third Parties in America: Citizen Response to Major Party Failure* (Princeton, NJ: Princeton University Press, 1984, second edition), p. 272.
8. Ibid., p. ix. For the concentration of TR's contributors, see Rhodes Cook, "Money Woes Limit Anderson, Third Party Presidential Bids," *Congressional Quarterly Weekly Report* (Vol. 38, No. 33, August 16, 1980): 2376.
9. John Samples, "The Failures of Taxpayer Financing of Presidential Campaigns," Cato Policy Analysis (Washington, DC: Cato Institute, November 25, 2003), pp. 7–8.
10. Campaign Finance Institute, "Participation, Competition, Engagement: How to Revive and Improve Public Funding for Presidential Nomination Politics," (Washington, DC: Campaign Finance Institute, September 2003), p. 7.
11. "Number of Federal PAC's Decreases," News Release, Federal Election Commission, July 10, 2007.
12. Kathleen M. Sullivan, "Against Campaign Finance Reform," *Utah Law Review* (1998), n.p.

13. Stephen Ansolabehere, John M. De Figueiredo, and James M. Snyder, Jr., "Why Is There So Little Money in U.S. Politics?" *Journal of Economic Perspectives* (Vol. 17, No. 1, Winter 2003), p. 106.

14. "Number of Federal PAC's Decreases," Federal Election Commission.

15. *Buckley v. Valeo*, footnote 52.

16. Quoted in David B. Magleby, "Party and Interest Group Electioneering in Federal Elections," in *Inside the Campaign Finance Battle: Court Testimony on the New Reforms*, edited by Anthony Corrado, Thomas E. Mann, and Trevor Potter (Washington, DC: Brookings Institution, 2003), p. 164.

17. Anthony Corrado, *Campaign Finance Reform* (New York: Century Foundation, 2000), p. 93.

18. Burton A. Abrams and Russell F. Settle, "Campaign-Finance Reform: A Public Choice Perspective," *Public Choice* (Vol. 120, 2004), p. 380.

19. For checkoff rates, see Campaign Finance Institute, "Participation, Competition, Engagement," p. 51.

20. Ibid., p. xi.

21. Ibid., p. xvii.

22. Ibid., p. 57.

23. Ibid., p. 58.

24. Anthony Corrado, *Paying for Presidents*, p. 27.

25. Ibid., p. 31.

26. Richard Morin, "Who Supports Public Campaign Financing?" *Washington Post*, June 5, 2000.

27. John Samples, "Government Financing of Campaigns: Public Choice and Public Values," Cato Policy Analysis (Washington, DC: Cato Institute, August 26, 2002), p. 11.

28. Campaign Finance Institute, "Participation, Competition, Engagement," p. xvii.

29. Ibid.

30. Burton A. Abrams and Russell F. Settle, "Campaign-Finance Reform: A Public Choice Perspective," *Public Choice* (Vol. 120, 2004), p. 389.

31. John Samples, "The Failures of Taxpayer Financing of Presidential Campaigns," Cato Policy Analysis (Washington, DC: Cato Institute, November 25, 2003), p. 10.

32. Quoted in Brooks Jackson, *Broken Promise: Why the Federal Election Commission Failed* (New York: Twentieth Century Fund, 1990), p. 10.

33. Stuart Taylor, Jr., "The President's Least-Favorite Nominee," *National Journal*, February 26, 2000, p. 599.

34. Brooks Jackson, *Broken Promise*, p. 2.

35. Ibid., p. 23.

36. Ibid., p. 1.

37. Ibid., p. 8.

38. John R. Lott, Jr., "A Simple Explanation for Why Campaign Expenditures Are Increasing: The Government Is Getting Bigger," *Journal of Law & Economics* (Vol. 43, October 2000), p. 359.

39. Ibid., p. 371.

40. Ibid., p. 377.

41. Ibid., p. 385.

42. Bradley A. Smith, "Faulty Assumptions and Undemocratic Consequences of Campaign Finance Reform," *Yale Law Journal* (Vol. 105, January 1996), n.p.

43. Stephen Ansolabehere, John M. De Figueiredo, and James M. Snyder, Jr., "Why Is There So Little Money in U.S. Politics?" *Journal of Economic Perspectives* (Vol. 17, No. 1, Winter 2003), p. 116.

44. Filip Palda, "The Determinants of Campaign Spending: The Role of the Government Jackpot," *Economic Inquiry* (Vol. 30, October 1992), p. 627.

45. Ibid., p. 628.

46. Ibid., p. 627.

47. Stuart Taylor, Jr., "The President's Least-Favorite Nominee," *National Journal*, February 26, 2000, p. 598.

48. Bradley A. Smith, *Unfree Speech: The Folly of Campaign Reform* (Princeton, NJ: Princeton University Press, 2001), p. x.

49. Stuart Taylor, Jr., "The President's Least-Favorite Nominee," p. 598.

50. Kathleen M. Sullivan, "Against Campaign Finance Reform," n.p.

51. Quoted in Jennifer A. Steen, "Self-Financed Candidates and the 'Millionaires' Amendment," in *The Election After Reform: Money, Politics, and the Bipartisan Campaign Reform Act*, edited by Michael J. Malbin (Lanham, MD: Rowman & Littlefield, 2006), p. 207.

52. Abrams and Settle, "Campaign-Finance Reform," p. 390.

53. Quoted in Michael J. Malbin, "Assessing the Bipartisan Campaign Reform Act," in *The Election After Reform: Money, Politics, and the Bipartisan Campaign Reform Act*, edited by Michael J. Malbin (Lanham, MD: Rowman & Littlefield, 2006), p. 1.

54. Sidney M. Milkis, "Parties versus Interest Groups," in *Inside the Campaign Finance Battle: Court Testimony on the New Reforms*, edited by Anthony Corrado, Thomas E. Mann, and Trevor Potter (Washington, DC: Brookings Institution, 2003), p. 41.

55. S.J. Res. 2, 105th Congress, 1st Session.

56. Kathleen M. Sullivan, "Against Campaign Finance Reform," n.p.

57. Andrew C. Geddis, "Campaign Finance Reform After McCain-Feingold: The More Speech-More Competition Solution," *Journal of Law & Politics* (Vol. 16, Summer 2000), n.p.

58. Paul S. Herrnson, "Two-Party Dominance and Minor Party Forays in American Politics," in *Multiparty Politics in America*, edited by Paul S. Herrnson and John C. Green (Lanham, MD: Rowman & Littlefield, 1997), p. 26.

59. Gary C. Jacobson, "Practical Consequences of Campaign Finance Reform: An Incumbent Protection Act?" *Public Policy* (Vol. 24, No. 1, Winter 1976), pp. 2, 4, 5.

60. Ibid., p. 30.

61. John R. Lott, Jr., "Does Additional Campaign Spending Really Hurt Incumbents?: The Theoretical Importance of Past Investments in Political Brand Name," *Public Choice* (Vol. 72, 1991), pp. 87, 91.

62. Gary C. Jacobson, "Practical Consequences of Campaign Finance Reform: An Incumbent Protection Act?" *Public Policy* (Vol. 24, No. 1, Winter 1976), p 31.

63. Bradley A. Smith, "Some Problems with Taxpayer-Funded Political Campaigns," *University of Pennsylvania Law Review* (Vol. 148, No. 2, December 1999), pp. 605–606.

64. Ruth S. Jones, "State Public Campaign Finance: Implications for Partisan Politics," *American Journal of Political Science* (Vol. 25, No. 2, May 1981), p. 348.

65. Michael J. Malbin and Thomas L. Gais, *The Day After Reform: Sobering Campaign Finance Lessons from the American States* (Albany, NY: Rockefeller Institute Press, 1998), pp. 67, 70.

66. For a survey of the experiences in Arizona, Maine, and Massachusetts, as well as other aspects of the campaign-finance question, see *Welfare for Politicians? Taxpayer Financing of Campaigns*, edited by John Samples (Washington, DC: Cato Institute, 2005).

67. Robert J. Franciosi, "Is Cleanliness Political Godliness?: Arizona's Clean Elections Law after Its First Year," (Phoenix, AZ: Goldwater Institute, November 2001), p. 5.

68. Ibid., p. 3.

69. Ibid., p. 16.

70. Ibid., p. 2.

71. Kenneth R. Mayer and John M. Wood, "The Impact of Public Financing on Electoral Competitiveness: Evidence from Wisconsin, 1964–1990," *Legislative Studies Quarterly* (Vol. 20, No. 1, February 1995), p. 70.

72. Ibid., p. 84.

73. Ibid., p. 71.

74. Ibid., p. 70.

75. Ruth S. Jones, "State Public Campaign Finance," p. 342.

76. John Samples, "Government Financing of Campaigns: Public Choice and Public Values," Cato Policy Analysis (Washington, DC: Cato Institute, August 26, 2002), p. 5.

77. Michael J. Malbin and Thomas L. Gais, *The Day After Reform: Sobering Campaign Finance Lessons from the American States*, pp. 135–36.

78. Ibid., p. 145.

79. Quoted in Anthony Corrado, *Campaign Finance Reform* (New York: Century Foundation, 2000), p. 35.

Chapter 6

The State Feeds the Party and the Party Feeds the State

Every four years, the Democrats and Republicans hold stage-managed conventions that have all the excitement of an ESPN2 rerun of a synchronized swim meet. These propaganda-heavy borefests, which are carried by the television networks, if with increasing reluctance, are now paid for by the taxpayer, thanks to one of FECA's grosser miscalculations.

Under the Federal Election Campaign Act of 1974, Republicans and Democrats — the language used therein was "major parties," defined as those which received more than 25% of the nationwide popular vote in the previous presidential election — were eligible to receive a grant of $2 million to cover the costs of their quadrennial convention. Minor parties could receive a fraction of this amount, depending on the vote they received four years prior — as long as it was above 5% but below 25%. New parties are out of luck: no pot of gold awaits them at the beginning of the rainbow. This sum of $2 million, to be adjusted for inflation every four years, was expected to pay most of the conventions' bills; the remainder were to be picked up, or so the intention was, by state and local governments. The theory — or the baseless hope — was that by substituting government subsidy of conventions for the previous mishmash of party funds and private support, the parties would no longer be beholden to greedy special interests. After all, the federal government is above the fray, beyond mere sectarian bickering. To be funded by Washington means that one has achieved a kind of transcendental objectivity. Nothing purifies a corrupt institution quite like an infusion of federal cash. That, anyway, was the theory.

In practice, the national party convention policy has been wasteful, ineffectual, and increasingly senseless. The amount of the subsidy has proved

J.T. Bennett, *Not Invited to the Party*, DOI 10.1007/978-1-4419-0366-2_6,
© Springer Science+Business Media, LLC 2009

inadequate. Private financing has overwhelmed public funding. The same old greedy special interests that used to underwrite the parties are still doing so. Corporate funding now dominates convention budgets. Third parties and independents are getting the shaft, as always. The fiction that conventions are mass gatherings of democratic deliberativeness is so ludicrous that not even FECA's staunchest defenders believe it. Indeed, these defenders speak, cautiously, of scrapping the subsidy. But they don't go beyond speaking about it. For nothing is quite so permanent as a good government program that has been hijacked by cynical politicians.

Convention subsidies have risen sharply, though they have not kept pace with the opulence of these spectacularly meaningless affairs. The bicentennial year of 1976, when the available pot of convention cash was $2 million per party, was the last year in which either party convention had even the merest shroud of mystery or brief jolt of excitement. Since then, the conventions have been monumental bores with about as much spontaneity as an Olympics opening ceremony. They have also gotten more expensive. In 1980, the Democrats and Republicans received $4.4 million for their midsummer gatherings. In 1984, the Democrats took in $8.1 million for their convention from the PECF and the Republicans, proclaiming "Morning in America," received a like amount. In 1988, each party was gifted with $9.2 million from the taxpayers. In 1992, both received $11 million, and in 1996 the Democrats, unanimously renominating Clinton at perhaps the least suspenseful convention in the history of politics, received $12.4 million while the Republicans, grimly falling in line behind the dour Bob Dole, took in the same. In 2000, the parties received tax-funded alms of $13.5 million each to pay for their conventions. In 2004, it was $15 million, and in 2008 the amount was $16 million.

Yet in relative terms, the public subsidy has shrunk. In 1980, for instance, the total of private contributions (which are channeled by corporations through host committees and devices called "municipal funds") to the party conventions was $1.1 million, or 13% of the federal convention subsidy. In 1984, private contributions had risen to $6.7 million, or 41% of the feds' contribution. Corporate donors outstripped the (involuntary) taxpayer donors to the Democratic and Republican conventions in 1996, when they supplied $38 million to the televised celebrations of duopoly, or 155% of the federal contribution. In 2000, private funding had risen to $56.2 million, or 208% of federal funding, and in 2004 those figures were $100 million and a whopping 333%.[1] By 2008, the respective figures had climbed to $118 million and 369%. The federal subsidy, once thought critical, was increasingly marginal.

In addition, the "growth in private contributions has largely gone to pay for items that are essentially the same as ones that historically have been considered as 'convention expenses' by the FEC."[2] These funds didn't go to tourism promotion or other ancillary goals of the convention. Rather, they underwrote the convention itself: its infrastructure, its communication facilities, its utilities, its production, and, most importantly, its servility toward the television industry. Host committees, and not the feds, foot the bill for "the redesign and construction of convention hall facilities, lighting and electrical work, communications and audio systems, convention transportation services, and security services."[3] Even the erstwhile requirement that the companies filling the host committee's coffers be in some way "local" has been scrapped. The original intent of the FECA has been betrayed, or perhaps just forgotten. So what's the point of keeping it alive?

To combat this terrifying menace of private money, the Campaign Finance Institute's task force recommended that government reseize the conventions. "Beginning in 2008," the task force demanded, "all convention expenses should be paid from federal grants, state and local government sources, and money to be raised by the national party committees within federal election ('hard money') contribution limits."[4] This would be a partnership, in other words, in which the first-mentioned feds take the senior role, supplemented by the affected state and local governments, and the parties, the junior partners, ante up a stake befitting their collaborative role.

Corporate and private sources would be permitted only to "promote the city as a site for a convention" and "facilitate commerce during the convention."[5] These were the purposes on which the FECA had originally envisioned private monies might be spent, but even the denser PAC directors and government-affairs officers of *Fortune* 500 firms realized the limited possibilities of paying for "Welcome to Houston!" kiosks and guides to "New York's 100 Best Restaurants" or "Do's and Don'ts with San Diego Prostitutes." The real action, and access, is in providing state-of-the-art, top-of-the-line, world-class communications facilities and propagandizing opportunities for the parties. So the corporate interests, naturally, seized on these.

Moreover, "a grant from the US Department of Homeland Security" should pay for law enforcement and security needs.[6] In a previous book (*Homeland Security Scams*) I have explained how "homeland security" has become one of the most lucrative pork-barrel scams in our history. Rural towns use homeland security loot to buy firetrucks, colleges use it to police parking on campus, and any critic of government spending who dares question "homeland security" is suspected of harboring closet sympathies for al-Qaeda. The very words *homeland security* are the modern equivalent of *Open Sesame*: they magically bring access to untold billions of taxpayer dollars, to be spent in a mind-bogglingly unaccountable manner. So it was only a matter of time before the party conventions hit upon the homeland security formula for quick cash – even though the expenditures are about as security-related as Mitt Romney's blow-drier.

The lion's share of convention-related spending is for "convention facility and production" – in other words, the manufacture of images, glamour, and whatever artificial "suspense" can be ginned up. Even party officials admit to the wearying phoniness of the convention. As former Democratic National Committee Chairman Don Fowler says, "Conventions used to be a way of selecting, inspiring enthusiasm about, and defining the candidate. Now directors, speechwriters, coaches, makeup, lighting, and design people are used to build the candidate politically and put an American flag behind it."[7] Why the American taxpayer should shell out for even a portion of this is a mystery – and unfortunately, it promises to be an enduring mystery, since the parties in Congress show no sign of wanting to stop the federal subsidy of the parties in convention.

In all, the PECF has spent $152 million on party conventions since 1976. Yet is it any coincidence that the great conventions of modern times – the 1948 Democratic convention, with the walkout by the Dixiecrats and the bitter fight over civil rights; the 1964 Republican convention in San Francisco, when the Goldwaterites overwhelmed the party establishment; the 1968 Democratic convention in Chicago, when Mayor Daley's finest throttled hippie protesters as the protesters chanted, "The whole world is watching!"; and the 1972 Democratic convention which repudiated the Daley-Humphrey Old Guard and nominated South Dakota Senator George McGovern – all happened *before* the federal government started underwriting these things? In what ways, exactly, has federal sponsorship of conventions improved conventions? Made them more democratic? More open? More interesting?

Only once – in 2000 – did a party other than the Republicans or Democrats receive so much as a dime to pay for its convention. That was the year in which the Reform Party, orphaned by the capricious Ross Perot, was split apart when populist-conservative columnist and former White House aide Pat Buchanan sought and received the nomination over the vocal opposition of some Reform Party founders and their curious ally, the physicist John Hagelin, who believes that by "Yogic flying" – the transcendental meditator's method of levitation – world peace might be achieved. Whatever the truth of this claim – is it any more preposterous than Bush's assertion that Iraq was packed with weapons of mass destruction, or the Democrats' belief that national healthcare will put an end to sickness, disease, and loneliness in America? – the Reform Party convention of 2000 did chew up $2.5 million of taxpayers' money.

"Conventions are critical presidential campaign events," notes the Campaign Finance Institute Task Force on Presidential Nomination Financing. To which the bemused reader can only respond, "Huh?" Since when? Not since 1976 has there been enough drama in a major party convention to keep an insomniac awake. They are stage-managed, dully choreographed affairs that use network television to present the nominees of the two major parties as men (at least so far) with the courage of Sergeant York, the intellect of Albert Einstein, and the moral fiber of a strange cross between Abraham Lincoln and Mother Teresa – compassionate, soulful, but willing to drop the bomb if necessary. The conventions, which once served an authentic deliberative – if frantically, sometimes comically deliberative – function, bringing together delegates from the far-flung states to palaver and bargain and tussle over who would be the party's next presidential standard-bearer, are now tedious public relations exercises. If the parties wish to retain them, fine. That is their right. But they also serve to prop up the parties, to advertise them once every four years as the only two choices from which an American is permitted from the political menu. Their subsidization is a flat-out government grant of privilege.

Federal sponsorship of these propaganda broadcasts is nowhere even hinted at or dreamt of, let alone mentioned, in the US Constitution, the purported governing document of the United States. Not that many of Washington's activities *are* mentioned in the Constitution, but still, it doesn't hurt to use that oft-forgotten document as the yardstick against which we measure any federal law.

Justifications for public subsidy of the conventions range from the crafty and disingenuous to the just plain porky. The conventions are said to be "major economic events for the host city and its surrounding area."[8] This is incontrovertibly true – conventions are boom times for hotels, taxicabs, and prostitutes – but since when is the capacity of the local Radisson or the volume of business done by miniskirted hookers a concern of the federal government?

In his partial dissent from *Buckley v. Valeo*, Chief Justice Warren Burger worried that "once the Government finances these national conventions by the expenditure of millions of dollars from the public treasury, we may be providing a springboard for later attempts to impose a whole range of requirements on delegate selection and convention activities. Does this fore-shadow judicial decisions allowing the federal courts to 'monitor' these conventions to assure compliance with court orders or regulations?"[9]

The answer – so far – is Not Yet.

But subsidy always comes with strings. It is not hard to imagine a minor party qualifying for convention monies, à la the Reform Party in 2000, and then running afoul of the feds by, say, discriminating against gays in delegate selection (as with a Christian Right party) or discriminating against whites (as with a radical minority party). You may disagree with the biases of these hypothetical parties, but how free and unfettered is a system in which the federal government would dictate delegate selection rules to ostensibly independent parties?

Third parties consistently get the short end of the stick. Even the stickiness: In 1980, John Anderson had to sue just to be able to send out campaign mailings at the same rate (3.1 cents per piece of mail) as the major party committees enjoyed in sending out their pro-Carter and pro-Reagan missives. Prior to the ruling, the Anderson camp was being charged 8.4 cents per piece.

As it is with postal rates, so too with the mandatory television appearances envisioned in numerous reform proposals. Campaign finance reformers have suggested "free" television time for candidates, which in practice translates to compulsory airing of candidates of the duopoly, whether television station managers (and viewers) want to broadcast and watch the clichémeisters or not. The details of such proposals vary, though most "would make the political parties responsible" for allocating time among the candidates.[10] The *two* political parties, that is: as with public financing and ballot access, the gift of free television would in all likelihood be parceled out according to performance in the previous election, and so the Republicans and Democrats would have another tool of self-perpetuation.

We can take a lesson here from the Commission on Presidential Debates, which the Democrats and Republicans created in 1987 when the League of Women Voters, which had organized the three previous series of presidential debates, proved intractable and unwilling to completely kowtow to the parties' wishes. The new commission, subsidized by corporations currying favor with the two parties, has managed the debates in every presidential election since 1988.

It has, naturally, discouraged third-party participation. Ralph Nader of the Greens and Reform Party candidate Pat Buchanan were kept offstage in 2000 by the commission's arbitrary declaration that a candidate had to be pulling down 15% in public-opinion polls in order to be admitted to the "debates," which are really more like heavily scripted sound-bite fests anyway. Incredibly, the commission barred Ross Perot from the debates in 1996, despite his remarkable 19% showing at the polls in 1992. It's a wonder such candidates are even allowed on the ballot anymore – though the ballot-access squeezers go as far as the lax Supreme Court will permit them.

The brazenness of the parties in demanding, indeed orchestrating, their own subsidization by the central government is part of a pattern that is moving political scientists to reconsider the very idea of what a political party is.

The seminal document in this sea-change bore the unpromising title "Changing Models of Party Organization and Party Democracy: The Emergence of the Cartel Party." The authors were Richard S. Katz of Johns Hopkins University and Peter Mair of the University of Leiden in the Netherlands, the venue was the scholarly journal *Party Politics*, and the insights were astonishingly keen. The nub of their argument was this: "that the recent period has witnessed the emergence of a new model of party, the cartel party, in which colluding parties become agents of the state and employ the resources of the state (the party state) to ensure their own collective survival."[11]

The political party, in the classic formulation, is a private organization of citizens who work together, "participate in politics, make demands on the state, and ultimately attempt to capture control of the state by placing their own representatives in key offices." Parties are creatures of civil society, not the state, though they provide the "essential linkage,"[12] the bridge, between citizen and state. In the phrase of Ingrid van Biezen of the University of Birmingham and Petr Kopecky of the University of Leiden, associates of Katz and Mair, "parties have traditionally been understood in terms of their *permanent linkage with society* and their *temporal linkage with the state*. Parties neither depended on the state for their resources and legitimacy nor were they managed or controlled by the state."

But this has changed in recent years; indeed, it has been reversed, or so contend the authors, into a situation in which "parties are now perhaps best understood in terms of their *temporal linkage with society* and their more *permanent linkage with the state*."[13] State and party have entered into a kind of symbiosis, each drawing upon the other for survival, for enrichment. Parties learned to use the state to further their interests, to protect their turf, to fatten on tax dollars and manipulate the state's laws to cripple or even criminalize opposition to their protected status. The party as an artifact of civil society is being replaced, argue Katz and Mair, by "parties becom[ing] part of the state apparatus itself."[14] They have, according to van Biezen and Kopecky, "gradually and consistently moved away from civil society towards the state, becoming ever more strongly entrenched within state institutions."[15]

Rather than contend for temporary control of or influence within the state, political parties in the United States and throughout the world have figured out how to connect a freeflowing pipeline from the state treasury into their own coffers. The "provision and regulation of state subventions to political parties," write Katz and Mair, "now often constitute one of the major financial and material resources" of those parties. This was not somehow done to the parties without their knowledge; they actively sought and received the state assistance. Critically, "because these subventions are often tied to prior party performance or position, whether defined in terms of electoral success or parliamentary representation, they help to ensure the maintenance of existing parties while at the same time posing barriers to the emergence of new groups."[16]

The implications of this profound shift are ominous for liberty and democracy: "The state . . . becomes an institutionalized structure of support, sustaining insiders while excluding outsiders. No longer simple brokers between civil society and the state, the parties now become absorbed by the state." They are "semi-state agencies."[17]

Yet the Out Party, the loser in any particular election, need not fear being cut off from the succor of the state. For this is a cartel, assert Katz and Mair, in which the leading parties share resources and band together to exclude challengers to their hegemony. It is not a one-party state, à la the old Communist Bloc in Eastern Europe, but a cozy cartel of ruling parties, of "inter-party collusion" in which "the differences in the material positions of winners and losers have been dramatically reduced."[18] What matters is being part of the cartel, which in the United States consists of the Democratic and Republican parties.

The mass party of old, the lumbering and awkward but still private creation of civil society, financed itself through membership fees or donations from supporters both modest and wealthy. It often published its own newspaper or newspapers, thereby raking in subscription fees. Certainly graft played a role, if often unacknowledged, in its ledger. But it fed on private donations, private money, private concerns. The state was not its benefactor.

The cartel party, rather than being an assemblage of citizens, an association of like-minded (or not) persons, is a "partnershi[p] of professionals" who are never really either In or Out but always on the payroll of the cartel. The parties they serve are strictly limited, for in the modern view, "the essence of democracy lies in the ability of voters to choose from a fixed menu of political parties."[19] Those out of the cartel are out of luck. And they are kept out by a mammoth wall constructed of ballot-access laws and the restriction of subventions to established parties meeting certain carefully chosen thresholds of support. The Outs start at such a huge competitive disadvantage as to make their penetration into the cartel — or, more provocatively, their destruction of the cartel — all but impossible. Not only is the playing field not level — the playing field is actually off-limits, by law, to those potential players not able to jump through regulatory hoops. Out parties are victims of a self-reinforcing cycle in which the established parties buttress their position through subsidy and regulation, and those not in the cycle are hung out to dry.

Sound familiar?

The parties within the cartel collude. They want to keep the subsidies washing over them and keep those grubby minor parties from sharing in the booty. Or the power. The cartel parties are bought and paid for by the state, which their functionaries and political glitterati take turns helming. They need not establish deep or lasting relationships with voters because their patron is the state, not the citizenry. Any connection the parties once had with ordinary people is frayed beyond recognition. The volunteer licking stamps and passing out handbills has gone the way of the horse and buggy. The party pro, versatile as he is unprincipled, has taken her place.

In return for funding, naturally, the parties are "legitimate objects of state regulation to a degree far exceeding what would normally be acceptable for private associations in a liberal society."[20] It's the price you pay: he who is a dependent on the state is a slave of the state. The party that is funded by the state and that uses the state to ward off challengers is in turn a mere ward of the state, subject to its regulations, its edicts, its orders. Independence is a massive price to pay, but the managers of the cartel are not the sort of robust men and women who enjoy independence anyway.

Instead, they are classic rent-seekers, searching for ways to manipulate and cadge special favors from the state. The "subsidy system," as one political scientist explains the cartel party critique, "is likely to be structured in ways which favor the established parties." New parties or dissident parties are discouraged by finely calibrated thresholds for subsidy; the result is "a life-support system for ageing [sic] parties which obstruct[s] the natural, organic development of the party system."[21]

The cartel party is hardly a phenomenon limited to the United States. In many of the new democracies of Eastern Europe, Africa, and Latin America, the parties "often originate within the state and reach out only minimally towards society."[22] These parties have not turned to the state for nourishment after long years of private funding; no, they were conceived in the state, gestated within the womb of the state, born in a state hospital, and raised in a state nursery. Is it any wonder that they reverence the state? Why wouldn't they? What sort of man, after all, vilifies his mother? And to these new parties, the state is Holy Mother.

Mair explains that "the increasingly top-down style of party organizational life . . . may also be said to have coincided with correspondingly greater emphasis on the linkage between party and state."[23] Engaged citizens have disengaged; many have come to see the parties as amoral instruments by which largely indistinguishable sets of interest groups contend for power. But the parties are doing just fine without these foot soldiers of politics. They have found a new lifeline: the state, which subsidizes their offices, their conventions, even their candidates. The mass party is a thing of the past; they are now, as Katz and Mair argue, virtually "part of the state."[24] They have left civil society far behind. Or, rather, they have left it on the other side of the fence.

Today, the state is "a means by which parties can help ensure their own persistence and survival."[25] Katz and Mair wonder if parties are tending toward a convergence: "All parties in any given country are obliged to conform to the national rules regarding state subventions and to the increasingly pervasive party laws; all face the increasing communality of circumstances associated with communicating through the broadcast media rather than their own idiosyncratic modes of revenue raising; and, within the wider area, all rely increasingly on the professional skills and expertise of the same group of marketing managers and consultants."[26] So the parties, facing the same pressures, the same rules and regulations, take on the same aspect. They begin to look alike, especially on the inside. Their outside aspects may differ, but in their guts, they are much the same. And one characteristic they share is an aversion to competition: "once in power, the elected representatives [of the major parties] can – and do – manipulate the laws governing the electoral process to their advantage and against weaker parties. Examples include laws governing ballot access, internal party operations, and campaign finance. Under these circumstances, successful minor party challenges are all but impossible."[27]

State subsidy of political parties was a post-World War II, Cold War-era policy innovation. The first states to finance parties were Costa Rica (1954) and Argentina (1955). Germany was the European pioneer in 1959 – or perhaps we should say West Germany, for in Stalinist East Germany, the party-state financial link was as crude and obvious as the Berlin Wall. Sweden

(1965), Finland (1967), and Norway (1970) brought the trend to Scandinavia, the United States hopped on board in 1974, along with several of the nations of Western Europe, and then the newly liberated countries of the Eastern Bloc (with the singular exception of Latvia) took up the practice of party-funding soon after achieving independence. Russia, interestingly, spends relatively little in subsidizing parties, permitting private interests to fund the vast majority of party politics, and its threshold of eligibility for minor parties is quite low. (In one of those signs-of-the-times facts, "the most elaborate rules concerning what kind of funding can be used for which purposes," according to Jon Pierre, Lars Svasan, and Anders Widfeldt in the journal *West European Politics*, belong not to regulation-crazed Sweden or trains-running-on-time Germany or one of the Eastern nations stumbling out of Communism but rather the United States. Morever, "The most extensive monitoring" of subsidies "is exercised in the United States and Germany."[28])

Provision for parties is increasingly a feature of constitutions in democratic states — as it was not in the republican Constitution of the United States of America. About three-quarters of new democracies constitutionally enshrine — or should it be entomb? — parties, while about half of older democracies do so. This difference, say Ingrid van Biezen and Petr Kopecky, is "probably a legacy of an historical conception of political parties as private and voluntary associations."[29]

Typically, a party's subsidy is linked to its electoral showing in the previous election, a seemingly "fair" measure of support that has the estimable bonus, for the establishment parties, of strengthening the status quo. The thresholds vary: in most countries, a party becomes eligible for a subsidy with an electoral performance of somewhere around 5% in the most recent election. The eligibility rules almost invariably rule out subsidy for some or most minor parties and for any spontaneously developing party or independent candidacy. Indeed, the very concept of an "independent" candidate or party is an anachronism in this setting. Typical of countries that try to make some provision for smaller parties is Hungary, in which one-quarter of the available monies is distributed equally to those parties that have won seats in parliament, while the other three-quarters are doled out in proportion to votes won in the most recent election. Even here, despite the nod to "fairness," the big get bigger and the small fight to keep from shrinking.

The arguments for state sponsorship of parties abroad is much the same as it is in the United States: "public" money, or money taken from taxpayers, is somehow "cleaner"[30] than private money. Public money is said to cleanse the political system, driving out the pollution of private money. A healthy democracy is a thing to be desired, and aren't all things to be desired proper objects of government charity?

Once freed from the necessity of carrying water for big contributors, political parties would deliberate, collectively, on big-picture questions, reaching policy conclusions untainted by filthy lucre. Yes, there were nay-sayers who charged that these subsidies were "implemented with the explicit intention of stifling political competition" and were "one of the key weapons wielded by established parties to freeze out new challengers."[31] What cynics!

Even more chutzpah was displayed in advancing another argument: that turning over financing of parties to the government would "facilitate a more equal level playing field by enabling new, small and less resourceful parties to compete on a more equitable basis with the dominant and financially more privileged ones."[32] This is on a par with believing that giving Mr. Fox parietal control over the baby chicks will ensure a long and healthy life for the little darlings. New parties in a state-managed and funded system have lifespans approximate to that of the baby chicks – if they are lucky.

Besides giving the state entrée into the regulation of both the major and petty affairs of the parties, one serious problem with such constitutional protections, as van Biezen and Kopecky point out, is that "pluralism, political participation and competition in contemporary democratic constitutions are often defined almost exclusively in terms of party."[33] Political action outside the parties – which was, after all, how such American movements for abolition, taxpayer rights, civil rights, peace, women's rights, and others were conducted – is unthinkable. Undoable. Unprotected. You must work within the party system, which means you are dependent on the state, a government grantee, a tamed and neutered party hack. It's hard to see how any noble or high-minded movement can develop from such a rotten base.

In her study of the extent to which public subsidization of parties institutionalizes the party system, Johanna Kristin Birnir notes that "state funding creates a barrier to entry for parties that have not received state support. The core of funded parties has an advantage that accumulates between elections and makes new entry increasingly difficult."[34] In the new democracies (Albania, Bosnia, Bulgaria, Croatia, the Czech Republic, Estonia, Hungary, Latvia, Lithuania, Macedonia, Moldova, Poland, Romania, Russia, Slovakia, Slovenia, and Ukraine) in her study, Birnir found strong support for the hypothesis that "Parties that do not receive state funds and have little or no sources of private or member funding cannot compete and are effectively excluded."[35] Given that in many countries public funding of parties is coupled with strict limits on private funding (in Mexico, for example, by law a party can raise only 10% of its monies from private sources), the fix, it would seem, is in.

Countries *without* public subsidy of parties exhibit much greater "electoral volatility"[36] in Birnir's study. Politics are more fluid, more open: new parties emerge with greater frequency and to greater effect; the status quo is not frozen. "[B]etween two and three more parties enter systems without public funds than systems where parties are publicly funded," writes Birnir.[37] Public funding therefore restricts choice; it acts as a barrier to new parties, to outsider participation, to a full and fair civil life. Because "the rules governing funding" are "determined by the people who stand to gain from restricting state funds to large legislative parties only," the game is rigged.[38] Subsidizing political parties is an egregious example of the establishment giving itself two extra queens, four extra rooks, and a passel of bishops and then fearlessly wiping out the friendless pawns across the board.

Political parties are directly funded by the central state in about three-quarters of democracies. The region with the lowest incidence (56%) of such funding is Africa; that with the highest (91%) is the new democracies of the former Communist Bloc in Europe. Among the few established democracies that are holdouts against this immense cooptation of parties by state and state by parties are Switzerland, India, and Jamaica; they are joined in this circumstance by such newer states as Latvia, Botswana, Mauritius, and Senegal.[39] A reading of the US Constitution and assorted Founding documents and philosophers might suggest that the United States of America would also grace that list, but that was long ago and far away – as far away as Swiss democracy.

The cooptation of the Eastern European parties is especially sad. In the heady first draft of freedom in Eastern Europe, the people expressed themselves politically in many and vivid ways. The Polish elections of 1992 featured 131 parties, the Czechoslovakian elections had 80. The natural state of things is to have many parties, many candidates, many voices: the Poles had no need to whittle the choices down to just two, the Coke and Pepsi of politics. The Polish and Czech examples would seem to demonstrate, as political scientist Kay Lawson of the Sorbonne wrote in her essay, "The Case for a Multiparty System," "If, then, it is natural to have many parties, there must be very good reasons for passing laws that discourage parties so drastically as to produce just two capable of waging effective campaigns for office."[40]

Just what these reasons are the duopolists never bother to explain. Oh, they'll mutter some platitudes about consensus and responsibility and avoiding fractiousness, but few have the heart to defend a system that begins with 300 million Americans and gives them a choice of George W. Bush and John Kerry. They are, however, appropriately dull symbols of the cartel party in action – the sort of men who rise to the top in subsidized parties.

Among the case studies in this rapidly growing field is Ingrid van Biezen's work on the financing of parties in Spain and Portugal, both of which emerged from right-wing dictatorships into Western democracies in the 1970s. And in both countries, "public funding plays a critical role in the financing of political parties."[41] In Spain, funding is tied to votes in the previous election, which means, as in the US system, that the two major parties (the Socialist Party and the Popular Party) receive the lion's share of the loot. In fact, they receive a share disproportionate to their vote totals, placing smaller parties at an even sharper competitive disadvantage. The main Spanish parties are now state dependents, for all intents and purposes; the only Spanish party "capable of generating large sums of money from private contributors" is the Basque National Party, an ethnic-regional party which has no US analogue.[42]

Pity the parties of Spain and Portugal, so recently born into newly democratic nations but so quickly tamed. They have weak connections with civil society, as van Biezen shows, and instead are virtual creations of the state. Up to 85% of the treasuries of Spanish and Portuguese parties comes directly from the state. The lesson the author draws from their cases is that "financial dependence on the state has indeed enshackled the organization as with iron chains."[43] And it has forced new democracies such as Spain and Portugal into frozen party systems that may have limited popular appeal. Subsidized parties in emerging democracies have extremely limited private financial support, and their membership lists, to the extent that such things even exist, are often shorter than Barry Bonds's list of teammates who liked him. "The financial link with society is generally much more weakly developed" when new parties receive infusions of government cash, writes van Biezen.[44] The monetary incentive to build connections with citizens and business leaders is absent: the state will provide, so why bother soliciting real live people as donors?

Ingrid van Biezen goes so far as to argue that political parties, "traditionally voluntary private associations," are now more like public utilities.[45] The party is no longer seen as an outgrowth of civil society, a loosely bound network of citizens come together in common and voluntary political cause. Rather, it is "an essential public good for democracy"[46] which is an organ of the state: subsidized by government, regulated by government, dedicated to government. Autonomy? A thing of the past. The party today belongs to the state. (In a curious way, it is the virtual consecration of political parties by political scientists that paved the intellectual way for this transformation.)

This would have been news to the American Founders, who distrusted party and the spirit of faction, but in our topsy-turvy world the central tenets of their political faith (federalism, small-r republicanism, separation of powers, avoidance of foreign wars) are dross while their antitheses are gold. Political parties are vital, key, essential, the cornerstones of democracy; one never hears denunciations of "faction" or "placeseeking" in our world, anymore than judges don wigs or men refrain from voting for themselves out of modesty. In 1942, the political scientist E.E. Schattschneider wrote in his classic *Party Government* that "modern democracy is unthinkable today save in terms of political parties."[47] It follows, or so it seems, that that whose absence is unthinkable must be subsidized by the state, nourished and fed and guided as an essential good, a public utility, a ward of the state on whose very existence the state depends. The end of this party-worship is the cartel party, the party as creature of the state. Such a party may be well-endowed, but it can never be a vessel for liberty.

Notes

1. Campaign Finance Institute, "Participation, Competition, Engagement: How to Revive and Improve Public Funding for Presidential Nomination Politics," (Washington, DC: Campaign Finance Institute, September 2003), p. 69.
2. Ibid., p. 71.
3. Anthony Corrado, "Public Funding of Presidential Campaigns," in *The New Campaign Finance Sourcebook*, edited by Anthony Corrado, Thomas E. Mann, Daniel Ortiz, and Trevor Potter (Washington, DC: Brookings Institution, 2005), p. 191.
4. Campaign Finance Institute, "Participation, Competition, Engagement," p. xix.
5. Ibid., p. 74.
6. Ibid., p. xix.
7. Ibid., pp. 72–73.
8. Ibid., p. xviii.
9. Chief Justice Warren Burger, "Public Financing" in *Buckley v. Valeo*, 424 U.S. 1 (1976), 4c, http://caselaw.lp.findlaw.com.Chief Justice Burger.
10. Corrado, *Campaign Finance Reform*, p. 113.
11. Richard S. Katz and Peter Mair, "Changing Models of Party Organization and Party Democracy: The Emergence of the Cartel Party," *Party Politics* (Vol. 1, No. 1, 1995), p. 5.

12. Ibid., pp. 6–7.
13. Ingrid van Biezen and Petr Kopecky, "The State and the Parties: Public Funding, Public Regulation and Rent-Seeking in Contemporary Democracies," *Party Politics*, p. 237.
14. Richard S. Katz and Peter Mair, "Changing Models of Party Organization and Party Democracy: The Emergence of the Cartel Party," *Party Politics*, p. 14.
15. van Biezen and Kopecky, "The State and the Parties," p. 236.
16. Katz and Mair, "Changing Models of Party Organization and Party Democracy," p. 15.
17. Ibid., p. 16.
18. Ibid., pp. 16–17.
19. Ibid., pp. 21–22.
20. Quoted in Ingrid van Biezen and Petr Kopecky, "The State and the Parties: Public Funding, Public Regulation and Rent-Seeking in Contemporary Democracies," *Party Politics*, p. 237.
21. Jon Pierre, Lars Svasand, and Anders Widfeldt, "State Subsidies to Political Parties: Confronting Rhetoric with Reality," *West European Politics* (Vol. 23, No. 3, July 2000), p. 3.
22. van Biezen and Kopecky, "The State and the Parties," p. 237.
23. Peter Mair, "Party Organizations: From Civil Society to the State," in *How Parties Organize: Change and Adaptation in Party Organizations in Western Europe*, edited by Richard S. Katz and Peter Mair (London: Sage, 1994), p. 7.
24. Ibid., p. 8.
25. Ibid., p. 7.
26. Ibid., p. 11.
27. Ibid., p. 61.
28. Jon Pierre, Lars Svasand, and Anders Widfeldt, "State Subsidies to Political Parties: Confronting Rhetoric with Reality," *West European Politics*, pp. 9, 12.
29. van Biezen and Kopecky, "The State and the Parties," p. 247.
30. Susan E. Scarrow, "Party Subsidies and the Freezing of Party Competition: Do Cartel Mechanisms Work?" *West European Politics* (Vol. 29, No. 4, September 2006), p. 619.
31. Ibid., pp. 621–622.
32. Ingrid van Biezen, "Political Parties as Public Utilities," *Party Politics* (Vol. 10, No. 6, 2004), p. 707.
33. van Biezen and Kopecky, "The State and the Parties," p. 240.
34. Johanna Kristin Birnir, "Public Venture Capital and Party Institutionalization," *Comparative Political Studies* (Vol. 38, No. 8, October 2005), p. 918.
35. Ibid., p. 921.
36. Ibid., p. 931.
37. Ibid., p. 932.
38. Ibid., p. 934.
39. van Biezen and Kopecky, "The State and the Parties," p. 245.
40. Kay Lawson, "The Case for a Multiparty System," in *Multiparty Politics in America*, pp. 59–60.

41. Ingrid van Biezen, "Party Financing in New Democracies: Spain and Portugal," *Party Politics* (Vol. 6, No. 3, 2000), p. 329.

42. Ibid., p. 332.

43. Ibid., p. 339.

44. Ingrid van Biezen, "Political Parties as Public Utilities," *Party Politics* (Vol. 10, No. 6, 2004), p. 711.

45. Ibid., p. 701.

46. Ibid., p. 702.

47. Ibid., p. 704.

Chapter 7

2008: The Year of Change – Or Plus Ca Change … ?

Early indications were that 2008 might be a banner year for third parties. It wasn't. In fact, it was downright disappointing. And although the excitement surrounding the historic Barack Obama campaign was partly responsible for that, the usual suspects – ballot access, unfair subsidies, and two-is-company, three's-a-crowd debate rules – played their roles in the farce as well.

The nation, souring on a war of choice in Iraq that had no end in sight, had rejected the Republicans in 2006 and given control of the US House of Representatives to the Democrats, despite widespread skepticism that the Democrats represented a real alternative. The indispensable Richard Winger crunched the numbers and found that in 2006, a full 5% of the votes for the "top office" on each state ballot – usually governor or US senator – went to independents and minor-party candidates. This was the second-best midterm showing since 1934: the best had been the previous midterm election in 2002, when the comparable figure was 5.3%. The worst midterm total was in 1954, at the height of the Red Scare, when only 0.6% of the votes for the top office went to non-Republicans/ Democrats, while the best showing – a remarkable 16.3% – was in 1914, as Teddy Roosevelt's Progressive "Bull Moose" Party, the Socialist Party of Eugene V. Debs, and the Prohibition Party polled well.[1]

Two US Senators were elected in 2006 as independents – the socialist Bernie Sanders of Vermont and Connecticut's Joseph Lieberman, who had been defeated in his state's Democratic primary. Both caucused with the Democrats when the Senate convened in 2007.

J.T. Bennett, *Not Invited to the Party*, DOI 10.1007/978-1-4419-0366-2_7,
© Springer Science+Business Media, LLC 2009

Down Texas way, always a tough state for independents, Lone Star voters were treated in 2006 to a four-way gubernatorial race that, for once, offered genuine choices. Carole Keeton Strayhorn, a Republican former mayor of Austin who opted out of the GOP primary, polled 18% of the vote in the general election. More flamboyantly, the irreverently witty singer-mystery novelist Kinky Friedman ran a lively race that caught the imagination of the state's counterculture and its middle class. Kinky was polling near 25% at one point; he appeared to have a real shot at pulling off a Jesse Ventura-like out-sider victory. In November, candidate Kinky won 12.5% of the vote – still an impressive number for a singer whose politically incorrect songs, such as "Asshole from El Paso," have insulted much of the state's population. Kinky is considering another race for governor in 2010, though he learned his les-son from Texas's strict laws protecting the duopoly. "God probably couldn't have won as an independent," he told the *Fort Worth Star-Telegram* in 2007.[2] If he runs again, it will probably be in the Democratic primary.

By early 2007, disillusionment with the new Democratic Congress was already setting in. Elected to end the war in Iraq, House Speaker Nancy Pelosi (D-CA) and the Democratic leadership did nothing of the sort. Pork, not peace, was their concern.

A Rasmussen Poll of May 2007 found that a strong majority (58%) of Americans surveyed believed the United States needed a competitive third party. Only 23% said that it did not. Moreover, time was on the side of the third-party enthusiasts: they were most common among those under 40 and least common among those over 65 years of age. The rejection of the Republican/Democrat stranglehold on American politics seemed to be on the horizon. But would that horizon be visible in 2008?

Again, signs were favorable. As *Ballot Access News* noted in March 2008, the percentage of voters refusing to register with either of the major parties (26.5) had hit its highest level in 80 years. Independents now made up almost one-fourth of the nation's voters (24.82%), while 1.63% were affili-ated with minor parties. The percentage of Democrats continued to drop, from 47.76 to 41.66% between 1992 and 2008, while Republican registra-tion (dropping from 32.97 to 31.89% over the same period) was off slightly.[3] People, especially young people, were abandoning the Democrats, but they were not falling into the arms of the Republicans. They were strik-ing out as independents.

Most ominously for the Demopublican duopoly, on the two most glaring issues come Election Day 2008 – the $700 billion bailout of Wall Street and the ruinous Iraq War, which had entered its sixth year – the major parties were in substantial agreement: they favored these policies, with some differences at the margin concerning the war. Yet a decided majority of the public opposed both the bailout and the war. Four serious minor-party and independent candidates were on the side of the public on these two issues. If ever the time was right for a revolt against the duopoly, 2008 would seem to be the year.

It didn't happen.

The potential for a popular challenge to the status quo was evident in the GOP primary campaign of Texas Republican congressman Ron Paul, who ran a staggeringly successful campaign on the web – if not in the voting booth.

Ron Paul was no stranger to third parties, although he had chosen to make his mark within the Republican Party – often to the dismay of its leadership. Paul, a physician who had graduated from Duke Medical School and served in the Air Force before settling in the Houston area, was first elected to Congress in an April 1976 special election. He was defeated that November but came back to win the seat in 1978 and serve four terms as that Washington rarity: a principled man who votes his convictions, even if they might prove harmful to his continuance in office. Rep. Paul compiled a voting record that was a taxpayers' dream: he opposed water and transportation projects, defense and welfare bills, and federal spending on everything from education to NATO. True to his libertarian philosophy, he criticized the federal war on drugs. And yet he survived politically, admired by many for his consistency, until in 1984 he lost the Republican primary for US Senate to future Senator Phil Gramm.

Out of office, Rep. Paul explored political options that took him outside the two-party system. He obtained the Libertarian Party's nomination for president in 1988 and ran a vigorous, if only partially successful, campaign, receiving 432,179 votes. He returned to the Republican Party, won a tough election race in 1996, and has since acted as a libertarian voice in the decidedly unlibertarian confines of the US House of Representatives.

When Rep. Paul announced the formation of an exploratory committee to assess the prospects of a candidacy for the GOP presidential nomination in February 2007, the news barely made the wire services. America's press was obsessed with far more important matters: the nocturnal doings of airhead heiress Paris Hilton, the romance of Brad Pitt and Angelina Jolie. Who cared about a long-shot antiwar libertarian who was demanding, absurdly enough, that the Republican Party return to constitutional values and a limited-government philosophy? Who could possibly be interested in a 71-year-old, soft-spoken member of Congress who explained his operating principle as "no government intervention, not in personal life, not in economic life, not in affairs of other nations"?[4]

Paul, whom the *Washington Post* sneeringly dubbed "The Gentleman from the 19th Century," opposes not only bailouts of Wall Street and automobile manufacturers: he even opposed federal subsidy of those people displaced by Hurricane Katrina. "Is bailing out people that choose to live on the coastline a proper function of the federal government?" he asked. "Why do people from Arizona have to be robbed in order to support the people on the coast?"[5] He voted against the issuance of congressional medals to the most sacred of sacred cows – Pope John Paul II and civil-rights pioneer Rosa Parks – and proposed instead that every member of Congress contribute $100 from his or her own wallet to pay for the medals. No one took him up on the offer. It's so much easier and far more satisfying to spend other peoples' money.

Yet, by May 2007 Ron Paul was blowing the likes of Rudy Giuliani and John McCain out of the cyber-water: he had far more friends on MySpace and Facebook, far more hits on You Tube and Google, than did the interchangeable establishment candidates.

His exchange with former New York City Mayor Giuliani in the South Carolina Republican Party debate of May 15, 2007, introduced a national audience to his iconoclastic views. Instead of dishing out the usual pabulum when the subject of terrorism came up, Rep. Paul said, "They attack us because we're over there. We've been bombing Iraq for 10 years." He refused to back down when Giuliani called his view "absurd" and demanded that Paul "withdraw that comment."[6] How dare Ron Paul stray from the carefully marked pathway of conventional opinion!

Said Paul to Fox News: "I want to be president because I have this dream. I'd like to reinstate the Constitution and restore the Republic."[7] Seemingly from out of the woodwork came thousands of others who shared that dream.

Rep. Paul, who eschewed federal matching funds as inconsistent with his principles, astonished the political world with his fund-raising – much of it done outside the campaign, by young supporters such as Vijay Boyapati and Trevor Lyman, who coordinated "money bombs" by which the doctor's grassroots admirers combined to fill his coffers with more money than his campaign could find time to spend.

One such "money bomb," detonated on November 5 and timed to coincide with Guy Fawkes Day (apparently borrowing from 2005's popular antiauthority movie, *V for Vendetta*), pulled in $4.2 million, a one-day GOP fund-raising record. The GOP, however, was not amused. Fox News attempted to bar Dr. Paul from one debate, and the chairman of the Michigan Republican Party, Saul Anuzis, argued that he should be kept off the stage because of his antiwar views.

By December 17, 2007, the *Washington Post* was no longer mocking Paul as a relic from the nineteenth century; he was now "Ron Paul, beacon to disaffected Americans and accidental instigator of one of the more memorable grass-roots campaigns in history."[8] In just six months, he had raised an astounding $25 million and had a fatter bank account than John McCain.

The tremendous enthusiasm for Paul online and in the hinterlands did not translate to votes, or at least not enough votes to contend for the Republican nomination. In addition to a total fund-raising take of $35 million, Paul did win 1.2 million votes and second-place finishes in some caucus states (Nevada, Montana). For a time, he threw a real scare into the already nervous Republicans when he seemed to entertain the possibility of traveling once more down that lonesome third-party path.

Though Paul eventually disdained the third-party route, turning down overtures from the Libertarian and Constitution Parties, he remained an advocate of opening up American elections to fresh voices and perspectives. In Congress, he again sponsored a ballot-access bill that would bar states from requiring more than 1,000 signatures for independent or minor-party (that is, parties that have not qualified for the ballot) candidates for the US House of Representatives. The Paul bill, which in previous incarnations was sponsored by Democrats John Conyers of Michigan and Tim Penny of Minnesota, has been voted on once: on July 30, 1998, it was buried by a vote of 363–62. Members of the House, it seems, are not eager to throw open the locked doors of the ballot.

Even with Ron Paul out of the race, Americans dissatisfied with the Tweedledum and Tweedledumber choices of the two major parties had serious alternatives to the status quo.

The candidate who assumed that he had the best chance of inheriting Paul's supporters was Bob Barr, the former Georgia congressman who had been a particular burr under Bill Clinton's saddle and a major figure in the House impeachment of the 42nd president. Barr, who had once licked whipped cream off a well-endowed woman's chest at a charity event – perhaps showing just how far he'd go to raise money for a good cause – left the GOP in 2006 and joined the Libertarian Party. Although he was distrusted by some long-time Libertarian activists for his one-time staunch support of the drug war, Barr was an articulate spokesman for limited government. He had name recognition, he had an appeal to right-wing Republicans who might be dissatisfied with GOP nominee John McCain, and he wound up the Libertarian candidate for President of the United States.

Ralph Nader, the venerable activist for consumer causes and tireless advocate of a more open democracy, ran once more, but this time Nader eschewed the faction-ridden Green Party and ran as an independent. Thus Nader was challenging not only the two-party system but even the very idea of parties themselves, hearkening back to the ideas of the Founders, who had worried that parties were corrupt vessels. Nader's campaign was very much in the spirit of *The Federalist Papers* and *Cato's Letters*, which had warned against turning over government to selfish and self-seeking party men.

To his great credit, Nader has tried to make ballot access (as well as access to the debates) an issue, though in this, as in other matters, the mainstream media ignore legitimate issues in favor of horserace journalism and breathless stories about which celebrities are supporting which of the major-party candidates. Brad Pitt's political preferences, it seems, are news; the shenanigans of officials in Texas and Oklahoma to limit the choices of voters is not.

During the campaign, Nader liked to tell the story of his meeting with editors of the *Washington Post*. He asked them why they weren't covering his campaign. Because, they smugly replied, you have no chance of winning. "Then why are you covering the Nationals?" he asked, in a reference to the cellar-dwelling major-league baseball team in the nation's capital.[9]

The Pooh-Bahs at the *Post* had no response, of course, because there is no response. But the *Post* kept on not covering the Nader campaign, or those of Barr and the two other outsider candidates, Cynthia McKinney and Chuck Baldwin, which, whatever one might think of their various views and platforms, at least offered food for thought rather than empty platitudes and pompous banalities, á la Barack Obama and John McCain.

Nader, in his list of "Twelve Issues that Matter for 2008," included "Put an end to ballot access obstructionism."[10] His solution is uniform laws throughout the states. There is, however, no guarantee that a uniform federal law would make things easier for insurgents – indeed, given the margin of defeat for the Paul-Conyers-Penny bill, it is easy to imagine the Democrats and Republicans in Congress ganging up to build an even *higher* wall for third parties and independents to climb. Nevertheless, Nader has raised this issue more than any other political figure in memory. Unlike many of those who appropriate the name and capitalize the first letter, he is a true democrat.

The Green Party chose as its standard-bearer another former Georgia member of Congress, Cynthia McKinney, who had compiled a leftish voting record in her Washington stint and who hoped to tap into discontent on the left with the me-tooism of the Democrats.

The fourth serious minor-party candidate in 2008 was Chuck Baldwin, pastor of the Crossroad Baptist Church in Pensacola, Florida, and one-time president of the state's Moral Majority chapter. Baldwin ran as the candidate of the Constitution Party, a religiously tinged "right-wing" party that advertises itself as pro-traditional morality and antiwar. He learned the hard lessons that any third party candidate learns. As Baldwin told an interviewer from the Center for Public Integrity,

> The ballot access is a major issue and it takes a lot of money to get on the ballots in the various states. Then after you've done all that hard work and you get your candidate on the ballot, then the news media will turn around and reject you from the national forums, the national debates, national exposure. They'll use the excuse, "You're not pulling enough percentage when we have these public opinion polls." Of course, they turn around and, by ignoring you and not giving you access to the people, they contribute to the low poll numbers. So they are manipulating the polling data. They're manipulating the election. They don't want anyone outside of the two major parties to have a voice.
>
> The reason for that is, of course, the two major parties are pretty much two peas in a pod. They're pretty much the same. As Pat Buchanan said, 'Two wings of the same bird of prey.' They like it that way. It's easier to manipulate the election that way. If all of a sudden you had three or four strong candidates in a race bringing independent and fresh ideas, who knows? The great American people out there, the rabble across the country, may actually elect someone who is not approved by the elites. They can't have that.[11]

Baldwin got something of a boost when Ron Paul endorsed him on September 22, 12 days after a press conference at which Paul, in an ecumenical mood, gathered Ralph Nader, Chuck Baldwin, and Cynthia McKinney for a Washington, DC, press conference at which the candidates agreed on Paul-esque issues ranging from ending the Iraq War to protecting the Bill of Rights to challenging the Federal Reserve. Libertarian nominee Bob Barr, though scheduled to participate, backed out of the press conference for what appeared to be reasons of personal pique – he wanted Paul's endorsement alone rather than as part of a blanket "vote third party" endorsement. Paul rather pointedly announced his support for Pastor Baldwin after that, though it seems not to have done Baldwin all that much good.

The insurgents peaked, appropriately, around Independence Day 2008. A CNN poll of July 2 had Ralph Nader running at 6%, or well above his best-ever showing, and Bob Barr at 3%. In a Zogby Poll of July 6, Barr was pulling down 6%, far and away the highest a Libertarian Party candidate for president had ever polled.[12]

As in previous years, the candidates soon got bogged down in the quicksand of ballot-access petitioning, and even after strenuous effort got them on most ballots, the major-party controlled debates commission pulled up the drawbridge and kept them far from the castle.

First, the ballot battle.

As Richard Winger detailed in a 2006 monograph published in *Election Law Journal*, independent and third-party candidates "for federal or state office were involved in at least 42 ballot access lawsuits" in 2004, making it the most litigious of the quadrennial presidential election years since 1976.[13]

This is not to say that 2004 was a banner year in the courts: in the highest profile such case, *Nader v. Keith*, the Seventh Circuit refused to order the state of Illinois to place Ralph Nader's name on the ballot. Judge Richard A. Posner, who in recent years has become something of a celebrity due to his prolific writings on everything from plagiarism to terrorism, wrote the opinion, displaying an almost breathtaking ignorance of the history of ballot-access laws while writing in his usual authoritative I-know-everything-under-the-sun style. For instance, Judge Posner opined, without evidence, that lenient ballot laws lead to a "multiplication of parties." Yet as Winger writes, "when one looks at the data, one finds that the number of parties was smallest during the years when there were no government-printed ballots." Indeed, during "the years of lenient ballot access (1889–1930), there were never more than nine parties. In the years of severe ballot access (1964–1996), the highest number of parties was eleven."

Facts, to Judge Posner, were an inconvenience that would not get in the way of his usual pontificating. He believes that minor parties are bad for democracy – they would make our political life "more ideological"[14] says this son of members of the American Communist Party, again without bothering to prove the assertion – so he acts as the judicial protector of the two-party system.

Candidate Nader was also the subject of an outrageous injustice when he was not only thrown off the ballot in 2004 (thanks to the Democratic hacks working on behalf of John Kerry) but also ordered to pay the $81,102 in court costs associated with the case. The presiding judge of the state's commonwealth court, in throwing Nader off the ballot, made much of the fact that Nader's petitions contained a few obvious joke names – Mickey Mouse, Fred Flintstone – as if such names do not pop up in every set of petitions that any candidate files. The court struck out 32,455 signatures from the

Nader petitions, which left him with just 18,818 valid names, far shy of the required 25,697.[15]

Clearly some of the rejected signatures were forgeries. But as John Murphy, the Pennsylvania coordinator of Nader's campaign, noted, "Only 1.4% of the signatures were rejected as forgeries! The other signatures were all rejected because of poor handwriting, or because a husband filled in the address for both he and his wife or because they forgot to include their middle initials or they signed their name as William Smith then printed it as Bill Smith or forgot to include the date!"

Murphy observed in a 2005 speech at the state capitol that the magnitude of the (anti-democratic) Democratic effort to bar Nader was evidence enough that Nader belonged on the ballot: "When eleven lawyers show up in a courtroom in order to keep a candidate off the ballot, that is proof positive that you have matched the statutory requirements to be a nonfrivolous candidate with community support which is what ballot access laws were really intended to ensure!"[16]

The Democrats were terrified that their lackluster nominee, John Kerry, would lose the Keystone state – which he did not, as he defeated Bush by 144,000 votes. So they filed twelve simultaneous lawsuits to keep Nader off the ballot!

Nader's basic democratic rights had been violated – and he was forced to pay the very people who had acted to violate those rights. As this book went to press, Nader's request for a reconsideration of the case had been rejected by the Pennsylvania Commonwealth Court; he was appealing the matter to the state supreme court.

In 2008, Ralph Nader did achieve ballot status in Pennsylvania, as did Bob Barr. Chuck Baldwin and Cynthia McKinney did not. But once again, challengers to the status quo had to spend far too much time and energy and money merely to get on the ballot.

The quartet of major minor-party and independent candidates failed to appear on the following 2008 ballots: Barr – Connecticut, Louisiana, Maine, Oklahoma, West Virginia, District of Columbia; Nader – Georgia, Indiana, North Carolina, Oklahoma, Texas; Baldwin – Arizona, California, Connecticut, Georgia, Indiana, Maine, New Hampshire, New York, North Carolina, Oklahoma, Pennsylvania, Texas; McKinney – Alabama, Alaska, Connecticut, Georgia, Idaho, Indiana, Kansas, Kentucky, Missouri, Montana, New Hampshire, North Carolina, North Dakota, Oklahoma, Pennsylvania, South Dakota, Texas, Vermont, Wyoming. Little wonder that independents made a poor showing.

Oklahoma took the prize as the most restrictive state of 2008, as none of the four main insurgents made the ballot. The Sooner State combines high signature requirements (46,324 to qualify a party for the ballot; 43,913 to qualify an individual) with too-soon filing deadlines (May 1 for a party, July 15 for an individual). This is a shame, given Oklahoma's history as a state welcoming of populists, from early twentieth-century Senator Thomas P. Gore to the 1960s–1970s Senator Fred Harris. The Libertarians, at least, did their best to liberate Oklahoma. Richard Winger estimates that since its birth in 1972, the LP has spent half a million dollars in getting on, or failing to get on, the Oklahoma ballot. So in September 2007 the Libertarians, with the help of other free-elections advocates, launched an Oklahoma Ballot Access Reform (OBAR) initiative that would have given Oklahoma voters the chance to reduce the state's ridiculously difficult path to ballot access. Instead of pegging access at the level of 10% in the last gubernatorial or presidential election, the initiative would have permitted parties that received 1% of the vote for any statewide office to achieve access. New parties would need to collect 5,000 signatures to make the ballot instead of the current 5% of the total votes cast in the last election (which works out to about 50,000).

OBAR had a strong kickoff and received favorable publicity from the *Daily Oklahoman*, the Oklahoma City-based biggest newspaper in the state. Alas, the state is also brutally hard on those who would place initiatives before the voters: 74,117 signatures were necessary, and the petitioners fell far short.[17] As in 2004, the presidential ballot was the exclusive province of the Republicrats in Oklahoma. Ralph Nader? Bob Barr? Greens? Constitutionalists? These were mere rumors, shadows that never fall within view of the voters of Oklahoma. After all, who wouldn't be satisfied with a choice between Barack Obama and John McCain?

Connecticut is also on the wall of dishonor, as only native son Nader qualified for the ballot in 2008. Other states in which three of the four main third-party and independent candidates failed to appear on the ballot were Georgia (which Barr and McKinney had each represented in Congress); Indiana (home of Socialist Eugene V. Debs, one of the most successful of all third party vote-getters); notoriously unfriendly to third parties North Carolina; and Texas, where, as we shall see, Democrats and Republicans don't have to follow the rules to achieve ballot status, but third parties surely do.

Certain of the other failures were due to poor ideological fits (the leftist McKinney in Idaho, for instance) or internecine battles within the parties, as when the California affiliate of the Constitution Party, the

American Independent Party, nominated Alan Keyes instead of Chuck Baldwin, who had defeated Keyes at the Constitution Party's national convention.

Barr made the notoriously difficult Ohio ballot thanks to a ruling of US District Court Judge Edmund Sargus. In 2006, a court had struck down Ohio's restrictive ballot-access law, which would have required third-party candidates to secure a near-impossible 40,000 signatures to make the 2008 ballot. In the place of this stricken standard, Ohio Secretary of State Jennifer L. Brunner determined in 2007 – seemingly through a mysterious process resembling sortilege, although the official explanation was that the magic number equalled one-half of 1% of the total number of voters in 2006 – that 20,114 signatures would be required to reach the ballot in 2008. The Libertarians fell far short of that number, submitting 6,545 in March 2008. So the party took the matter to court, Barr campaign manager Russell Verney complaining that "Ballot restrictions are designed to prevent competition for the Democrats and Republicans."[18]

Verney was right, though that is seldom an effective defense in a court of law. Yet Judge Sargus ordered Secretary of State Brunner to add Barr to the ballot. As Richard Winger noted at the time, "This is the first time any party, other than the Democratic and Republican Parties, will have been on the ballot in Ohio since 2000."[19] As far as can be determined, not a single citizen of Ohio complained that the ballot was cluttered up with too many choices.

The most amusing ballot-access story of the season came from Texas, where Bob Barr learned that rules are more flexible when broken by major than by minor-party candidates. Since 2005, Texas law has required the parties to submit "written certification" of the names of their presidential and vice presidential candidates "before 5 p.m. on the 70th day before election day." In 2008, that set the deadline at 5 p.m. on August 26th. Due to the somewhat later than usual national conventions, the Democrats and Republicans had yet to formally endorse candidates Obama and McCain by August 26. (They were both nominated within the next week at their party conventions in Denver and St. Paul, respectively.) The Libertarians, however, had placed Bob Barr's name on the Texas ballot, which meant that according to a strict reading of the election law, the Libertarian should have been the only candidate listed on the November ballot in Texas.

Surprise, surprise, surprise: the Texas Secretary of State ordered the names of Obama and McCain placed on the ballot, law be damned. But for once, a minor party turned the tables on the big boys. Bob Barr filed suit in the Texas Supreme Court in Austin to remove Obama and McCain from the Texas ballot. "The seriousness of this issue is self-evident," his lawsuit asserted. "The hubris of the major parties has risen to such a level that they do not believe that the election laws of the State of Texas apply to them."[20]

The Barr campaign was not defending Texas election law; rather, it was highlighting the hypocrisy of those who use such draconian laws to bar competition. "We agree that unreasonably early deadlines are absurd," said Barr campaign manager Russ Verney. "We've run into them in states like Oklahoma, West Virginia, and Maine during our fight for ballot access across the nation. But if third parties are required to adhere to the law, then we expect the same for the candidates of any other party. Maybe this will show Republicans and Democrats what it is like to be on the wrong side of ballot access laws."[21]

Chiming in was the chairman of the Texas Libertarian Party, Pat Dixon, who said, "Libertarian principles require personal responsibility for your acts and failures. Obama and McCain failed to meet the deadlines. They must follow the law like everyone else."[22]

Guess again. Without an explanation, the Texas Supreme Court on September 23 rejected Barr's suit. It essentially ignored the letter of the law and placed the names of Obama and McCain on the ballot. This brought howls of protest from the Libertarians. "We are naturally disappointed that the Supreme Court has refused to enforce the law against Republicans and Democrats in this case, when courts have repeatedly enforced the law against Libertarians," said Pat Dixon.[23] Wes Benedict, executive director of the Texas LP, also pointed out the glaring double standard: "Third parties, including the Libertarian Party around the country, have been held to a higher standard. When we miss a deadline, we've been disqualified from the ballot."[24]

Any wagers on whether or not Barr, Nader, Baldwin, or McKinney would have been granted such an indulgence? Coincidentally, the Texas ruling came less than three weeks after a US District Court judge ruled against Bob Barr's challenge to West Virginia's unreasonably early petition deadline. The Mountaineer State required minor parties to submit 15,118 signatures by August 1. (The Republicans and Democrats were automatically on the ballot, as was the Green Party, due to the showing of its West Virginia affiliate, the Mountain Party, at the last election.) The Libertarians came up with 13,171 autographs on petitions by that date, and followed those up with another 10,652 later in the month. US District Judge John T. Copenhaver Jr. dismissed the suit, harrumphing that "It was [the Libertarian Party's] lack of reasonable diligence that ultimately thwarted their effort to gain ballot access here."[25]

One might say the same of the Republicans and Democrats in Texas. But as on George Orwell's *Animal Farm*, some animals are more equal – or more reasonably diligent – than others.

Barr, who appeared on 45 state ballots, also failed to make the Maine ballot when his campaign filed 3,200 signatures by the August 8 deadline, or 800 short of the legal requirement. The Barr campaign filed suit to extend the deadline, but its case was rejected. Maine is traditionally a hotbed for anti-establishment candidates: it has elected two independent governors in the last four decades (James Longley and Angus King) and gave Ross Perot a whopping 30% of the vote in 1992. Yet as Richard Winger notes, it is a tough state in which to qualify for the ballot. Signature gatherers "must submit petitions to the town clerks, then go back again and collect them and deliver them to the Secretary of State."[26]

Ralph Nader made the Maine ballot, however, and in fact it was his best state in 2008, as he attracted about 1.5% of the vote. Who knows how many more votes he might have attracted had the articulate Nader appeared in those soporific and slogan-dominated snoozefests known as the presidential debates?

The Nader camp complained long and loudly about their exclusion from the debates, but to no avail. The major parties, which effectively control the debates, recall what happened when gadfly Ross Perot gained entry to the stage in 1992, and they are not about to risk giving a huge boost to another independent candidate.

The Commission on Presidential Debates (CPD) once again was in charge of deciding which candidates Americans would get to see and hear, and once again it decided that two was plenty. The CPD's cochairmen are Frank J. Fahrenkopf Jr. and Paul G. Kirk Jr. – former chairmen of the Republican and Democratic National Committees, respectively. How convenient! No wonder Barr, Nader, and the rest hadn't a prayer of crashing the party. The CPD's nine-member board of directors includes politicians (retired Republican senators Alan K. Simpson of Wyoming and John C. Danforth of Missouri), fixtures on nonprofit and philanthropic boards (Antonia Hernandez, Caroline Kennedy, Dorothy Ridings), an educator (H. Patrick Swygert,), a billionaire (Howard Buffet), and Democratic political activists (Newton Minow, Michael D. McCurry).[27] What it does not contain is anyone associated in any way with third party or independent political activity.

The commission set its hurdles, in its usual high-handed and arbitrary manner, just high enough to include the major candidates and exclude anyone else. The CPD requires debate-worthy candidates to appear on enough ballots to have a mathematical chance of winning the race, by which standard Barr, Nader, McKinney, and Baldwin easily qualified, but it also insists that they poll at least an average of 15% in five national public-opinion surveys before the debates – an almost impossible bar to surmount. Barr and Nader could plausibly argue that if they had a chance to debate, their post-debate poll numbers would flirt with, if not exceed, 15%, but the Catch-22 of the situation cruelly shuts them out.

The CPD sponsored three presidential debates and one vice presidential debate in 2008. Those who stayed awake for the three McCain-Obama debates witnessed two candidates who agreed with each other on the vast majority of the issues raised, from what to do about Georgia (the one near Russia, not the one that contains Atlanta and Savannah) to whether or not to bail out Wall Street to the tune of $700 billion (for starters). Nader, Barr, Baldwin, and McKinney would have offered dissent from this cozy twosome, but they were not allowed anywhere near the stage.

The CPD claims to be protecting the American public from fringe candidates who would waste their valuable time, but when in mid-August 2008 Zogby International polled that same American public it found that 55% of likely voters wanted Bob Barr included in the presidential debates and 46% of likely voters wanted Ralph Nader in the fray. Majorities of every listed demographic group – men, women, big city dwellers, suburban dwellers, married, and single people – supported Barr's inclusion, while in Nader's case voters were split almost evenly down the middle. By large margins, independents wanted Barr (69%) and Nader (59%) in the discussion. Even Republicans – whose candidate it was generally believed Barr's candidacy would hurt most – favored Barr's participation by 50–41%.

Pollster Zogby summed up his findings: "This election will be won in the political middle, and independent voters are the major prize up for grabs. It looks like independents want a full debate this fall to get a wider range of views and voices out onto the table."[28]

The voters got no such thing. The CPD knows best.

Nader and Baldwin did participate in a third-party candidates debate on October 23 in Washington that was broadcast on C-SPAN2 and received the microscopic ratings typical of that network. More ideas were exchanged in that single debate than in all the CPD debates put together. Which is why, perhaps, the CPD had no intention of letting Ralph Nader and Chuck Baldwin crash the party.

Nor did the outlier candidates in 2008 benefit in any significant way from the quadrennial giveaway of taxpayers' dollars.

Ralph Nader and Cynthia McKinney received federal matching funds under FECA during the primary season to the tune of $881,494 and $5,148, respectively. Bob Barr refused any subsidy, in keeping with the Libertarian Party's principles, and Chuck Baldwin likewise did not receive one red cent of government money to pay for his campaign. The real contrast, however, was between Barack Obama and John McCain.

Both candidates declined public financing in the primaries, thus freeing them from spending limits. But in the general election, the Republican took his $84.103 million subsidy from the Presidential Election Campaign Fund, thereby shutting off the private-money option. Democrat Obama, however, became the first major-party candidate to opt out of the system in the fall election, freeing himself to raise as much money from private sources as his adept managers could raise. By declining the $84 million he was free to raise several times that amount – and he did, as his campaign, during the primary and general election, received, from all sources, a record $639 million.

Candidate Obama had piously pledged in the previous year that "If I am the Democratic nominee, I will aggressively pursue an agreement with the Republican nominee to preserve a publicly financed general election."

As the song goes, money changes everything. Obama, awash in donations, the vast majority of them from big-money contributors, went back on his word. He did not "aggressively pursue" any such agreement. As John McCain charged, "He has completely reversed himself and gone back, not on his word to me, but the commitment he made to the American people."[29]

The Obama-infatuated media never called the Illinois senator on his reversal, or his blatant untruth, to be more precise. It is impolite to badger a saint about his hypocrisy. As a result of Obama blowing off the public-financing dollars, he "outspent Mr. McCain by the biggest margin in history," wrote Karl Rove, the former Bush operative, in the *Wall Street Journal*.[30]

This was, as the Center for Responsive Politics notes, the first time that the general-election candidates for president of the United States spent, in sum, more than $1 billion. The fund-raising breakdown shows that that the Democrat and Republican accounted for $999 million, which is somewhat more than half the total – in fact, it is somewhat more than 99% of the total. According to the Center for Responsive Politics's webpage (http://www.OpenSecrets.org), the funds raised during 2008 presidential campaign by each candidate were: Barack Obama, $639 million; John McCain, $360 million; Ralph Nader, $4 million; Bob Barr, $1 million; Chuck Baldwin, $239,000; and Cynthia McKinney, $188,000.

While John and Cindy McCain's seven houses were the source of much mirth, some envy, and considerable grumbling over conspicuous consumption, McCain's "candidate self-financing" line on the Center for Responsive Politics rundown of how the candidates raised their money features a big fat zero. Barack Obama, too, failed to contribute to himself, but when $639 million is washing into your campaign treasury it's understandable that one might ask "Why bother?" Bob Barr donated $1,000 toward his effort, but the only candidate who took advantage of the *Buckley v. Valeo* right to unlimited self-financing was Ralph Nader, who spent $42,456 of his own money on his campaign. Nader, to his credit, put his money where his mouth was.[31]

Karl Rove, in his analysis of where the money came from to pay for the candidates in 2008, quotes the campaign-finance expert Michael Malbin dismissing as a "myth" the claim that Obama's crusade was propelled by small donors. In fact, 74% of Obama's money came from contributors who gave more than $200. Thirty-plus years after the landmark campaign finance reform, all the contribution limits and taxpayer subsidies have failed utterly to "cleanse" the system. If anything, they have further sullied it.

On the bright side, though, the 2008 election may have rung the death knell for public financing in the general election. Rove predicts that "No presidential candidate will ever take public financing in the general election again and risk being outspent as badly as Mr. McCain was this year."[32] Unfortunately, given contribution limits that clip the wings of financial angels, the likelihood of a non-billionaire third-party or independent candidate taking flight will remain a longshot even in that changed environment.

Despite the appalling imbalance in funding, ballot access, and debate appearances, as the general election rolled along a few rays of hope shone through for non-establishment candidates. The Democrats, after all, had nominated an inexperienced Chicago politician, US Senator Barack Obama, whose voting record was, arguably, the most liberal in the United States Senate. The Republican nominee was Arizona Senator John McCain, an angry old man who had alienated the GOP base by his apostasy on immigration and campaign-finance reform. He was also a vocal, even belligerent supporter of the vastly unpopular Iraq War of George W. Bush, and in a campaign appearance had even cheerfully speculated that US troops might occupy Iraq for 50 or 100 years. What did he care?

Yet for all the imperfections of the Demopublican pair, the odds were stacked so steeply against the other candidates that none of them ever really achieved traction.

Ralph Nader did the best of the lot, tallying 738,475 votes, compared to 465,650 in 2004 and 2,882,955 in his highwater campaign of 2000, the year he won 2.7% of the nationwide popular vote and "cost" Al Gore the election in the mythos of the Democrats – as though all votes belong to the two major parties, and anyone else with the effrontery to run is "stealing" votes from titans such as Al Gore and George W. Bush.

Bob Barr failed to catch the Ron Paul wave. His campaign manager, Perot veteran Russ Verney, told Dave Weigel of *Reason* during the LP convention in Denver that the Barr effort hoped to raise $30 million; it fell about $29 million shy of that goal.[33]

Barr polled 518,087 votes, or the second-highest total in the LP's brief history, though that half-million plus was much less than optimistic Libertarians had predicted and not much more than half of the party's best showing, the 1980 candidacy of California attorney Ed Clark, which was fueled by billionaire running-mate David Koch's wallet. Barr exceeded 1% in Indiana – he was the only minor-party candidate for which Hoosiers were permitted to vote. Barr's 29,186 votes, or 1.1% of the popular vote in the state, exceeded Barack Obama's margin of victory over John McCain, which was 26,163. Now, it is extremely unlikely that those Barr voters would all have voted McCain had the LP been kept off the ballot – many were probably antiwar conservatives and libertarians who'd have voted for Obama as the lesser of two evils – but the Republicans took notice of the Barr tally. Had Indiana decided the election, as Florida did in 2000, Barr would have been hung in effigy and crucified on talk radio just as Ralph Nader was in that earlier campaign.

One lesson the LP seems to have drawn is that, as vice presidential nominee Wayne Allen Root said, they need a new Koch. (Not to be confused with New Coke.) It is a sad lot to which we have fallen in this country when in order to mount a serious electoral challenge to the establishment you have to search, wish for, or beg a billionaire to run on your ticket and shower you with money. But that is what we have come to only 220 years after the ratification of the US Constitution.

The Green Party, with nominee Cynthia McKinney, polled 156,654 votes, which was more than the total of 119,859 that the half-hearted candidacy of David Cobb attracted in 2004. But McKinney's total was less than 10% of what Green candidate Nader won in 2000 – a precipitous decline.

Finally, Chuck Baldwin, the pastor who won Ron Paul's endorsement, tallied 196,461 votes in 38 states. Paul himself, whose name was placed on the ballot by supporters in Montana, won 2.2% of the vote in the Big Sky State, which was the best showing in any state by a third-party candidate in 2008. Had he run as a Libertarian or Libertarian-Constitution fusion candidate, there is little doubt that he'd have tallied at least 2% nationally, and possibly quite higher. The financial meltdown against which Paul had warned began shortly before Election Day, and the war whose passionate opponent he was, was going disastrously as well. On paper, the prospects had seldom looked better for a strong showing by a minor party. But until the legal advantages that the two parties have built into the system are repealed, it is improbable that a third party campaign in the United States will make the transition from looking good on paper to doing well at the ballot box. The losers in all this are not so much the candidates, who are often admirable examples of American idealism, but the American people. Three hundred million people. Two choices. It just doesn't add up.

Notes

1. Richard Winger, "Minor Party and Independent Vote for Top Offices Is 2nd Best Mid-Term Result Since 1934," *Ballot Access News*, December 1, 2006.
2. Interview with Kinky Friedman, *Fort Worth Star-Telegram*, August 23, 2007.
3. Richard Winger, "26.5% of Voters Are Not Registered Dems or Reps," *Ballot Access News*, March 1, 2008.
4. Michael Brendan Dougherty, "Lone Star," *American Conservative*, June 18, 2007, p. 7.
5. Libby Copeland, "The Gentleman from the 19th Century," *Washington Post National Weekly*, July 17–23, 2006.
6. Jose Antonio Vargas, "An Also-Ran in the GOP Polls, Ron Paul Is Huge on the Web," *Washington Post*, June 16, 2007.
7. "Lone Star," *American Conservative*, p. 7.
8. "Ron Paul: The Libertarian Surprise," *Washington Post*, December 17, 2007.
9. Chico Harlan, "Nader on Nats," *Washington Post*, September 18, 2008.
10. Ralph Nader, "Twelve Issues that Matter for 2008," Fund-raising Letter, March 2008.
11. Interview with Chuck Baldwin, http://www.buyingofthepresident.org, May 20, 2008.
12. Richard Winger, "Zogby Presidential Poll of July 6," http://www.ballot-access.org, July 7, 2008.
13. Richard Winger, "How Many Parties Ought To Be on the Ballot?: An Analysis of *Nader v. Keith*," *Election Law Journal*, Vol. 5, No. 2, 2006, p. 170.
14. Ibid., p. 172.
15. Kate Zernike, "Court Strikes Nader from Pennsylvania Ballot," *New York Times*, October 14, 2004.
16. "Remarks of John Murphy, Pennsylvania Coordinator of the 2004 Ralph Nader Campaign, at the Kickoff Rally for the Voter's Choice Act," September 24, 2005, http://www.paballotaccess.org.

17. Richard Winger, "Libertarian Party Tackles Oklahoma," *Ballot Access News*, September 1, 2007.

18. Bob Driehaus, "Court Orders Ohio to Include Libertarian Party on Ballot," *New York Times*, July 19, 2008.

19. Richard Winger, "Ohio Victory," *Ballot Access News*, August 1, 2008.

20. Scott Shephard, "Bob Barr Wants McCain, Obama Off Texas Ballot," *Atlanta Journal-Constitution*, September 16, 2008.

21. "Bob Barr: The Lone Candidate in the Lone Star State," http://www.thelibertypapers.org, August 28, 2008.

22. "Bob Barr Wants McCain, Obama Off Texas Ballot," *Atlanta Journal-Constitution*.

23. "Barr Loses Bid to Keep Obama, McCain Off Texas Ballot," *Houston Chronicle*, September 23, 2008.

24. Christy Hoppe, "Court Denies Libertarian Bob Barr's Effort to Kick McCain, Obama Off Texas Ballot," *Dallas Morning News*, September 23, 2008.

25. "Judge Tosses Barr's W.Va. Ballot Access Lawsuit," *USA Today*, September 7, 2008.

26. Richard Winger, "Bob Barr Fails to Make Ballot in Maine," http://www.ballot-access.org, August 18, 2008.

27. Commission Leadership, http://www.debates.org, December 2, 2008.

28. "Zogby Poll: Majority Want Libertarian Bob Barr Included in Presidential Debates," press release, August 15, 2008.

29. Michael Luo and Jeff Zeleny, "Obama, in Shift, Says He'll Reject Public Financing," *New York Times*, June 20, 2008.

30. Karl Rove, "McCain Couldn't Compete with Obama's Money," *Wall Street Journal*, December 4, 2008.

31. Center for Responsive Politics, http://www.OpenSecrets.org.

32. Karl Rove, "McCain Couldn't Compete with Obama's Money."

33. Dave Weigel, "Bob Barr Looks Back," http://www.Reason.com, November 24, 2008.

Chapter 8

Taking the Party Outside: Do Other Democracies Treat Third Parties and Independents Any Better?

For decades, Americans spoke proudly of living in the capital of the "Free World," whose antithesis was the Soviet Union and its captive nations – the communist bloc. We were a representative democracy; they were a dictatorship. We protected the right to speech and dissent; they clamped down on any expression not authorized by the central authorities. We had free elections; they had sham elections in which the Communist Party won by nearly unanimous votes – because the Communists were the only party allowed on the ballot. In every way, citizens of the United States were freer than citizens of the Soviet Union.

So in surveying the situation for third parties in democracies outside the US, it might behoove us to begin with our former opposite number, or at least its historic core – Russia.

The late and unlamented Soviet Union had the most restrictive ballot access laws on the books this side of Oklahoma. No, to be fair, they were even stricter than those of Oklahoma. Only the Communist Party candidate was permitted on the ballot in the USSR, though voters theoretically had the right to cross his or her name out. Few subjects of the Soviet Union did so. It could be hazardous to your health.

Post-Soviet Russia tore down those barriers, so that by the 1990s, as communism sat like trash in the dustbin of history, it really was harder for a candidate to make the ballot in Oklahoma than in Moscow. Until 1999, as Regina Smyth writes in *Candidate Strategies and Electoral Competition in the Russian*

J.T. Bennett, *Not Invited to the Party*, DOI 10.1007/978-1-4419-0366-2_8,
© Springer Science+Business Media, LLC 2009

Federation (2006), "all candidates running in a single-member district, regardless of whether or not they affiliated with a political party, needed to collect signatures from 1% of the voters in the district."[1] Paying for signatures was a common practice. In 1999, a new path to the ballot was opened: a deposit that was refundable only to those who garnered at least 3% of the vote. The purpose, writes Smyth, was to "diminish the number of contestants while still retaining the advantage for governing parties."[2] So the new democrats of Russia were learning their lesson quickly: to fortify one's power, make it more difficult for challengers to arise.

But still, new parties formed in the dawn of post-communist Russia. Twenty-six parties made the ballot in 1999, and the number remained fairly steady even after the introduction of the nonrefundable deposit law.

So in the first decade of the twenty-first century, President Vladimir Putin, acting perhaps under the illusion that he was governor of Oklahoma, supervised construction of several additional electoral barriers:

- The signature requirement for officially registering a party was boosted from 10,000 to 50,000.
- Parties could not be represented in parliament unless they achieved 7% of the vote.
- Independent candidacies for parliament were barred.[3]

As expected, competition was diminished. Though the system retained a certain fluidity, it became that much harder for a new party to emerge to take on the ascendant parties. Russian elections were still a far sight freer than those of the Soviet Union of Stalin and Brezhnev, but small parties were treated just as brusquely and contemptuously as their counterparts are treated in many American states. It was an inauspicious time for Russian democracy.

It was also a betrayal of a pledge made two decades ago by democracies of all kinds: old, young, and even imaginary. In its dying days, the Soviet Union became signatory to one of the major pieces of international diplomacy regarding the rights of out-of-power parties to contest elections. So, too, did its rival across the sea sign this document, and thereby hangs a tale of international hypocrisy.

For the United States was also among the signatories in June 1990 to the Copenhagen Document of the Helsinki Accords. Officially known as the Document of the Meeting of the Conference on the Human Dimension of the Commission on Security and Cooperation in Europe, this landmark agreement of the states of Europe – both of the West and the in-the-process-ofdisintegrating communist states of the East — expressed a "conviction that full respect for human rights and fundamental freedoms and the development of societies based on pluralistic democracy and the rule of law are prerequisites for progress in setting up the lasting order of peace, security, justice and co-operation that they seek to establish in Europe."[4]

Now, you might ask why the United States of America, which the last time we checked a map was nowhere near the continent of Europe, was a key player in this meeting. Thousands of US soldiers stationed in Europe under the NATO alliance would be your answer. Representatives from across the continent (and even beyond) participated in the Copenhagen conference. They came from Austria, Belgium, Bulgaria, Canada, Cyprus, Czechoslovakia, Denmark, Finland, France, the German Democratic Republic (East Germany), the Federal Republic of Germany (West Germany), Greece, the Holy See, Hungary, Iceland, Ireland, Italy, Liechtenstein, Luxembourg, Malta, Monaco, the Netherlands, Norway, Poland, Portugal, Romania, San Marino, Spain, Sweden, Switzerland, Turkey, the Union of Soviet Socialist Republics, the United Kingdom, and the US of A.

The states represented agreed on a number of "fundamental freedoms" of the citizen vis-à-vis the state, among them religious, legal, and political liberties. Among the political freedoms agreed to was "a clear separation between the State and political parties; in particular, political parties will not be merged with the State."[5]

One wonders if the diplomats who agreed to this language knew anything of the nuts and bolts and wire-cutters of election law. For in the United States, its federal elections shaped by FECA and the PECF, its state ballots controlled by the reigning parties, there is about as much separation between the Republicans/Democrats and the government as there would be between an All-Pro cornerback and an exceptionally slow Pop Warner league wide receiver. As for the European signatories, they have, with few exceptions, moved rapidly since the collapse of Communism toward the "cartel party" model discussed earlier.

But the document is violated even more egregiously by several nations, the United States especially, a bit further on down the list of protected "freedoms," where the signatories agree to "respect the right of citizens to seek political or public office, individually or as representatives of political parties, without discrimination."[6]

Without discrimination? Tell that to Ohio!

In the next section of the Helsinki Accords the European and American signer-nations pledge to "respect the right of individuals and groups to establish, in full freedom, their own political parties or other political organizations and provide such political parties and organizations with the necessary legal guarantees to enable them to compete with each other on a basis of equal treatment before the law and by the authorities."

This is violated so routinely by the state legislatures, the US Congress, and the Federal Election Commission as to boggle the imagination. Yes, third parties in the US are not suppressed with the ruthlessness and thoroughness of the old Soviet bloc, but nor do they enjoy anything like the freedoms supposedly guaranteed by the Copenhagen document. True, neither "violence nor intimidation bars the parties and their candidates from freely presenting their views and qualifications," but that prohibition is supposed to apply to "administrative action"[7] as well, and few nations anywhere in the world outside the worst despotisms can claim to harass minor party and independent candidates with as much administrative vigor as do the governmental bodies of the United States.

Something was rotten in Denmark when that concordat was signed, and it wasn't the pretty rhetoric but rather the galling gap between publicly professed principles and messy law.

The hypocrisy was too rich to believe. Political leaders unsympathetic to the United States have had a field day ever since in pointing out the chasm between US rhetoric and US reality. In 2005, the former president of Iran, Ali Akhbar Hashemi Rafsanjani, said, "There is only a veneer of democracy in the United States, and we have a real democracy. … Election laws are so complicated in your country that people have no choice but to vote for one of the candidates who are with one of the two parties." As Richard Winger has noted, in that same year of 2005 the Iranian ballot had seven presidential candidates — this occurred 1 year after Ralph Nader exhausted his modest resources in trying to make the ballot, fighting the legal challenges of John Kerry and the Democrats at every turn.[8]

In March 2007, the Office for Democratic Institutions and Human Rights, which was created to oversee compliance with the noble sentiments of Helsinki/ Copenhagen by the signatories, chastised Pennsylvania — that's Pennsylvania, USA — for its Sisyphean ballot requirements.

This ought to have been an embarrassment: a respected international human-rights organization calling out an American state for violating basic electoral rights that the United States government had pledged to uphold. But the duopoly was unmoved. Pennsylvania did not bat an eye. Some things — maintaining two-party dominance, for instance — are more important than mere principles.

This is not to say that the other nations of the West, or of the broader democratic world, have lived up to words of Helsinki.

In her study of why certain "West European right-wing extremist parties have performed better at the polls than others,"[9] political scientist Elisabeth Carter provides a useful survey of the continent's electoral laws. Carter's findings confirm certain long-held suspicions about the effects of electoral systems on minor parties while challenging other assumptions.

For instance, of the 14 countries in her study (Austria, Belgium, Britain, Denmark, France, Germany, Greece, Italy, Netherlands, Norway, Portugal, Spain, Sweden, and Switzerland), only France and Britain distribute legislative seats via majoritarian, or winner-take-all, formulae, which of course are supposed to advantage the two-party system. In Britain, the parliamentary seat goes to the candidate who tallies the most votes in a district, even if he or she achieves only a plurality. France employs a double-ballot scheme. In the first ballot, a candidate must win a majority of votes cast in order to win the seat; failing that, a second ballot is taken, in which all candidates who earned a vote total equal to 12.5% of the electorate (rather than 12.5% of votes cast) participate. The winner of this second ballot is awarded the seat, even if he or she fails to gain 50% of the vote.

In the other dozen countries under examination, parliamentary seats are divvied up by proportional formulae; while the details vary widely, these formulae usually provide that even parties that fail to win majorities or pluralities in any electoral districts pick up seats in the national legislature.

Political scientists generally hold that majoritarian formulae discourage people from voting for third (or fourth) party or independent candidates. "Don't waste your vote!" has many translations; it remains an effective bar to those contemplating such a vote.

Yet the evidence gathered by Carter is mixed. In majoritarian-system France, the primary "right-wing extremist party," the National Front, has shown strength at the polls. Tapping popular discontent over immigration and law and order, the National Front "has encountered success at the polls even though the institutional environment in which it has competed has been relatively restrictive."[10] Indeed, in 2002 its controversial leader, Jean-Marie Le Pen, finished second in the first round of balloting for president and wound up with 17% of the vote in the second round.

The National Front elected various officials, including several mayors in cities with native-immigrant tensions, though the usual internecine fights have since splintered the party and sapped some of its strength.

Yet the other West European country that distributes seats by majoritarian calculus, Great Britain, has exceptionally weak "right-wing extremist" parties, the most notable being the British National Party, or BNP. Minor parties with similar agendas have fared badly in some proportional-formula countries, too, among them Germany, Greece, the Netherlands, Portugal, and Spain, while other such parties have done comparatively well under the proportional-formula systems of Austria, Italy, and Norway. Indeed, the mean "right-wing extremist party vote" was highest in Italy (21.6% between 1994 and 2001) and Austria (14.8% in 1979–2002) and lowest in Britain (0.2% from 1979 to 2001, and 0.7% in 2005).[11]

Now, local conditions obviously account for some of the differences between countries. The parties in Carter's study naturally do better in nations in which Third World immigration has become a hot issue, notably France and Italy. As the immigration issue takes up more of the political radar screen in Britain, one might expect a right-wing party to do better, though the BNP has accumulated such racist baggage as to make its emergence as a significant political player extremely improbable.

In Germany, by contrast, the parties under discussion bear, whether fairly or not, the stigma of Nazism, so that one suspects that no matter how contentious an issue immigration becomes, or no matter how third-party friendly the proportional formula may be, parties of the extreme right will, for the foreseeable future, lag badly in Deutschland.

(Parenthetically, Carter's definition of "right-wing extremist party," which raises any number of red flags, is open to debate. The British National Party has a reputation for racism, for instance, while in Italy the Lega Nord, or Northern League, is a popular party in the northern party of the country that speaks not to racial but to regional concerns. It is federalist in the old American sense of devolutionist, and to tag it as extremist, let alone right wing, is problematic, if not extremely unfair. Carter might as well have substituted "populist" for "extremist" and not let slip her own political biases.)

In any case, having failed to find a strong correlation between electoral systems and the success of right-wing extremist parties, Carter moved on to electoral laws, and found that access to state subvention (and access to the media) is a better predictor of success for these parties.

To take the latter first, Carter finds that "the fortunes of the West European right-wing extremist parties are indeed related to the media access laws present in the various countries."[12] As a rule, such parties tend to do better in nations that, by law – that is, by force of the state – ensure access to the media for smaller parties. For instance, in Denmark, every party that is eligible for the ballot – Denmark has fairly strict ballot access rules – receives an equal amount of free media, which is the only media game in town, since political advertisements are verboten. In countries such as Greece, the Netherlands, and Austria, by contrast, the allocation of media time is determined, to an extent, by the number of seats a party has in parliament. Woe unto the new party, or the party without parliamentary representation. At least on television, the new party wears a cloak of invisibility.

The strongest influence upon a right-wing extremist party's vote, found Elisabeth Carter, was the size and availability of state subsidies. There is a sense in which this measures the extent to which the "cartel party" system holds in various countries. If a party is dependent upon the state, it becomes, in some insidious way, a creature of the state. This is no less true of third, fourth, and fifth parties than of major parties, but of course the systems are usually rigged so that the ruling parties split the bounty and the smaller entities scramble for crumbs.

Carter measures both the access to and the size of state subventions. Austria, for example, has both "easy" access to subsidies (a party must have tallied at least 1% of the vote in the previous election) and "generous" subsidies. Its most popular party fitting Carter's definition, the FPO, regularly scored over 20% in elections during the 1990s. Denmark and Germany also hit the daily double of "easy" and "generous" subsidies, but while in Denmark a series of right-wing parties has polled around 10%, the main right-wing extremist German parties, the Republikaners, the National Democrat Party, and the German Peoples' Union, have not done well. Again, this may well be due to the very special circumstances of Germany, where parties of the extreme right will for some years to come fall under the dark cloud of suspicion due to the Nazi era and, in the case of the National Democrats and German Peoples' Union especially, because of racist or anti-Semitic associations.

The only country in which access to state subvention of political parties is "very hard" is Britain, which requires parliamentary representation for a subsidy of any kind. Parties of the extreme right have done poorly in Britain, as they have in Spain, which falls under the "hard" category.

Concludes Carter: "generous levels of state subventions and easy access requirements are associated with high right-wing extremist party scores, whereas modest levels of state subsidies and access requirements that are difficult to satisfy are linked with low right-wing extremist party scores."[13] This seems commonsensical, but it is good sometimes to have common sense verified. When a third party has access to money and media, it does better, on average, than when such a party does not have access to these goods.

The nations of Western Europe also handicap third parties and independents, though few do so as cripplingly as does the United States. As Elisabeth Carter found, Norway, Portugal, Spain, and Sweden are the countries in which it is easiest for political outliers to gain ballot status. Spain requires merely that a candidate be nominated by a registered political association; Norway and Portugal require that parties submit 5,000 signatures in order to appear on the ballot. In all three countries, "registration is continuous"[14] – a party is not kicked off the ballot if it fails to meet a baseline vote total. Sweden requires 1,500 signatures to register a party, though parties tallying less than 1% of the vote must reimburse the state for the cost of producing paper ballots.

The other ten West European countries in Carter's study threw up obstacles of varying height to small parties. In each case, the party or the candidate had to submit signatures and/or pay a deposit before every election in order to ensure the presence of the party or candidate on the ballot.

The toughest ballot nuts to crack are in Austria, Denmark, and the Netherlands. Austria requires both a substantial non-reimbursable deposit and between 200 and 500 signatures per district. Denmark demands that parties which have no representation in the national legislature submit petitions containing signatures equal to 1/175th of the votes in the most recent election, or about 20,000 in sum. The Netherlands earns a "hard" rating from Carter for its not insignificant required deposit.

Petitions and deposits can be formidable barriers to the ballot, but they are not the whole story. For example, the British National Party (and "extremist" parties of the left, too) polls poorly, but the leading right-wing parties of "hard" Austria have done well over the last two decades. Clearly ballot access is not the only explanation for a minor party's success or failure – though note that Austria's hurdles are still much more easily surmounted than the hurdles to ballot access for minor parties in such American states as West Virginia, Ohio, and Oklahoma.

Perhaps not coincidentally, Norway, with its easy ballot access, has seen in recent years a minor party, the FrP, or Progress Party, come in from the fringes to become, at this writing, the second-largest party in the country. Begun as something of an anti-tax protest movement in 1973, when it actually elected four members to the Storting, the Norwegian parliament, the Progress Party rode a populist wave in the late 1980s to become a significant force in the nation's politics. In 2005 it elected 38 members to the 169-member Storting, becoming in the process the leading opposition party in Norway. (The ruling Arbeiderpartiet, or Labour Party, currently has 61 members.)

Progress is a "classical liberal party," according to its chairwoman, Siv Jensen.[15] In this sense it is closer, perhaps, to the Libertarian Party of the USA than it is to, say, the Republicans, though it has achieved a presence in Norway that the American Libertarians can only dream about.

Would this have been the case had Norway barred the ballot door to minor parties? Ask the Libertarians or Ralph Nader, who have played upon anti-establishment populist themes with considerable skill but little electoral success.

The failure of a viable third party to compete regularly in US elections is thrown into stark relief when one looks at nations with relatively similar methods of apportioning legislative seats.

In one comparative study of the party systems of Canada, India, Great Britain, and the United States ("The Formation of National Party Systems: Federalism and Party Competition in Canada, Great Britain, India, and the United States"), authors Pradeep Chhibber and Ken Kollman note that while the four countries under study all have "single-member, simple-plurality voting systems for the lower houses of parliament,"[16] the non-US trio each have active, even vigorous regional parties while the United States, in obedience to the previously discussed Duverger's Law, is stuck with two national parties.

Rendered graphically, the differences are striking. Using the generally recognized measure by political scientists Markku Laasko and Rein Taagepera to calculate the "effective number of parties"[17] in a given system, the authors show that while the number has fluctuated in each of the countries under examination, it has generally hovered around three in Canada and Great Britain from the late nineteenth century through the beginning of the twenty-first, while in India it has ranged between four and seven over the last half-century. The United States, by contrast, while it had a lively and vigorous multiparty system for much of its first seven score years, fell into a steady and boring two-party rut by 1920, and nothing has disturbed it since.

Centralization of power is a prime reason for the stability of the two-party system in America, argue the authors. Their thesis: "Voters are more likely to support national political parties as the national government becomes more important in their lives."[18] As political power is transferred from the provinces to the central state, "voters will naturally have more incentive to try to influence politics at higher levels,"[19] and parties will respond to national, rather than local, questions. It is, for Americans of federalist sympathies, a bitter pill to swallow: the United States, born in a federalist matrix, is a centralized state, and the parties have responded to that; meanwhile, such countries as India, Canada, and Great Britain have multi-party systems, or at least active third parties, because those parties respond to local interests and local pressures, whether in Quebec or Scotland or West Bengal. America, home of federalism, could learn a thing or two about decentralizing power – and protecting the liberty of parties – from the countries of the Crown, even Great Britain, which alone of the quartet has never been federal, though in the 1990s it devolved power to the regions, fueling nationalist movements in Scotland and Wales. Give people a taste of self-rule and they will usually develop a healthy appetite for it.

In India, the ruling Congress Party, which dominated politics in the decades following the achievement of independence in 1947, was gradually challenged by a Socialist Party and conservative parties (Jan Sangh and its successor, the Bharatiya Janata Party) as well as numerous ethnic and religious-based parties. The Indian lower house, the Lok Sabha, typically comprises more than five parties of varying strength. Indian politics have a strong regional component, so the system has not ossified into a duopoly. The country's cultural, religious, and linguistic diversity perhaps guarantees a fragmentary political life, despite the best efforts to centralize power under Prime Minister Indira Gandhi. It should be noted, however, that other countries exhibit diversity – Delta Mississippi and interior Alaska are, after all, part of the same country – within a two-party system.

Chhibber and Kollman note that the Indian government is "less involved in economic decisions that affect voters at the local level than are national governments in Canada, Great Britain, and the United States." The national tax burden upon citizens is far lower in India than in the other three nations, and the "national bureaucracy"[20] is considerably less expensive and intrusive in India. States in India retain genuine responsibilities and authority – rather as the American states did before the consolidation of the United States in the 1930s.

How strange it is to use the United States as the standard of political consolidation! The United States, however, "has had probably the world's purest two-partism since the 1930s,"[21] when the New Deal centralized authority in Washington, D.C., where it has remained, seemingly invulnerable to the usual political vicissitudes. Pre-New Deal, other parties, amplifying other voices, other perspectives, existed, even thrived, in a minor way. But that, in terms of America's past, is ancient history. One other point, which resounds from earlier chapters of this book: Chhibber and Kollman write that "it is almost certainly the case that the United States has the most onerous ballot access rules – at the state level – compared with those in the other three countries. These differences," they add, "could go some way toward explaining why the United States has fewer parties than the other countries."[22]

Nor have regional or state-level parties arisen in the US, unlike in India, partly for structural reasons (single-member, first-past-the-post elections; the necessity of putting together a national coalition to win presidential elections) but also because of "the United States national government's domination of the states on economic policies"[23] – in other words, the centralization of a once decentralized republic.

In Canada, matters were and are different. A regional party such as Social Credit could dominate a province (Alberta) in the 1930s because provinces had "real authority over economic policies."[24] Even today, the Parti Québécois remains a major player in Quebec affairs – and national affairs – even though it has a real presence only in a single province.

The first major Canadian party, the Liberal-Conservatives, forerunners of the Conservative Party, dates to the 1850s. The opposition parties took longer to coalesce into what became the Liberal Party. (If only for the sake of colorful language, one regrets that an early opposition party, the Clear Grits, a band of free-traders of libertarian bent out of Upper Canada, did not endure.)

Regional parties have occasionally asserted themselves, not only in Quebec but in the western provinces, most spectacularly with the Social Credit Party of Alberta. This party, which at times aspired to be a non-party, was an outgrowth of the United Farmers of America, an agrarian movement born on the plains of Alberta, a resource-rich province of western Canada which was, at that date, something of a colony of the national government. The UFA base was small landholders and farmers, and from 1921 through 1935 the movement dominated Alberta: during the years of UFA rule, the main opposition party, the Liberals, attracted just 26.2% of the votes in provincial elections.[25]

Although elsewhere in Canada a two-party system was developing, Alberta seemed to be producing something closer to a non-party system, as most debates took place within the UFA, which held that the "natural harmony of group interests" in Alberta precluded class-based parties.[26] Canadian political scientist C.B. MacPherson, in his study, *Democracy in Alberta: Social Credit and the Party System* (1953/1968), theorized that Alberta's socioeconomic homogeneity retarded the growth of a duopoly.

In any event, the UFA evolved into the Social Credit movement in 1935. Social Credit was a populist-tinged tendency which was not seeded in the wheatfields of the prairies but was imported from England. Inspired by Major C.H. Douglas, an English engineer, the party put forth a somewhat fanciful and unworkable monetary program in service of a far-reaching societal reform that would, in theory, lead to the flourishing of the individual in a world increasingly marked by conformity.

Whether it was utopian idealism or economically illiterate nonsense, Social Credit formed the basis of the dominant party in Alberta, even after Social Credit and its leader, E.C. Manning, denounced Major Douglas in 1947 for his increasingly anti-Semitic views.[27] The party collapsed in the 1960s; its followers tended to go to the Conservatives or, in later years, the Reform Party.

Unlike Social Credit, which was largely – though not entirely – confined to Alberta, the New Democratic Party (NDP), founded in 1961 as a labor-left party with western Canadian roots, is a national organization, as was the western-based Reform Party of the early 1990s, which spoke for western alienation from Ottawa in a voice similar to that of the Perot movement in the United States.

There are regional and historical reasons for the success of Social Credit and the Parti Québécois and the endurance of the NDP, but at least one administrative factor made it all possible: Canada has very easy ballot-access laws. Obtain a nominal 100 signatures (or 50 in more remote ridings) and pay a refundable filing fee of $1,000 (Canadian) and you are on the ballot. There are no legalistic hassles or challenges by a phalanx of lawyers to keep parties other than the Conservatives and Liberals off the ballot. A hopeful candidate does not need to pay professional petition circulators to hunt up thousands of signatures, only to see those signatures challenged by Democratic or Republican hacks. In Canada, a candidate, no matter her party, begins on a footing of legal equality with the big boys.

Great Britain, too, has modest signature requirements (only ten names), though its requisite deposit (of £500) is forfeited if the candidate does not win at least 5% of the vote – a condition that is unquestionably a discouragement to minor-party candidates.

Yet the British, however unfriendly the system is in some ways to third parties, have generally had a pulse-bearing third choice since the rise of the Labour Party in the early twentieth century. Like Canada, Britain has two dominant parties but healthy alternative parties as well.

The primary British parties of the nineteenth century, the Conservatives and Liberals, were run by – and ran for office – men of means. Landed aristocrats, titled nobles, and men to the manor born supplied the bulk of each party's treasury. Spending limits enacted by the Corrupt and Illegal Practices (Prevention) Act of 1883 sought to hem in the influence of money in politics, but those limits merely transferred responsibility for footing the electoral bill from wealthy individuals to the burgeoning party bureaucracies and, by the early twentieth century, the "new plutocracy of successful businessmen and industrialists," as R.J. Johnston and C.J. Pattie wrote in their monograph on British party finances.[28] With the rise of the Labour Party, unions, bolstered by dues from their members, became the seedbed of a new, frankly class-based party.

Liberals became the live third-party option after the emergence of Labour as the binary partner of the Conservatives in 1922, though for a decade or so Great Britain had a real three-party system before the Liberals collapsed. They revived, somewhat at least, in the 1960s, and in the years since the Social Democrats and Liberal Democrats have played the part of a third force. Moreover, localist or regional parties such as the Scottish National Party and Plaid Cymru in Wales became significant presences in the outlying regions of Great Britain by the 1970s, giving a distinctly decentralized flavor to British elections in the years since.

Great Britain took a step toward the subsidization of its parties with the 1918 Representation of the People Act — so bland and vanilla a title that it makes recent whitewashed nomenclature such as the Patriot Act and the Million Moms March seem positively incendiary in name. The Representation of the People Act made the state responsible for various election-related expenses previously borne by the parties; it also inaugurated a postal subsidy for candidates.

Yet while Great Britain doles out the usual subsidies to political parties via grants to members of parliament, local councillors, and their organizations, as well as in-kind subsidies for certain campaign expenses, it has yet to enact a full-fledged subsidization of campaigns for the House of Commons. In 2007, Justice Secretary Jack Straw threatened to mobilize the Labor Party behind such a program, but the movement has yet to pry open the exchequer. The Conservative Party has been a stalwart opponent on Thatcherite free-market grounds. Straw also met principled opposition from Roger Gough, research director for governance of the British think tank Policy Exchange, who said of Straw's threat, "The root cause of British political finance is … diminishing popular support for parties. If we go further down the road of state funding, we risk exacerbating the long-run trend from parties as popular, democratic institutions into top-down bureaucracies."[29] The cartel party has yet to dominate Britain. But the fight is not over.

Across the channel, France took the concept of strange bedfellows to new heights of perversity when it came to protests against the subsidization of its political parties.

Under the Fifth Republic, which came into life in 1958, the French adhered to a fairly strict separation of party and state that lasted until 1988. A law of 1901, which remained in effect as the Fifth Republic matured, limited party dues to 100 French francs, a modest sum upon which a party could not build a solid financial base. Presidential candidates were eligible for reimbursement of certain expenses, free television time, and government-provided election posters. Candidates for the National Assembly who tallied more than 5% of the vote were also reimbursed for various paper and publicity-related expenses – though France being France, land of etatism, "uncontrolled placarding"[30] was discouraged by restricting campaign posters to designated areas. Heaven forbid that telephone poles be defaced by the mugs of political candidates!

Periodic proposals for the state to fund the parties had run into crippling opposition by none other than that noted non-defender of a free market in political ideas … the French Communist Party! As scholar Thomas Drysch wrote in his study of French political finance, the 1979 attempt by Prime Minister Raymond Barre to fund French political parties out of the national treasury was defeated by the "strong resistance of the Communist Party against public party funding. The Communist Party was not plagued by any financial worries, because of their adequate legal and illegal financial sources, and they threatened to use all of the means of propaganda at their disposal to brand public party funding a self-service of the parties at the taxpayers' expense."[31]

What a delicious irony this was! The French Communists upholding laissez-faire principles – albeit in part because of their "illegal financial sources," which included money from the Soviet bloc.

The Socialists, reliant on Communist votes, reluctantly went along with their more doctrinaire Marxist brethren in their opposition to public funding of parties and squelched the plan, for a time.

Advocates of such funding finally prevailed when on March 11, 1988, law number 88-227 established a system of government funding for the parties as well as reimbursement for candidates. The bill passed over the opposition of the Communists – whose sugar daddies to the east were about to go sour – and the "right-wing" National Front – the two most popular "minor" parties. In an additional act sure to give free-market partisans a severe case of cognitive dissonance, the Communists refused any public subsidy in 1989 on principle, though as Thomas Drysch adds, "Having noticed the obvious disadvantage attached to such behavioural purity, the PCF accepted its share of public funds in 1990."[32] Adherence to limited-government principles, the Communists discovered, has its price.

The 1988 law, and subsequent modifications, legalized individual donations to parties of up to, at present, 7,500 euros (or 4,600 in election years). Yet the primary burden of party funding has fallen on the beneficent central state. The parties receive state subsidies in proportion to, first, the number of votes they attracted in the most recent general election, and second, their representation in the National Assembly and Senate. To ensure obedience to official feminist doctrine, party subsidies are docked by a set percentage if the party in question does not comply with "gender parity" requirements.

As it happens, the Communists and the National Front were right, at least from the point of view of self-interest, in opposing the party-subsidy system. For instance, in 2003, the major parties were lavishly funded – the ruling Union pour un Mouvement Populaire received 33.4 million euros (minus a "gender parity" penalty) and its partner in quasi-duopoly, the Parti Socialiste, took in 19.6 million euros courtesy of the taxpayers. The National Front, by contrast, received 4.6 million euros and the Parti Communiste Francais was given 3.7 million euros. As Thomas Drysch notes, the formula for distribution of the funds discriminates against smaller parties and "has served to stabilize the established party system, since it benefits the large parties."[33]

As the cartel party has battened on the public purse across the globe, just how attached have parties become to the subsidies on which they feast? Canadians found out in late 2008.

Conservative Party Prime Minister Stephen Harper was feeling his oats after a victory in the October 14 parliamentary election, in which his party solidified its plurality – but not, crucially, majority – in Parliament. The global economic crisis was in its early stages, and Harper crafted a set of proposals designed to meet, or at least appear to meet, that crisis. He proposed to sell off government assets, ban strikes by public employees until 2011, and –in the most fiscally marginal but politically controversial step – end the government subsidy of Canadian parties.

You'd have thought Prime Minister Harper had called for replacing the maple leaf with the silhouette of Lucifer. The opposition, fearing a cut-off from the public trough, erupted with indignant denunciations of Harper's plan.

"This is huge. This is audacious and outrageous. This means war," screeched Pat Martin, an NDP member of Parliament from Winnipeg.

"If they want to do that it is a denial of democracy," whined Denis Corderre, a Liberal Party MP from Quebec.[34]

Canadian parties are annually given $1.75 from the public treasury for every vote they attract in a federal election. (The $1.75 is indexed for inflation; at press time it was about $1.95.) That amounts, in the larger budgetary scheme of things, to relative peanuts: $28 million. A lot of peanuts, yes, but then the state has the appetite of a million elephants.

The peanuts mean more to some parties than to others. For the year ending September 30, 2008, for instance, the government subsidy accounted for 35% of the Conservative Party's total funds ($10.5 million of $30.2 million). The comparable figures were much higher for the Green Party ($1.3 million out of $2.8 million raised, or 46%); the New Democratic Party ($5.06 million out of a total of $10.16 million, or 50%); the Liberal Party ($8.75 million out of $14.35 million, or 61%); and the Bloc Québécois ($3.03 million out of $3.86 million, or 78%).[35]

The Conservatives, it is clear, could run a nationwide campaign on privately raised funds; the other parties would have a tougher time doing so. (The Bloc Québécois, of course, is limited to Quebec.) The Conservatives are in good shape fiscally, if not always electorally or intellectually. The Liberals, NDP, the Bloc Québécois, and the Greens need bank loans to run their campaigns, and these loans are made in the confidence that the parties will be able to repay the loans with their government subsidy checks. Take away the checks and the banks might balk.

If there is one thing that the NDP, the Liberals, and the Bloc Québécois can agree on in parliament, it's that the stream of public monies must keep flowing into their coffers. (The Greens have no parliamentary representation.) So the leaders of the three opposition parties began serious discussions about calling for a vote of no-confidence in the Harper government, which would have dissolved it only two months after the most recent election.

Harper and the Conservatives backtracked like a Willie Mays racing to the warning track to catch a fly ball. They ceased their attack on party subsidies and doused the political fire before it consumed their government. They were, from the point of view of many Canadians, right on the issue, though they handled it in a way that turned off even many of their supporters. As Mike Brock wrote in the conservative *Western Standard*, "Philosophically, I am completely on board with the idea of cutting subsidies to the parties. But that being said, the Conservatives were not taking an ideological stand on fund-raising. They were simply trying to bankrupt the opposition."[36] For instance, the Conservatives did not call for lifting donation limits, which would have facilitated private fund-raising by the parties. Or as Progressive Conservative campaign chairman Norman Atkins said in 1990, looking back on his party's successful fund-raising efforts in the 1980s, "you can't run national campaigns on [the proceeds from] selling fudge."[37] From selling offices, perhaps – at least if you are a Chicago politician none too troubled by ethical considerations – but fudge, never.

As the Canadian case shows, parties have come to rely on state subsidies, rather as junkies rely on a fix. The parties of Austria and Sweden have also become state dependents, as political scientist Gudrun Klee of Germany's University of Oldenburg found in her comparative study of party finances in the two nations.

Given that legislative representation in those countries is based on the popular vote for parties rather than candidates, the state subsidies flow directly to those parties instead of the candidates – in fact, they are the lifeblood, not to mention the life, of the parties.

In Sweden, unlike in France, the Communist Party was a significant force in favor of the introduction of public financing in 1965. Prior to that time, party finances in Sweden were an entirely private matter, but the ruling Social Democratic Party, whose ideology seemingly denied the legitimacy of any private matter (other than sexual behavior), enacted "a subsidy scheme ... designed to assist only parties with considerable support" – that is, the Social Democrats above all. The formula for assistance was tweaked in 1972 as a way of paying off the Communists for their support; henceforth, parties whose vote exceeded 2.5% in one of the previous two elections – a threshold that guaranteed a grant to the Swedish Communists – were eligible for government monies.

In Austria, the public financing of political parties had deeper roots. Austrian states had subsidized parties (paying a set number of schillings for each vote) for years, so that when the question of a nationwide system of government funding came up in 1975, there was "no general debate on the principle."[38] It carried easily.

As in Sweden, the system is set up to give an artificial boost to the major parties. Minor parties (those receiving at least 1% in national elections) do receive reduced funding from the state treasury, though only in election years. The formula was jiggered in 1987 after the emergence in the 1980s of the Green Party and the rightist FPO, as the majors feared that these two ideologically based parties were growing at too rapid a pace. In addition, a new subsidy was introduced in 1989 that was tied to a party's membership in the Nationalrat, the Austrian legislature.

As is the case elsewhere, writes Professor Klee, in both Sweden and Austria "the respective subsidy scheme operates to the advantage of the established parties."[39]

One might think that in Germany, with its nightmarish experience of the merger of the Nazi Party and the state, wise and cautious statesmen would seek to ensure a clear separation of party and state. The Basic Law of the Federal Republic of Germany (West Germany) did not provide for subsidy of political parties, and in fact, as Hans Herbert von Arnim of the Post-Graduate School of Administrative Sciences in Speyer, Germany, writes, in 1948–1949, "the idea of public political financing did not even occur to anyone." It was "considered to be a constitutionally dubious practice," says von Arnim, and the Federal Constitutional Court ratified that assumption when it ruled that "the parties are responsible themselves for the financial expenditures associated with their organizations and activities."

Hessian Prime Minister Georg-August Zinn said flatly, "the idea of the state supporting the parties financially was completely unimaginable."[40]

In time, the unimaginable became all too easy to imagine.

The Party Finance Act of 1959 authorized grants to the parties "which by 1964 reached the astronomical sum of … one German mark per voter," as John Brady, Beverly Crawford, and Sarah Elise Wiliarty wrote in *The Postwar Transformation of Germany: Democracy, Prosperity, and Nationhood* (1999).[41] The Bundestag predictably limited eligibility to those parties represented in the Bundestag, though the Constitutional Court ruled that this discriminated against minor parties. The years since saw a tug of war between the Bundestag and the Court over the treatment of minor parties: the former disdained them, the latter tried to offer some protection.

Base payments, or sockelbetrag, are provided today to German parties based on their showing in elections to the Bundestag, the European Parliament, and Landtag (state parliaments). This system artificially favors established parties. The extent of public financing in Germany is regarded as generous (or spendthrift, depending on one's point of view), but lost in the shuffle are the outsiders, the dissidents, those who stay outside the main German parties. As Professor von Arnim concludes, "Small and new parties … are increasingly strangled financially with the growing amounts of public financing for parties, party groups/caucuses, and party foundations."[42]

But where is this not the case? It is almost inconceivable that the parties dominant in a legislature will not see to it that any public subsidies are steered to themselves and not to potential challengers. If major parties have the power to enrich themselves, or to keep others off a ballot, they will do so. That, it seems, is a truism that crosses state borders.

Notes

1. Regina Smyth, *Candidate Strategies and Electoral Competition in the Russian Federation: Democracy without Foundation* (Cambridge: Cambridge University Press, 2006), p. 79.
2. Ibid., p. 80.
3. Richard Galpin, "Putin machine squeezes opponents," BBC News, http://news-vote.bbc.co.uk, November 27, 2007.
4. "Document of the Copenhagen Meeting of the Conference on the Human Dimension of the CSCE," Washington: United States Commission on Security and Cooperation in Europe, 1990, p. 2.
5. Ibid., p. 3.
6. Ibid., p. 5.
7. Ibid., p. 6.
8. Quoted in Richard Winger, "How Many Parties Ought to be on the Ballot? An Analysis of *Nader v. Keith*," *Election Law Journal* 5 (2006), pp. 183–184.
9. Elisabeth Carter, *The Extreme Right in Western Europe: Success or Failure?* (Manchester: Manchester University Press, 2005), p. 146.
10. Ibid., p. 194.
11. Ibid., p. 159.
12. Ibid., p. 176.
13. Ibid., p. 192.
14. Ibid., p. 163.
15. "A Norwegian Thatcher?" Interview with Siv Jensen, Standpoint.online, December 2008.
16. Pradeep Chhibber and Ken Kollman, *The Formation of National Party Systems: Federalism and Party Competition in Canada, Great Britain, India, and the United States* (Princeton: Princeton University Press, 2004), p. 3.
17. Ibid., pp. 5–9.
18. Ibid., p. 222.
19. Ibid., p. 78.
20. Ibid., pp. 200–201.
21. Ibid., p. 173.
22. Ibid., p. 233.
23. Ibid., p. 182.
24. Ibid., p. 191.
25. Maurice Pinard, *The Rise of a Third Party: A Study in Crisis Politics* (Montreal: McGill-Queen's University Press, 1975), p. 43.
26. C.B. MacPherson, *Democracy in Alberta: Social Credit and the Party System* (Toronto: University of Toronto Press, 1953, second edition 1968), p. 47.
27. Ibid., p. 212.

28. R.J. Johnston and C.J. Pattie, "Great Britain: Twentieth Century Parties Operating Under Nineteenth Century Regulations," in *Campaign and Party Finance in North America and Western Europe*, edited by Arthur B. Gunlicks (New York: toExcel, 2000/1993), p. 126.

29. "Spending Arms Race by the Political Parties 'A Myth,'" Press release, Policy Exchange, April 23, 2008, http://www.policyexchange.org.uk.

30. Thomas Drysch, "The New French System of Political Finance," in *Campaign and Party Finance in North America and Western Europe*, p. 160.

31. Ibid., p. 156.

32. Ibid., p. 170.

33. Ibid., p. 173.

34. David Akin and Elizabeth Thompson, "'Stephen Harper Is Playing Silly Politics': Grits Accuse Harper of Playing Politics with Fiscal Update," http://www.canada.com, November 26, 2008.

35. Ibid.

36. Mike Brock, "Stephen Harper: The Party Never Really Started," http://www.westernstandard.ca, November 30, 2008.

37. William T. Stanbury, "Financing Federal Politics in Canada in an Era of Reform," in *Campaign and Party Finance in North America and Western Europe*, p. 68.

38. Gudrun Klee, "Financing Parties and Elections in Small European Democracies: Austria and Sweden," in *Campaign and Party Finance in North America and Western Europe*, pp. 181–182.

39. Ibid., p. 186.

40. Hans Herbert von Arnim, "Campaign and Party Finance in Germany," translated by Arthur B. Gunlicks, in *Campaign and Party Finance in North America and Western Europe*, p. 203.

41. John Brady, Beverly Crawford, and Sarah Elise Wiliarty, *The Postwar Transformation of Germany: Democracy, Prosperity, and Nationhood* (Ann Arbor: University of Michigan Press, 1999), p. 102.

42. Hans Herbert von Arnim, "Campaign and Party Finance in Germany," in *Campaign and Party Finance in North America and Western Europe*, p. 210.

Chapter 9

Conclusion: Pulling the Plug?

No matter how low an estate the political parties may occupy in the public estimation, they remain sacred cows to large parts of the American journalistic and political establishment. To these mandarins, anything that weakens party control – that is, Republican-Democratic control – of American politics is also sapping the life from the American republic. Any measure that transfers greater authority over political life to the two parties, on the other hand, is an unadulterated good, much to be desired.

The poster boy for the duopoly's boosters is David S. Broder, the seemingly eternal columnist for the *Washington Post*. Broder is perhaps the journalist whose views most closely mirror those of the sober and responsible element of the American political establishment. He decries partisanship but reveres parties; he frets over the erosion of party loyalties, as though the emergence of the independent voter is a development to be lamented. Oh, for those golden days of the party-line voting robot!

Broder issued the first of his calls to arms – moderate, straitlaced calls, befitting his persona – in defense of the two-party system in his 1971 book, *The Party's Over: The Failure of Politics in America*.

Don't get the wrong idea from the title. The failure of politics was the failure of parties, and the author was determined to see both succeed. "[W]e can make government responsible and responsive again, only when we begin to use the political parties as they are meant to be used," wrote Broder. "And that is the thesis of this book."[1]

As they were meant to be used. Did Broder mean by this "as crowbars with which to force open the public treasury"? No. How about "as a means of seizing and wielding power"? Negative. Instead, David Broder sees political

J.T. Bennett, *Not Invited to the Party*, DOI 10.1007/978-1-4419-0366-2_9,
© Springer Science+Business Media, LLC 2009

parties as essential to a democratic republic and mourns their decline, their erosion, and wishes to strengthen them. "[T]he political party," he declares, is "the one instrument available to us for disciplining government to meet our needs."[2] Disciplining government. Now there's a twist! Government, of recent decades, has been more likely to discipline us.

Broder mourns divided government as "the opposite of responsible government"[3] and a condition devoutly to be wished to be missed. In fact, divided government has been a blessing over the last generation: the Republican Congress of the mid-1990s acted as a brake on Bill Clinton's Democratic liberalism and gave us a balanced budget, while the Democratic Congress of George W. Bush's last two years perhaps kept him from waging even more pre-emptive wars and from further shredding the Bill of Rights in the name of "homeland security."

Broder's was the establishment mindset of the early 1970s, before Watergate gave even the courtiers a temporary dose of cynicism. His model of "responsible party government" was in Nelson Rockefeller's New York, where Rocky, with a compliant Republican legislature, virtu-ally bankrupted the state with profligate (and often off-budget) spending. (It would take a liberal Democrat, Hugh Carey, to finally end the "days of wine and roses," as Carey announced in a sobering inaugural address.) Rockefeller also pushed through draconian drug laws which, among other outrages, set the punishment for selling two ounces of marijuana as equal to that for second-degree murder, with a minimum of 15 years to life. This fueled the budget-busting growth in the state's corrections industry, which, it must be admitted, partakes of the "discipline" so admired by Broder. As if that weren't enough, Rockefeller, entranced as he was by modernist art and architecture, oversaw the eviction of thousands of Albany residents from their homes – he used eminent domain the way other men used tissue paper – so that a legendarily ugly government mall could be built on the ruins.

Broder marvels at Rocky's accomplishments, but then he wrote in 1971, before the due bills came in. New York, he enthused, was "probably the best laboratory experiment in responsible party government one can find."[4] Broder has an interesting idea of what constitutes responsible party government. For Rockefeller blocked the emergence of a party primary system in the state because he knew that rank-and-file Republicans, if given the chance, would rebel against the spend-it-all and jail-'em-all liberalism of himself and US Senator Jacob Javits. He is, unintentionally, the father of the Conservative Party, which was started by conservative Republicans frustrated that

Rockefeller's "responsible" government kept them from running candidates against Rocky in the GOP primaries.

Broder, Mr. Responsible, also urges the consolidation of local governments and reducing the number of elected officials – proposals which in fact make government and governors *more* distant and *less* responsive. "In state government," he writes, "we need to reduce the number of elected officials," extend the terms of governors, and reduce the size of legislatures.[5] This is, essentially, a wet dream of professional politicians who fear no one so much as an enraged, or engaged, electorate.

We see in this very influential book the genesis of the FECA reforms. Broder urges public financing of candidates and wants to see "channeling much more of the money (including, in my view, all general election spending) through the respective party committees, rather than through individual candidates' treasuries."[6] In other words, the federal government is to direct taxpayer dollars to the parties, which then dole them out to those candidates who most docilely support the party agenda.

He chides ticket-splitters and people who say "there is no difference between the parties." Poisonous cynics! How dare they see no difference between, in the previous election, the pro-Vietnam War, pro-welfare state Democratic candidate Hubert Humphrey and the pro-Vietnam War, pro-welfare state Republican Richard M. Nixon. Far better, he writes, "to give a temporary grant of power to one party at a time, rather than dividing responsibility so skillfully between the parties that neither can govern."[7]

Power to the parties! That was Broder's cry in his impeccably establishmentarian voice. The parties did not disagree. In fact, they took him up on it. And the armor of protections enjoyed by the Democrats and Republicans are a legacy of this way of thinking.

Is there a way out? Is Broderism our only choice? Are we doomed to the duopoly? Must FECA and petty ballot laws forever shape our politics?

Not necessarily. There are paths that lead toward a freer, less regulated, more open, less duopolistic system.

For instance, Theodore J. Lowi, the John L. Senior Professor of American Institutions at Cornell, has been a thoughtful maverick in his profession: a political scientist who is also an activist in efforts to build a centrist third party.

Lowi eschews the number-and-equation dominated discourse of contemporary political science for bluntly stated opinion: "One of the best-kept secrets in American politics is that the two-party system has long been braindead – maintained by a life-support system that protects the established parties from rivals," he writes. "The two-party system would collapse in an instant if the tubes were pulled and the IVs were cut. And until then, the dominant two parties will not, and cannot, reform a system in which they are the principal beneficiaries."[8]

Not for Lowi any misty-eyed paeans to the venerable two-party system. Nor does he accept the canard that the Democrats and Republicans are the logical culmination of 200 years under the US Constitution. "Interestingly enough," he notes, "although many scholars present the two-party system as being inevitable, it has never been left to accomplish its wonders alone. It has been supplemented by primary, ballot, campaign finance, and electoral rules that are heavily biased against the formation and maintenance of anything other than the two-party system."

Lowi notes the sacred-cow status of the two-party system within academia and journalism. "With religious zeal," he writes, "the high priests of the two-party system have preached the established faith and their students who become leading journalists, spread the two-party dogma to the great unwashed."[9] If David Broder is the chief dogmatist, he has plenty of company in the mainstream media.

Lowi is, politically, something of a progressive. He was involved in the early efforts to create a centrist party with folks like former Connecticut Governor Lowell Weicker, who had been a liberal Republican US Senator before bolting the party. So Lowi's prescriptions are not always strictly limited to repealing favors and privileges for the two major parties. He argues, for example, that the heterogeneity of modern American life has rendered single-member geographically based districts anachronistic, a dubious proposition, and he therefore proposes that all members of the House be elected at-large statewide. Try running that one by the residents of Northern California or Western Massachusetts or Upstate New York or other culturally distinct regions that would be overwhelmed in such state-wide elections, so much so that, depending on the method used to count the votes, every single member of the congressional delegations of those states might come from a spot that represents about 10% of a given state's total area.

Nevertheless, Lowi, in his other recommendations, makes refreshing sense. Noting that third parties tend to be idea-based, even those reputedly centered around personalities (Perot, Wallace), he asserts that a greater prominence for such parties would mean a greater role for ideas in politics, and the emergence of genuine choices and alternatives to a status quo grown atrophied. Platitude-spouting pundits like to bemoan the lack of ideas in American politics: well, open it up to hitherto marginalized voices and that will all change. It's time, says Lowi, to pronounce an epitaph on "a party system that, on its own, would surely have crumbled a long time ago and remains vibrant only in the hearts of party practitioners and political scientists."

He concludes, "*It is time to deregulate American politics, letting it take whatever form it will.*"[10]

Lowi dreams of lawsuits challenging fusion laws, ballot access laws, and even single-member district elections for the US House of Representatives. These reforms are hardly un-American; indeed, in their concern for liberty and justice, they are quintessentially American.

The manifold ways in which the two parties have stacked the deck have been long evident. Some Populists, aware of the exterminationist intent of late nineteenth-century reforms, even proposed abolishing the Australian ballot. That is probably off the table at this point. But we do well to remember the history surrounding such reforms. We must shed our illusions, as Peter H. Argersinger says, that electoral laws that squeezed out challengers to the two-party system were "nonpartisan institutional reforms." Rather, as a Michigan Populist said of antifusion laws in 1895, they were "a step toward making the Australian ballot system a means for the repression instead of the expression of the will of the people."[11]

These measures were poison darts aimed at a vigorous multiparty system in which those who refuse to kowtow to Republican and Democratic bosses and bromides and clichés have a voice, a choice, a democratic outlet. The first step must be to remove the darts and drain the poison. Technological advances make a return to the pre-Australian ballot strip system unlikely, but they also render moot the already-ridiculous claim that without strict ballot access laws the number of candidates would exceed the voting machine's ability to list them. These laws must be repealed, state by state, and replaced with commonsense rules that permit the widest possible variety of candidates and parties to participate.

Coupled with a repeal of FECA, a lifting of the ceiling on campaign contributions, and the end to subsidization of the parties, candidates and conventions, we might see something resembling robust democratic debate break out.

That is no pipe dream of woolgathering radicals. In his book chapter "Institutional Obstacles to a Multiparty System," Richard Winger, the ballot access maven, has argued (with ample empirical evidence) that "minor parties win elections in states with favorable election laws and that they don't win elections in states with unfavorable laws."[12]

In his exhaustively researched style, Winger has looked at the major post-war third-party victories: governorships in Alaska and Connecticut won by well-known Republicans Walter Hickel and Lowell Weicker running on minor party lines in 1990; James Buckley's 1970 US Senate victory; earlier New York congressional wins by the leftist American Labor and Liberal Parties; the Senate and congressional victories of the independent socialist Bernie Sanders of Vermont; and Libertarian state legislative triumphs in Alaska and New Hampshire.

The "good" third-party states seemingly have little in common: they are urban and rural, western and eastern, ethnically diverse and almost all white. But they share relatively nonexclusive election laws. For one thing, they permit parties to nominate "recent converts" – unlike such states as California, which forbid parties from nominating candidates who have not been members of the party for a specified time. Several of the states (New York, Vermont, New Hampshire, Connecticut) permit fusion candidacies, or nomination by more than one party. Ballot access laws tend to be less draconian in the states with winning third-party candidates. "Good" minor-party states tend to allow parties to nominate all their candidates with a single petition; restrictive states often require separate petitions for each candidate, a nearly impossible task for many state legislature candidates. Filing fees, when high, can also be a deterrent to non-major party candidacies.

After surveying the fifty states, Winger concludes that "there is a high correlation between minor party victories and the characteristics of state election laws discussed above. The more favorable [that is – the less repressive] the state law toward minor parties, the greater the likelihood of minor party success."[13] The lesson is unmistakable: with a fair shake, minor parties can do far better than they do now. Perhaps they won't break up the duopoly, but they will enliven the debate and provide real choices. Alas, given that relaxation of these laws depends on the tender mercies of Republican and Democratic state legislators, reform seems a longer shot than betting the Texas Rangers to rip off five World Series titles in row.

But change is never impossible. Even David Broder isn't immune to it. A quarter century after his plea for a strengthening of the two-party system, he was back on the subject, this time worrying that the game was up. The title of his piece: "Is the Party Over?"

Auguries were in the wind. The final decade of the twentieth century was a time of deep popular disillusionment with the major parties. A July 8, 1992 *Washington Post* poll found that 82% of Americans agreed that "both American political parties are pretty much out of touch with the American people."[14] Moreover, "In poll after poll … [in the 1990s] nearly three out of every five respondents said they favor having a third-party alternative discussing issues and presenting candidates for offices, in opposition to the Republicans and the Democrats." In a throwback to the nonpartisan movement of Nebraska, a 1992 Louis Harris and Associates poll found that "38% wanted elections in which individuals ran without party labels."[15]

Yet, as political scientist J. David Gillespie opined in 1993, after surveying politics at the American margins, "the structural barriers placed on third-party participation in American politics have been more forbidding and debilitating than behooves the world's leading democratic nation."[16]

But despite those forbidding and debilitating barriers, Gillespie was writing at a moment pregnant with possibility. The first election of the decade had been a harbinger, as two third-party candidates won governorships in 1990: Walter J. Hickel of the Alaska Independence Party, and Lowell P. Weicker of A Connecticut Party. Of course it helped that Hickel and Weicker had greater name recognition than did their opponents in the three-way races: Hickel was a former Republican governor of his state, and Weicker had been a long-time Republican Senator from the Nutmeg State. They ran for reasons different from the idealism that usually motivates third-party standardbearers: they were ambitious, they had scores to settle, they sensed an opening and a path back to power. Hickel ran as the nominee of a secessionist party with a distinctly libertarian flavor, but the former Secretary of the Interior in the cabinet of President Richard M. Nixon was no firebrand advocate of extricating Alaska from the Union.

Nevertheless, the victories of Hickel and Weicker foretokened a revival of third-party fortunes in the 1990s, a revival that would take form most dramatically in the person of Texas billionaire H. Ross Perot. In 1992, Perot won 30% of the popular vote in Maine, 27% in Alaska, Idaho, Kansas, and Utah, 26% in Montana, Nevada, and Wyoming, and 25% in Oregon. Astonishing!

Writing in August 1996, as discontent simmered over yet another choiceless election, this one featuring incumbent Democrat Bill Clinton and the virtually lifeless Republican Senator Bob Dole, Broder predicted that Ross Perot's Reform Party was likely to replace one or the other of the major parties. The Republicans and Democrats, he wrote, have failed to "step up to the growing challenge of entitlement reform."[17] Unless they were to apply every ounce of statesmanship they possessed to taming Medicare and Medicaid and putting Social Security on a sounder footing, the death knell would toll for the GOP or the Democrats.

Well, the parties never did step up, but neither were they punished for yet another failure. Perot let the Reform Party die. The Democrats and Republicans push on.

Still, Broder's change of heart was striking, given his earlier fealty to the system. "I believe there is such a [third] party in the nation's near future," he declared. "I came into political journalism 40 years ago with a strong belief that the two-party system is a vital and irreplaceable bulwark of our system of government. I still believe that. But public dissatisfaction with the performance of the Democrats and Republicans is simply too great to be ignored."[18]

What Broder did not reckon with were the institutional barriers to the growth of new parties. But he was not alone in his sense that something might be aborning. In *Multiparty Politics in America* (1997), a collection that featured Broder's piece, editors Paul S. Herrnson and John C. Green wrote that "a small but vocal group of activists, scholars, and reform organizations are pressuring the federal, state, and even some local governments to revise their election codes in ways that would benefit minor parties at the expense of their major party counterparts. These reformers argue that without current restrictions on minor parties, from ballot access limitations to plurality elections, a multiparty system would emerge and flourish in the United States."[19]

Rather than tinkering with FECA, or augmenting it with a constitutional amendment overturning the Supreme Court's ban on expenditure limits, proponents of free and unfettered speech and open access to the ballot would repeal it. Their model, which has been dubbed "No Limits – Full Disclosure," would repeal public financing, permit unlimited contributions to candidates from any domestic source, and require only that all contributions be disclosed via the Internet.

Most approve of the mandatory disclosure requirements of FECA, on the grounds that voters deserve to know just who is funding the candidates. These make it so much easier to follow the money trail. Yet disclosure, as we have seen, can also invade the privacy of contributors or subject them to ridicule or reprisals. (As Kathleen M. Sullivan has suggested, exempting small contributors from disclosure requirements could obviate this potential problem.)

Freed of the regulatory burden, which historically bears hardest on those least able to afford the phalanx of lawyers necessary to its lessening, challengers and outsiders might have a shot. With more money – with higher campaign spending, not less, as cynical incumbents are wont to propose – the outsider voices might be heard. One thing is sure: fund-raising by outsiders would be a great deal easier.

Eliminating contribution limits, abolishing the tax checkoff, and ending government financing of federal elections would return us to a condition in which major party nominations went to people such as Dwight D. Eisenhower, Adlai Stevenson, Barry Goldwater, George McGovern, Richard M. Nixon – men who, whatever one might think of their politics – had substance and intelligence. Admittedly, the description applies to the first two men elected under FECA, Jimmy Carter and Ronald Reagan. But does anyone want to argue that the vast majority of post-FECA candidates – Walter Mondale, Michael Dukakis, the two Bushes, Bill Clinton, John Kerry – are of the same caliber of the earlier men?

Combine FECA repeal with an overhaul – a wide-scale repeal – of ballot-access laws and an end to party subsidies and the field opens up for vigorous, lively, contentious third-party candidacies that might finally offer alienated and bored and disgusted voters a choice, not an echo.

Economists Burton A. Abrams and Russell F. Settle ask, "Free markets and individual liberty have served the United States and its citizens well. Why adopt a nonmarket solution for running political campaigns?"[20]

An excellent question. If our citizens are cynical, our system sclerotic, and the parties uninspiring at best and corrupt at worst, why on earth would we wish to subsidize the parties, freeze the system at the status quo, and curtail choices for our citizens? Fair and just reforms are obvious, but it is just as obvious that the duopolists have no interest in rewriting the laws to make challenges to their power any easier.

Besides, as Jefferson told us, no man should be obligated to pay out of his taxes for the propagation of opinions he finds noxious.

Under the current arrangement of centralized power in Washington and a government that spends and taxes far more than would seem to be envisioned in the Constitution, the best campaign finance reform may be simple repeal. Perhaps the contrarians are right: we need more spending on campaigns, not less, at least if we are to decrease the shamefully high reelection rates of congressional incumbents and inject some ideas into the current morass.

But the best way to sharply reduce campaign spending in a constitutional way is to sharply reduce the powers of the central government and the privileges and subsidies it hands out. That would be the most radical – and most refreshing – reform of all.

Notes

1. David S. Broder, *The Party's Over: The Failure of Politics in America* (New York: Harper & Row, 1971), p. xvi.
2. Ibid., p. xx.
3. Ibid., p. 1.
4. Ibid., p. 187.
5. Ibid., p. 255.
6. Ibid., p. 256.
7. Ibid., p. 257.
8. Theodore J. Lowi, "Toward a More Responsible Three-Party System: Deregulating American Democracy," in *The State of the Parties: The Changing Role of Contemporary American Parties*, fourth edition, edited by John C. Green and Rick Farmer (Lanham, MD: Rowman & Littlefield, 2003), p. 354.
9. Ibid., pp. 354–355.
10. Ibid., p. 376. Emphasis added.
11. Peter H. Argersinger, "'A Place on the Ballot': Fusion Politics and Antifusion Laws," *American Historical Review* (Vol. 85, No. 2, April 1980), p. 159.
12. Richard Winger, "Institutional Obstacles to a Multiparty System," in *Multiparty Politics in America*, edited by Paul S. Herrnson and John C. Green (Lanham, MD: Rowman & Littlefield, 1997), p. 159.
13. Ibid., p. 169.
14. John F. Bibby and L. Sandy Maisel, *Two Parties. Or More? The American Party System* (Cambridge, MA: Westview, 2003), p. 21.
15. Ibid., pp. 86–87.
16. J. David Gillespie, *Politics at the Periphery: Third Parties in Two-Party America* (Columbia: University of South Carolina Press, 1993), p. vii.
17. David S. Broder, "Is the Party Over?" in *Multiparty Politics in America*, edited by Paul S. Herrnson and John C. Green (Lanham, MD: Rowman & Littlefield, 1997), p. 2.
18. Ibid., pp. 7–8.
19. Paul S. Herrnson and John C. Green, "American Party Politics at the Dawn of a New Century," in *Multiparty Politics in America*, edited by Paul S. Herrnson and John C. Green, p. 12.
20. Burton A. Abrams and Russell F. Settle, "Campaign-Finance Reform: A Public Choice Perspective," *Public Choice* (Vol. 120, 2004), p. 396.

Afterword

In the fall of 2007, a friend was circulating an initiative petition in Oklahoma that, if enough valid signatures had been gathered, would have placed on the ballot for the voters in that state an initiative that would have drastically lowered the number of voters' signatures necessary to qualify political parties not already recognized by the State of Oklahoma on the ballot for future elections there; in other words, political parties other than the Democratic Party and the Republican Party. My friend approached one man and asked him to sign, stating how Oklahoma had the most restrictive ballot access laws in the nation, to which the man replied, "I know, but I don't care."

Fortunately, that individual is in the minority. On the whole, it appears that the American people want more candidate choices on the ballot, not fewer, even though – for now – the vast majority of people don't ultimately vote for these candidates.

The Constitution of the State of Florida requires that every 20 years, the Florida Constitution Revision Commission review the Florida Constitution and propose changes to it that go before the states' voters for approval. In its 1997–1998 session, the Commission proposed to greatly ease ballot access requirements in Florida (which had been among the toughest in the United States). Specifically, the Commission proposed adding to the Florida Constitution "the requirements for a candidate with no party affiliation or for a candidate of a minor party for placement of the candidate's name on the ballot shall be no greater than the requirements for a candidate of the party having the largest number of registered voters."

In November 1998, the voters of Florida passed that proposed revision to that state's Constitution, making Florida among the easiest states in which minor parties can earn ballot access.

The Commonwealth of Massachusetts also had among the toughest ballot access laws in the United States, and, in 1990, the people of Massachusetts passed a citizen's initiative to lower the number of voter signatures that must be gathered for a minor party to get on the ballot in that state to 10,000.

When the question is put to them, the voters declare that they want more choices at the ballot box. They also want minor party candidates included in debates. Polls of the public continually show that a majority of respondents want minor party candidates included in political debates. Minor party candidates would certainly spice up the dialogue and make debates less tired sounding and scripted.

Ultimately, though, if Americans want more effective choices from which to choose come election time, this nation will have to enact electoral reform. The largest impediment to effective political competition to the Democrats and Republicans is the single-member legislative district and plurality elections in those districts. Political scientists say that the natural result of Single Member Plurality (SMP) voting is two dominant parties, both running for the center, trying to offend as few people as possible, in order to winner single-member district elections.

And, not only does our current SMP voting system discourage minor party and independent challengers, it discourages challengers of any sort. Commonly, roughly half of state legislator elections throughout the nation have only one candidate (the incumbent, of course) on the ballot.

For single winner elections, Instant Runoff Voting (IRV) could be used. It works as follows: instead of a voter having one vote to cast for no more than one candidate, a voter gets to rank candidates in order of preference (#1, #2, #3, etc. – as many or as few candidates for whom the voter wishes to express preferences). If a candidate receives a majority of first choice votes, that candidate wins. If not, the last place candidate is eliminated, with his or her votes transferred to each of those voters' next choice candidate. This process continues until a majority winner emerges.

IRV eliminates the spoiler effect and "wasted vote syndrome" associated with minor party and independent candidates. It might not make such candidates electable for more political offices than is the case today, but it would likely increase media coverage of them because more people would be interested in voting for them under IRV, and it would likely lead to inclusion of more minor party and independent candidates in political debates. IRV also reduces negative campaigning as candidates would be interested in getting voters' second and third choice preferences.

IRV has real political legs in the United States, as it has been adopted by cities such as San Francisco, Oakland, Minneapolis, Memphis, and Burlington, Vermont for municipal elections, by the States of Arkansas and Louisiana for voters who are overseas, and by the Republican Party of Utah for some internal elections. Its time has come in the United States, and, as its adoption spreads, doors will be opened, at least somewhat, for new voices on the American political landscape.

For the candidates of minor parties to truly become electable to public office in this nation, the adoption of proportional voting systems will likely be needed. The United States is in the clear minority of developed democracies in this world in not using proportional voting systems, which employ multimember districts to elect legislators and distribute seats in legislatures to candidates much more in line with the percentage of the vote that their party earned.

How are these reforms going to be enacted in a land in which legislatures are controlled by Republicans and Democrats? I suggest that the Initiative & Referendum (I&R) power that is currently given to the people in 24 states is how this will develop in the United States. Other states will adopt I&R along the way, or their legislatures will feel pressured to adopt electoral reform once it becomes popular in the states with I&R.

Electoral reform, which is farther along in Canada and the United Kingdom, will, I predict, eventually come to the United States. It will be a multi-decade process that the two older parties will fight tooth and nail (be wary about all the arguments that will be heard about "American Exceptionalism").

But, when that electoral reform does occur, the American people will have finally thrown off the yoke of the two older parties that is impeding our progress as a people.

William Redpath
Chairman, Libertarian National Committee
Washington, DC

Index

Printed in the United States of America